Guilty Pleasures

Guilty Pleasures

POPULAR NOVELS AND
AMERICAN AUDIENCES IN THE
LONG NINETEENTH CENTURY

Hugh McIntosh

UNIVERSITY OF VIRGINIA PRESS
CHARLOTTESVILLE AND LONDON

University of Virginia Press
© 2018 by the Rector and Visitors of the University of Virginia
All rights reserved
Printed in the United States of America on acid-free paper

First published 2018

9 8 7 6 5 4 3 2 1

Library of Congress Cataloging-in-Publication Data
Names: McIntosh, Hugh, 1978– author.
Title: Guilty pleasures : popular novels and American audiences in the long nineteenth century / Hugh McIntosh.
Description: Charlottesville : University of Virginia Press, 2018. | Includes bibliographical references.
Identifiers: LCCN 2018021875 | ISBN 9780813941646 (cloth : alk. paper) | ISBN 9780813941653 (paperback : alk. paper) | ISBN 9780813941660 (e-book)
Subjects: LCSH: American fiction—19th century—History and criticism. | American fiction—20th century—History and criticism. | Popular literature—United States—History and criticism. | Literature and society—United States—History.
Classification: LCC PS374.P63 M35 2018 | DDC 813./309—dc23
LC record available at https://lccn.loc.gov/2018021875

Cover art: Detail from "Between Performances. The Uncle Tommers' Christmas Dinner on the Road." *Puck* magazine, December 4, 1907. (Courtesy of the Library of Congress)

For my parents

Contents

Acknowledgments ix

Introduction: The Not-So-Great American Novel 1
1. *Uncle Tom's Cabin* and the Unprivileged Public Sphere 29
2. *Ben-Hur*: Spectacles of Belief 57
3. British Authorship, American Advertising 78
4. Questionable Americans Abroad 104
5. Unknowing American Realism: *Uncle Tom's Cabin* to Henry James, James Weldon Johnson, and James Baldwin 121

Afterword: The Novel and America Abroad Now 149

Notes 153
Bibliography 163
Index 169

Acknowledgments

I owe debts of gratitude to many teachers, colleagues, and readers who have helped this book along the way. First, my teachers at Northwestern: Julia Stern, Betsy Erkkilä, Jay Grossman, Tracy Davis, and Kate Masur. Although she arrived as I was packing my bags, Janice Radway also offered helpful advice in the early stages. The generous support of the Jay and Deborah Last Fellowship through the American Antiquarian Society, and the guidance from those I was lucky to meet there—Paul Erickson, Meredith McGill, Lisa Gitelman, Melissa Homestead, and Elizabeth Dillon—were crucial to this book's development as well. Two manuscript readers, Wesley Raabe and one who remains anonymous, provided extremely valuable feedback throughout the review process.

But no one deserves more thanks for this book than Anna, who makes my day, every day, and May and Brownie, whose oversized spirits remind me always why it's worth digging through history for signs of life that might surprise us.

Portions of chapter 1 were previously included in "Thrilling the Broken Nation," *ESQ* 58, no. 3 (2012): 338–74. Portions of chapter 3 were previously included in "Misreading and the Marketplace," *NOVEL* 49, no. 3 (2016): 429–48.

Guilty Pleasures

INTRODUCTION

The Not-So-Great American Novel

In many ways at once, late nineteenth-century American literary culture championed the idea that popular novels didn't need to be great. Critics, novelists, and everyday readers became adept at seeing vague auras where literary excellence might have been. According to the *New York Tribune*, Lew Wallace's best seller *Ben-Hur* (1880) was "not one of the great novels of English literature," but seemed to be divinely inspired, "permeated with the beatific spirit of the New Testament."[1] It was widely agreed that George du Maurier's *Trilby* (1895) "had not the staying power nor the ability for a classic."[2] But American audiences regarded it as a triumph of atmosphere: "that refreshing ozone," as one critic described it, "which was perhaps the book's greatest success."[3] The long reception of Harriet Beecher Stowe's *Uncle Tom's Cabin* (1852) took this distinction between aura and artwork to a remarkable extreme. Countless late-century voices would echo the claim that this archetypical American best seller was "less a work of art than of spirit."[4]

Guilty Pleasures argues that notions of less-than-great literature shaped a unique style of response in American popular culture. The readers, authors, and critics who wondered about the pleasures and potencies of best-selling novels were fascinated by amateur efforts that produced powerful effects. Reactions to this category of popular texts mixed a lack of respect for novels as finished products with reverence for the forces they seemed to embody: the presence of God, the essence of a national spirit, the ethos of revolution. The archive of criticism, rewriting, parody, and stage adaptation explored here reflects these especially torn perspectives, which questioned what it meant to be deeply attracted to a text that seemed, at the same time, unworthy of deference.

This ambivalence stood out against the language of intense emotion that so often characterized nineteenth-century novel reading. William Lloyd Garrison's description of *Uncle Tom's Cabin*, for example, invokes imagery of enthrallment that would have been familiar to any reader of contemporary literary reviews: "We confess," Garrison wrote, "to the frequent moistening of our eyes, and the making of our heart grow liquid as water, and the trembling of every nerve within us, in the perusal of the incidents and scenes so vividly depicted in her pages."[5] Alongside this kind of superheated consumption, however, other voices explored far cooler attitudes toward the books they enjoyed. There was certainly no shortage of readers bathed in tears, possessed by outrage, or overwhelmed by sympathy in nineteenth-century America; but a full account of popular reading in this period needs to acknowledge that melodramatic best sellers like *Uncle Tom's Cabin*, *A Tale of Two Cities* (1859), and *Ben-Hur* inspired as many lukewarm reactions as they did strong outpourings of feeling.

This became a matter of nationhood as well as aesthetics. Ambivalence about the amateur, the flawed, and the unfinished took on a special significance in American contexts, in a culture still very much preoccupied with the nation's relatively new place on the world stage. While prominent American literary figures such as Thomas Wentworth Higginson, William Dean Howells, and Albion Tourgée pronounced the need for professional authors who could write great and definitively "American" novels, many less official voices invoked the Americanness of the not-so-refined.[6] Critics admitted to being deeply and often mysteriously moved by novels they otherwise viewed as subpar. Parodists imagined well-known characters from British and American novels learning new lessons in the brashly commercialized culture of American cities. Stage adaptations of American works ridiculed their artistry while praising their moral superiority. Meanwhile, a wide range of authors applauded American settings and characters for conveying the essential goodness of the clumsy and the overreaching.

This exploration of the absence of greatness is worth remembering as a source of uncertainties and debates about what it meant to be part of a mass reading public but also, more broadly, about what it meant to participate in an American national community. The style of response considered here revolved around states of explicitly *conflicted* assent: interrogating the experience of enjoying a flawed novel, or the state of being part of a dubious—if not immoral—society. *Guilty Pleasures* examines this crossing of personal, cultural, and national consciousness, in which considering what it meant to be partially attached to a reading public sparked new ways of imagining partial bonds with the new nation. Like much recent work in novel history, then, this book is interested in how genre and geography become inextricably intertwined. In this case, a long-standing mark of the novel form—that it holds high themes in tension with humble forms of expression—took on a unique meaning in the late nineteenth-century transatlantic world, as the amateurism of popular narratives resonated with the discourse of new nationhood.

This overlap of reading and images of belonging to a national public had much to do with the massive expansion in American print and theatrical cultures that took shape over the nineteenth century. As novels began circulating by the millions, reaching a legitimately national audience, they offered readers a special opportunity to express their relationship to what "every" American seemed to be doing. This scale gave acts of reading a new relevance to constructs of national life. It allowed critics, for instance, to jump from discussing the aesthetic failings of *Ben-Hur* or *Trilby* to questioning more broadly the failures of American progress. It also helped acts of conspicuously consuming popular literature to express complex relations between individuals and the abstract social body. According to Henry James, one of the period's most astute observers of ambivalence as both an aesthetic and a national mood, seeing *Uncle Tom's Cabin* on stage could be experienced as a lesson in "detachment" from the American mass: "the point exactly was that we attended this spectacle just in order *not* to be beguiled, just in order to enjoy with ironic detachment and, at the very most, to be amused ourselves at our sensibility should it proved to have been trapped and caught."[7]

Scenes of cool reception like these shaped the novel's social meaning in ways that literary studies has, for the most part, missed. Historians of the novel have produced a remarkably thorough account of the genre's often conflicting communal roles, from its close ties to the language of human rights to its seemingly endless appetite for punishing characters who stray from social norms; from its relationship to scientific objectivity to its affinities with utopian thought.[8] Focusing on response in the age of mass print emphasizes yet another key role the novel played in American contexts: it sparked a wide range of creative expression that refused to give popular novelists the last word on the grand themes of their works. This couldn't have happened without the genre's *approachability*, its status of not only seeming to speak to everyone in the reading public but also being open to the *not* great. Studies of American literature have compellingly argued that certain plot conventions—the prodigal's story, the picaresque adventure, and the seduction tale—have had special relationships to American social thought.[9] To many nineteenth-century voices, however, what seemed most American about popular novels were not the stories they told as much as the amateurism they brought to the exploration of lofty subjects.

This tension between elevated themes and low discursive status created a culture not of low expectations but of uncertain expectations. The counterpart to the novel that didn't need to be great was a reader that remained on the fence, taking part without entirely buying in. To characterize such readers as acting "cool" might seem anachronistic, and to some degree it is: as scholarship on the origins of *cool* has shown, the term now carries connotations of oppositional—and often racially charged—insider knowledge that it did not take on until the twentieth-century vocabularies of jazz, beat, and sixties counterculture absorbed and transformed its meaning. By referring to the attitude that this book discusses as "cool," I do not mean to suggest that this later etymology applies to these nineteenth-century scenes of reading. I mean instead to invoke the general meaning that *cool* carried in this earlier period: a state of emotional detachment and reserve, a stance of resistance to external forces.[10]

Indeed, looking back to the late nineteenth-century usage of *cool* helps reveal how deeply the attitude of partial participation became intertwined with ideas about American identity. It is no accident that the stock American character that had for decades been known as the "cute Yankee"—so named for his bumbling, comedic attempts at acute reasoning—had been renamed the "cool Yankee" by the turn of the century. To rename the Yankee "cool" was to suggest that there was something typically American about a detached, unemotional orientation toward the world. The following will explore a few instances in which the term *cool* appeared directly in the context of popular reading: the cool Yankee character that became a standard addition to stage productions of *Uncle Tom's Cabin*, for instance, or a journalist referring to Lew Wallace as a cool author. But, more than these explicit points of connection, I am interested in the often unspoken attitudes about nationhood and detachment that informed both representations of the cool Yankee and imagery of popular reading.

The most often told story about coolness in twentieth-century America is one of slow decline: the movement from midcentury counterculture to what historian Thomas Frank refers to as the "conquest of cool" by corporate advertising in the seventies and eighties. American cool, its historians point out, has become nothing if not ambiguous, equally relatable to social dissent and the smooth functioning of consumerism's status quo. In looking at depictions of detached Americans, both in novels—in portrayals of American characters "reading" the social world—and around novels—as Americans conspicuously consuming popular books—*Guilty Pleasures* argues that this uncertainty has a longer social history than is often assumed. From the earliest notions that there was something fundamentally American about what James described as "ironic detachment," the idea cut two ways, undermining the potentially powerful force of passionate attachment even while opening up new possibilities for questioning and revising popular narratives. As best-selling books were deemed at once seriously flawed and deeply significant, acts of cool detachment could seem full of possibility. But what this possibility entailed was far from clear.

Approaching this trend from the perspective of cultural theory, we might say that this mystique surrounding cool detachment toward popular novels was a particularly American product of the Benjaminian moment. Walter Benjamin's wide-ranging analysis of nineteenth-century aesthetics has much more to say about visual art, urban space, and lyric poetry than narrative, but his speculations about the new possibilities opened up by mass-produced artwork and the growth of consumer culture are relevant to novel reading as well. To Benjamin, the nineteenth century marked a tipping point, as what he called the "nightmare" of modernity began to inspire a new vocabulary of utopian images and signs, forms of creativity sparked by the mixture of sacred and profane symbols in urban experience: paintings and sculptures accessed through mass reproduction rather than spaces of worship, department stores built to resemble cathedrals. Benjamin saw this nonintellectual, and often nonsensical, cultural activity as alive with an energy that countered the bourgeois notions of individualism and social progress he hoped would give way to more fulfilling social forms.

Benjamin's deep distrust for constructs of interiority perhaps explains why his encyclopedic discussion of nineteenth-century popular culture avoids the topic of best-selling novels. As literary scholars such as Terry Eagleton, Michael McKeon, and Nancy Armstrong have emphasized, the mainstream Victorian novel took the period's faith in individuality to a degree that seems almost pathological, celebrating at every turn visions of national flourishing rooted in the individualizing space of the home.[11] The notes and citations that Benjamin collected in the *Arcades Project* file labeled "The Interior" include comparisons between the nineteenth-century "addiction" to inner experience and a "prison" and a "spider web" filled with bodies drained of blood. He refers to the remarkable amount of violence toward pieces of furniture in Edgar Allen Poe's stories as a "struggle to awaken from the collective dream."[12] As if to stoke the fires of this dream, the most widely read nineteenth-century novels depicted individual acts of sympathy, resistance, and object choice as the forces impelling narratives toward endings that feature happy marriages and comfortable domestic space.

If popular novels moved away from what Benjamin would identify as revolutionary energy, resistance to them might be understood as attempts to tell a different story. But the not-so-great novel became provocative for different reasons than Benjamin might suggest. His often cited essay "On the Work of Art in the Age of Mechanical Reproduction" links the critical potential of mass-produced visual art to the way it presents signs invested with traditional authority—religious icons, for example—while draining from them the aura of traditional power. The mass-circulating form of the novel often functioned in a different way, not as artwork in which the aura of the otherworldly is conspicuously absent, but as texts invested with grandeur that didn't seem to match the inferior quality of their production. Packaging majestic themes in eminently approachable forms, the most widely available texts turned auras, atmospheres, and "permeating spirits" into subjects seemingly fit for amateurs to take on in public. The mass-circulating novel was less a sign of spiritual authority's absence than an invitation to reimagine its relationship to everyday life.

While cool reading reflected the disruptive momentum of the marketplace that Benjamin theorized, its mix of reverence and disrespect is not easy to square with his analysis. The attitude is similarly out of step with the most often discussed mode of aesthetic irreverence: the counterculture of "camp." As Susan Sontag claims in her influential 1964 essay, "Notes on Camp," the scenes of reception and refashioning that she categorizes as camp have roots in nineteenth-century popular reading. Sontag cites Oscar Wilde's mock callousness toward one of the most famous death scenes in the period's popular literature as an early sign of the attitude she intends to describe. Wilde's remark that "one must have a heart of stone to read the death of Little Nell without laughing" anticipated the idea that, as Sontag phrases it, there is such a thing as "a good taste of bad taste."[13] In the realm of attraction to objects that don't command respect, the distinction between cool and camp might be summed up as the difference between mass belonging and participating in a subculture. The sensibility that Sontag and others after her have explored draws on the insider knowledge of "good bad taste" to mark new forms of subculture within a larger community. Cool reading, on the other hand, didn't help delineate a state of full belonging to part of the national populace; instead, it expressed a partial relationship to the whole.

But the kinds of insider belonging performed as camp and the kinds of mass estrangement channeled through cool consumption are equally hard to pin down. As the boundary-pushing director Bruce LaBruce has recently claimed, the stylistic excesses of camp are now so ubiquitous that they have no clear value, shaping some of the most normative forms of entertainment and some of the edgiest statements of subculture. LaBruce calls for a view of camp that is more sensitive to both extremes, a view in which we differentiate between "good camp" and "bad camp."[14] I would suggest that much the same can be said for the kinds of partial attachments discussed here. Noncommittal, unserious, self-enclosed, unfeeling: the ways in which cool feeds into what Benjamin calls the isolating nightmare of the nineteenth century are not hard to see (consider, as a glaring example, the white readers who were able to treat *Uncle Tom's Cabin* as casual, light entertainment). Less obvious are the optimisms and critical refusals that lukewarm feelings about popular literature have helped express. Understanding the close relationship between not-so-great culture and its cool readers—both past and present—calls for becoming sensitive to both its negative and its potentially productive dimensions.

The first two chapters of this book focus on how the reception of blockbuster American novels—*Uncle Tom's Cabin* and *Ben-Hur*—became a sounding board for ideas about how novels that lack greatness might still have profound effects. The readers, critics, and rewriters these chapters discuss portrayed the not-so-great as characteristically American, and they imagined this trait as *enabling* engagement with popular texts that was creative precisely because it was only partially attached. Chapters 3 and 4 show how representations of transatlantic travel, of Americans in England and of British figures (and texts) in America, reinforced the idea that there is something American, and oddly appealing, about cool, partial attachments. The final chapter locates in twentieth- and twenty-first-century narratives the ongoing impact of the imagined connection between Americanness and the absence of greatness.

No example reflects the disruptive impact of this connection more than *Uncle Tom's Cabin,* the subject of chapter 1. *Uncle Tom's Cabin*'s reception history exemplifies both the potential cruelty of cool response and the power of popular audiences to reshape narrative in dramatically reductive ways. As cultural historians such as Eric Lott and Barbara Hochman have pointed out, the long afterlife of Stowe's novel on stage and in print projected a dizzying array of racist and sexist imagery onto the abolitionist text. Crying out against slavery in unmistakable terms helped *Uncle Tom's Cabin* define what it meant to be a nineteenth-century best seller; it also provided a hugely recognizable way to ridicule African American characters and reject the abolitionism the novel espoused. Chapter 1 shows that the antagonistic reaction to *Uncle Tom's Cabin* was not limited to the proslavery voices that railed against Stowe's book and the impresarios who cashed in on the novel's unprecedented popularity, turning it into a show dominated by minstrelsy and nostalgia for the "old South." *Uncle Tom's Cabin* also inspired a good deal of more subtle resistance, from loaded questions about its quality to the privilege of simply feeling detached from its depictions of cruelty.

But for other voices, treating *Uncle Tom's Cabin* as an amateurish text opened up ways to question and extend Stowe's strong claims for the divine power of feeling. True to sentimental fashion, *Uncle Tom's Cabin* located this extra-intellectual way of knowing in proximity to domestic space, feminine influence, and the innocence of childhood. Many ambivalent readers wondered what this divine power would look like if it weren't anchored to the home. My inquiry into *Uncle Tom's Cabin*'s reception history examines a variety of responses—from early reviews to late parodies, from Stowe's follow-up novel, *Agnes of Sorrento,* to Langston Hughes's "Colonel Tom's Cabin"—that pushed against the equation of whiteness, domesticity, and American progress. At the center of this story was little Eva, Stowe's version of the white redeemer. As Wilde claimed, laughing at Dickens's little Nell could be a sign of good taste; the treatment of little Eva illustrates how a similar figure of innocence and sacrifice could inspire disagreement about what it meant to "feel right," and what, if anything, this had to do with the United States. Paying attention to the irreverent side of the novel's reception helps extend the claim, made by book historians such as Claire Parfait, that *Uncle Tom's Cabin*'s circulation through so many vastly different formats and social settings made it an especially protean text.[15]

Uncle Tom's Cabin was unparalleled among nineteenth-century popular novels in many ways: its relatively bold treatment of race, for instance, and its direct involvement in a political crisis. But the broad outlines of its social presence reveal themes that return as reactions to subsequent best sellers explore the tension between novels' moral visions and the increasingly consumerist culture through which they moved. The 1880s *Ben-Hur* phenomenon made the gap between ethics and consumption especially plain. As chapter 2 discusses, Lew Wallace's narrative of ancient Israel began as an exercise in biblical history and ended as the most lavish, special effects–driven stage production of its time. *Ben-Hur* thus took shape across two strikingly distinct nineteenth-century genres, Christian historiography—which aimed first and foremost to facilitate faith—and sensationalism—conspicuously addressed to thrill for its own sake. And the narrative's uncertain genre status was made murkier by Wallace's self-fashioning as a naïve, amateurish author. A close look at the reception of both the novel and its stage adaptation shows how this odd mix of religious import and low expectations sparked discussions about an equally strange version of aesthetic detachment: the desire to become naïve enough to be moved by *Ben-Hur*.

Taking a transatlantic focus, the next two chapters deal more explicitly with the perception of amateurishness as an American aesthetic and coolness as a characteristically American attitude. Chapter 3 examines the conflicted American response to British literary celebrities, paying special attention to two parodies that depict Dickens's and Du Maurier's characters transplanted to Manhattan: Robert Henry Newell's *The Cloven Foot* (1870) and an anonymously authored sequel to *Trilby* (1895). These para-texts make fun of Dickens's and Du Maurier's investments in Britishness and authorial control by portraying their characters being carried away by American consumerism. Where reactions to *Uncle Tom's Cabin* and *Ben-Hur* often had much to say about the spirits animating these popular novels, the rewritings of Dickens and Du Maurier located a vague power in the expressiveness of American advertising. These responses worked to counter British views of US commercial culture as, ultimately, a disappointing development.

Instead, they suggested—in the noncommittal voice of satire—that relatively new forms of consumerism might pave the way for better communal bonds.

At the same time, representations of American characters in British settings helped define the partial participation that the cool Yankee came to signify. Examining depictions of Americans in England, from Tom Taylor's *Our American Cousin* (1858) to the London reception of Joseph Jefferson's *Rip Van Winkle* (1859), from Anthony Trollope's *The American Senator* (1876) to Mark Twain's *A Connecticut Yankee in King Arthur's Court* (1889), chapter 4 shows how not buying in was presented as an American characteristic. The cool Yankee traveler enjoys the local trappings of Englishness, such as teatime and foxhunts, while treating them as ultimately meaningless things. But in a way that resonates with the attraction to not-so-great novels, British observers find themselves unable to view these outsiders as missing the point entirely. With notable regularity, these depictions of Americans abroad are unclear about whether the inability to participate in national culture is irritating or appealing. Popular "Yankee abroad" literature is ultimately ambiguous, I argue, about the social value of American detachment.

The concluding chapter explores the role of the not-so-great American novel in shaping conceptions of serious authorship by tracking how three influential male writers—Henry James, James Weldon Johnson, and James Baldwin—explicitly defined their artistic ambitions against those of *Uncle Tom's Cabin*. Comparing these diverse reactions to *Uncle Tom's Cabin* highlights the multiple meanings Stowe's text carried, from a sign of naïve compassion to, in Baldwin's words, an artifact of "violent inhumanity." Reading these responses side by side also calls attention to the constellation of masculinity, realism, and notions of American emptiness that shaped early twentieth-century US literary culture, both for white authors staking claims to the privilege of universality and for black authors fighting an exclusionary public sphere. For James, Johnson, and Baldwin alike, Stowe epitomized the amateurism that American art would have to surpass in order to impact the world. But, in different ways for each, *Uncle Tom's Cabin* also represented a connection between the accessible and the elusive that a more male-centered, and more professional, American literature would need to capture.

These chapters tell a story in which a contradictory genre helped articulate a contradictory national mood—one equally informed by insecurity and grandiosity about America's cultural newness. The two-sided quality of the popular novel, which seemed open to both amateur efforts and magnificent effects, became especially relevant to those struggling to make sense of the murky ground between America's supposed lack of sophistication and high hopes for its global influence. Ultimately, the discourse of novel reading promoted the idea that American culture didn't have to be aesthetically respectable to have a powerful impact. And this idea had consequences, both in terms of how texts were consumed (in a conspicuously ambivalent and revisionist spirit) and in terms of how American belonging was imagined more broadly (as a site of partial, reserved assent).

As a whole, this book tracks a discussion that was informed by common traits of best-selling novels—their supposed lack of greatness, their close ties with consumerism—but kept spilling over into more abstract subjects: the value of American culture, the significance of mixed feelings, and the even less concrete notion of social possibility itself. At issue in the vocabulary of novel reading and coolness was an ongoing dialogue about how to imagine one's relation not only to a nation but also to a shared space that might have the power to transform the sympathies, attractions, and customs that shape everyday life. To call this a dialogue, though, is to overstate its clarity quite a bit. The noise and creativity that surrounded widely read novels contained far more imagery than conceptual content, more vague implications than explicit critique. Again and again, popular response returned to figures of unknowing, from the critic who can't understand why he is drawn to a best-selling text, to the audience member who feels detached and deeply engaged at once. This is distinctly anti-intellectual critique.

But, as Benjamin suggested, this might be the most important kind. Distrustful of human motivations, Benjamin argued that the historiography of innovative thought would do well to bypass people who had a clear sense of what they were saying and doing and focus instead on less conscientious moments of creativity, juxtaposition, and odd exuberance. This is one of the major reasons his eccentric philosophy has resonated with literary scholars of all stripes. But I would argue that nineteenth-century popular novel reading offers an especially rich archive of expression that resists the foundations of individual judgment and intellectual directedness which so often govern social criticism, then and now. The novels of the era helped make this possible by reflecting relatively weak modes of authority: the amateur, the not great. The expanding print and commercial culture that surrounded them played a crucial role as well, shaping a media landscape in which a wide array of anonymous reaction, parody, merchandising, and rewriting conspicuously refused to give popular novels the last word.

Groundbreaking work in the history of the book and sociology of texts has long demonstrated that readers help create the meaning of the books they consume. The culture of nineteenth-century popular narratives emphasizes as well how novels and their media contexts shape the meaning of reading. As Nina Baym shows in her richly detailed study of American novel reading before the Civil War, nineteenth-century periodicals promoted a loosely cohesive mode of aesthetic judgment, based largely on two questions: Does the plot hold the readers' attention? And, does the novel "accord with a vision of a morally governed universe?"[16] These criteria continued to loom large in the postbellum decades, but as novel reading grew into a mass phenomenon, a new implicit question began to hold more sway: In what ways can this novel's moral vision be supplemented, revised, or updated? The American reading public pushed this invitation to participation into the foreground by celebrating the not-so-great novel, and the culture industries helped make the question prominent by offering a wide range of timely avenues for revision and response, from giant posters on the streets of New York to the magazines that circulated in ever-larger volume and with ever-quicker speeds.

But while this book asks how readers and their social contexts impact the meaning of novels, it also examines the roles that popular writers play in shaping the attitudes with which they are received. As Baym argues, "ideas about the genre of the work at hand enter into that work at every phase of its history: into its creation by the writer, its presentation by the publisher, its reception by readers, and its assessment and transmission by critics."[17] This is entirely true of the nineteenth-century popular novel. Part of understanding the irreverence and even disrespect for authors that drove cool response is seeing how celebrity writers encouraged these reactions: for instance, how Stowe juggled extremes of humility and grandiosity, how Wallace presented himself as an amateur, and how Dickens was drawn to the aggressive readership he imagined taking place in the United States. Together, novelists and readers filled popular literature with ideas about weakened self-possession, as writers without a strong grip on what their texts meant catered to audiences unsure how to feel about their works.

In a way, *Guilty Pleasures* locates a cultural context in which "ideas about the genre of the work at hand" cut against the grain of the genre's larger formation. The links between the Victorian novel and the emergence of middle-class identities can make the form feel—as Armstrong in particular has asserted—almost ridiculously narrow minded. Nineteenth-century novels were so caught up in asserting the value of self-control, individualism, and national pride, Armstrong argues, that their figures of horror and monstrosity might be their only redeeming features.[18] We might imagine Benjamin making a similar claim: if the nineteenth-century's mainstream narratives were the stuff of his nightmares, he might have appreciated the monstrosities imagined within them and alongside them, in the creativity they made possible. This is why the fashion for treating novels coolly had significance beyond mere playfulness. While popular novels might seem narrowly and redundantly focused, they circulated in a culture reluctant to take them at face value.

While this study is meant as a contribution to genre history, I hope it points to questions that are relevant beyond considerations of the novel, especially when read against the twenty-first century's markedly nonliterary popular culture. While novels no longer have nearly as prominent a role in the most widely consumed strata of mass media, the attitudes that began to be articulated around best-selling books in the nineteenth century certainly do. As Alan Liu suggests in *The Laws of Cool,* opting in to mainstream culture ironically or under vague protest has become par for the course in the Internet age. Liu stresses the two-sidedness of coolness: a strong sense of detachment from the social value of the content they consume makes cool customers the ultimate audience for culture industries that do little to challenge business as usual. At the same time, Liu sees the attitude of cool as a faint reflection of a shared fascination with the unknown that might connect the work of cultural history with the "paradigmatic student we all know at the back of the lecture hall: slouched in his or her chair, feet up, dressed in a tee-shirt advertising an alternative or a heavy-metal band, headphones on, looking up at the ceiling or down at the ground."[19] In other words, the history of coolness might help articulate the disaffections of the present by linking them with those of the past.

The idea that studying the nineteenth-century novel could illuminate the present in this way ventures beyond genre history. But the novel has always been something more than a genre. It might be more accurate to think of the novel, as Armstrong does, not just as a literary form but also as a framework of modern experience itself: "The novel in this larger sense cannot be pinned down to any individual novel, tradition, or institution of the novel. The novel is more like a ubiquitous cultural narrative that not only measures personal growth in terms of an individual's ability to locate him- or herself productively within the aggregate but also and simultaneously measures the aggregate in terms of its ability to accommodate the increasing heterogeneity of individuals."[20] Seen this way, specific works like *Uncle Tom's Cabin* and *Trilby* appear as symptoms of a larger structure of meaning making. And what audiences do as they digest and resist these texts takes on special significance for those interested in what the monstrous unknown outside of individualist experience might look like.

By way of background, the rest of this introduction looks closely at three key nineteenth-century terms that will help contextualize the range of responses to popular novels: *greatness, sensation,* and *cool.* In different ways, each of these keywords pointed to assumptions that shaped the field of mass reading. First and foremost, the sentiment that best-selling novels didn't need to be great took shape alongside the now well-documented call for American authors to take up the mantle of greatness. Nationalist pleas for great novels, as scholarship by Lawrence Buell, Amy Kaplan, Mark McGurl, Nancy Bentley, and others has shown, imagined literary culture as a site of masculine ability, expansive analytical vision, and a resistance to the tastes of American mass audiences. To note and even approve of a popular novel's lack of greatness in this context was to highlight how it fell short not only in comparison to classic literary works but also to the ideals associated with novelistic excellence in the present. The not-so-great American novel was unmanly, insufficiently analytical, and not glorifying enough for its author—all qualities that contributed to its dismissal but also its mystique.

Transatlantic popular culture developed a term as well for the opposite end of the spectrum, the lowest common denominator of crowd-pleasing. *Sensation* became prominent in the 1860s as a name for what seemed like a new emphasis in popular novels—narratives like Wilkie Collins's *The Woman in White* (1859) and Mary Elizabeth Braddon's *Lady Audley's Secret* (1862) that depicted domestic space as rife with secret vices and crimes—but also a new kind of pandering to theater audiences. The productions that came to be known as "sensation" shows, like *The Black Crook* (1866), *Under the Gaslight* (1867) and *Ben-Hur* (1899), addressed themselves to sensory thrill through outsize displays of stage machination and special effects. *Sensation* didn't signify much new in terms of content; novels had dealt in the unseemly underbelly of everyday life for decades, and stagecraft had always addressed itself to thrilling the audience's senses. Rather, the term pointed out a new way of foregrounding mere entertainment *for its own sake* in conspicuously unapologetic ways. As Nicholas Daly's scholarship on sensationalism in 1860s London reveals, this was a buzzword closely linked with an emerging urban consumerism. But the term took on national connotations as well: examining the language of sensation in both the British and American press reveals how the term also came to be associated with the idea that U.S. culture was especially devoted to pleasing tasteless mass audiences.

While calls for great American novels and debates about sensationalism worked to define the extremes of cultural value, the shift from the "cute Yankee" to the "cool Yankee" marked a new way of thinking about American attitudes. The midcentury imagery of cute hinged on stereotypes of Americans as calculating, self-promoting, and commercially shrewd. The cool Yankee of later decades parodied shrewdness with a more consumerist twist. *Cool* entered into American slang as a term of metaphorical but also literal temperature: a cool person kept his or her head under pressure but also chose the right kind of clothing for summer heat. As a style of consumption and a stock American type, cool helped articulate a kind of detachment from one's immediate environment that had as much to do with object choice as it did temperament. The distant cousin of the ever-calculating cute Yankee, the cool Yankee held a portion of his or her awareness always in reserve, holding out hope for a more satisfying or rewarding scenario.

Cultural concepts like greatness, sensation, and cool are by nature imprecise. But getting a feel for their use helps put the contemporary response to popular novels in perspective. Roughly put, the artwork imagined in terms of greatness—most often, in American contexts, named as an ideal that had yet to be realized—would be awe inspiring. Sensation novels and plays would thrill the senses in ways as undeniable as they were undignified. The half in, half out, partially detached sensibility of coolness pushed toward thinking about popular novels that fell in between these two extremes. In the confused space between the great American novel and sensationalism, there was room enough to imagine how narratives that lacked the authority of greatness might, with the audience's help, critique norms of individualism and national progress in ways that so-called great novels couldn't.

SENSATION

The term *sensational* had been kicking around in popular culture long before it rose to prominence in the transatlantic 1860s. Early nineteenth-century critics might call a newspaper article sensational if it dealt with a salacious scandal or a novel or play sensational if it exposed some hidden vice, along the lines of George Lippard's *The Quaker City* (1845) or T. S. Arthur's *Ten Nights in a Bar Room* (1854). An event that drew huge crowds might also be described as making a sensation, the word signifying a certain kind of consumption as well as production: authors pandering to questionable tastes and crowds chasing the latest fad. The voices that made *sensation* a buzzword of the 1860s weren't naming new forms of content as much as a sharpening awareness of consumerism's place in popular culture. Plenty of critics denounced what they saw as the increasing shallowness of mainstream novels and plays. But many writers and theater impresarios embraced sensationalism as a valid genre, and audiences seemed to agree.

The discourse of sensation is especially relevant to nineteenth-century reading because it explored the idea that popular novels don't need to be great, and, perhaps, they shouldn't be. But, to understand the significance of sensation in American contexts, it pays to think beyond fiction. Because literary studies have defined the conversation about sensationalism, and because the writers most associated with the term in the transatlantic world were British—Wilkie Collins and Mary Elizabeth Braddon—the scholarship on the sensational 1860s has focused on England in ways that obscure the trend's national subtexts. But the writing on British sensationalism is absolutely right about the fashion's ties to a heightened awareness of consumerist culture. "On the cusp of the transition from early industrialist production toward consumerism and consumer society," Patrick Brantlinger writes, "sensation fiction seems to capitulate to the desires of the mass reading public in a self-conscious manner that distinguishes it from earlier writing and publishing practices."[21]

This culture of capitulation took different forms. In the realm of the popular novel, this meant books that seemed solely dedicated to superficial pleasure and spine-tingling thrill. The idea that the public would embrace a book only for the excitement it offered—and not for its moral value or sublimity—was incongruous enough in genteel circles that it sparked a lot of jokes. One *Harper's Weekly* cartoonist, for instance, made fun of the sensation trend in 1863 with a series of cartoons depicting well-dressed young women reading in interior spaces that showed their relative wealth. The humor revolves around the misalignment of class and gender expectations and the young readers' mode of consumption: they are enjoying "delightful horrors" instead of more decorous forms of fiction. Even in the midst of the Civil War, it was clear to American observers that popular culture seemed to be carving out new ways of catering to a mass audience's questionable tastes.

Like much of the critical response to this 1860s fashion, Henry James's long review of Braddon's works draws a strong line between sensation fiction and novels with social value. Braddon's *Lady Audley's Secret* and *Aurora Floyd* (1863) had found huge transatlantic success, drawing audiences in by depicting hidden crimes of seemingly respectable, middle-class characters. To James, Braddon's mass popularity is a kind of genre trespassing, the "assumption by a 'sensation' novel of the honors of legitimate fiction": "People talk of novels with a purpose," James continues, "and from this class of works, both by her patrons and her enemies, Miss Braddon's tales are excluded."[22] Enjoying mainstream success while falling outside of legitimate fiction with social purpose, sensation novels addressed a heterogeneous audience that didn't seem to care about the ultimate value of the books they read. Not only Braddon's many harsh critics, but also her patrons, James notes, were happy to see her novels as having nothing to offer but pleasure.

Outside of novel reading, sensation became closely tied to spectacle. One of the most discussed theatrical sensation shows bringing spectacle to the foreground was *The Black Crook*, a play that debuted in 1866 and featured a thin love plot fleshed out by lavish stage sets that moved and changed in dramatic "transformation" scenes, as well as a large cast of dancers in revealing tights. Around this same time, playwright and impresario Augustin Daly would make a name for himself as a purveyor of sensational special effects, from the train scene in *Under the Gaslight* to the hot-air balloon effects in *Around the World in Eighty Days* (1879). As early as 1864, though, the sporting and theater paper *Wilkes' Spirit of the Times* was proclaiming the noticeable shift in American theater audiences' tastes. The playgoing audience seemed to have "changed in its characteristics" lately, *Wilkes'* reported, "and goes in largely for the sensational in place of the legitimate."[23] The 1860s thus marked a turning point in which the sensational was articulated as a viable option—which readers and playgoers might choose over more legitimate authoritative, idealistic, or sentimental modes, depending on their mood. In other words, the fashion helped articulate the kind of consumerist culture in which we live and move today: a field of choice in which one of the most popular options is simply superficial pleasure.

The flamboyant showmanship of P. T. Barnum is often taken as the epitome of nineteenth-century American popular culture, but, in a way, sensationalism was the opposite of the Barnumesque. Barnum's New York museum attracted huge audiences by providing what cultural historian James W. Cook calls "playful frauds," exhibits that couched some of the pleasures of sensationalism—spectacle and mere amusement—in the language of genteel self-improvement.[24] With a wink to the audience, Barnum played at once to the attractiveness of thrill and voyeurism and the pretense of middle-class respectability. Sensationalists and their patrons, on the other hand, proudly claimed that self-improvement and respectability are not the only acceptable aims of cultural production. In the case of advertising, though, Barnum's innovative mode of self-promotion was a major influence on what came to be known as the sensational style. In the fashion for "sensation advertisements," the sensational and the Barnumesque crossed paths.

An 1863 *New York Ledger* article addressed this fad, discussing the array of "sensation posters" pasted along a board fence by City Hall Park. Sensation ads were distinguished not only by bright colors and huge type, but also by mystery. One giant poster simply says, "Autoperipatetikos," with no explanation. Another exclaims, "Zampilaerostation!" Another asks the viewer, "Why Will Ye Die?" This kind of capitalizing on mystery had been a strategy of Barnum's for years (perhaps the most famous example is his brick man promotion, in which he paid a man to rearrange a pile of bricks in a cryptic way in front of his museum, apparently drawing a large, curious crowd). Where sensation fiction and sensation theater helped establish a more consumerist culture, sensation advertisements attempted to make commerce itself a source of fun. A successful sensation ad campaign would create far more excitement than the product in question could without the aura of mystery: "Sozodont!," one of the biggest and most well-known sensation ads of the 1860s, turned out to be a new kind of toothpaste.

The best-selling books in nineteenth-century America were not sensational; they didn't proudly declare their distance from social relevance. Quite the opposite: *Uncle Tom's Cabin*, *A Tale of Two Cities*, *Ben-Hur*, Edward Bellamy's *Looking Backward* (1888), and *Trilby* each met the reader with a clear purpose, whether this be promoting abolition, critiquing capitalism, strengthening religious faith, or cautioning against the excesses of aestheticism. But the culture of sensationalism had many direct ties to the reception of these popular favorites. The producers of *The Black Crook,* for example, would go on to stage a lavish version of *Uncle Tom's Cabin.* The dramatization of *Ben-Hur* would become the nation's most visible example of a special effects–driven sensation play. Parodies of Dickens's work would imagine how his characters might react to a sensational ad campaign in New York. These various links begin to suggest how the discourse of sensation shaped the ambiguity between moral engagement and self-indulgence that made nineteenth-century novel reading such a contradictory cultural space.

But discussions of the sensational are most relevant to understanding the attitudes surrounding popular fiction for what they suggest about consumerism and the not-so-great novel. The responses to fiction that *Guilty Pleasures* explores furthered and revised the challenge to ideals of literary greatness that sensationalism represented. One American theater critic put this challenge bluntly in 1887, reviewing a sensation play that failed to deliver on its promise of extravagant special effects. The reviewer reported that, by missing the opportunity to thrill the audience, the play "ended as tamely as a Howells novel."[25] This dig at William Dean Howells, one of the biggest proponents of a potentially great American literature, makes it seem liberating that sensation falls squarely outside of the erudite approaches to art he represents. With the sensational seen as being outside the legitimate, many then wondered if this illegitimacy might point the way to a more modern, and more fulfilling, popular creativity. Part of an increasingly consumerist mainstream culture, sensationalism made it possible to think about the lack of greatness as a point of pride.

Equally important here are the national associations that the sensational carried. While the novelists who came to be known as sensation writers were mostly British, the larger cultural trend that the label represented—the celebration of the crowd's unrefined tastes, the flamboyance of advertising media and stagecraft, and the receptivity to shallow fads—read as American in the transatlantic world. A comic poem that ran in London's *Punch* magazine (not to be confused with New York's *Punch*) in 1861 shows both the extent to which sensation meant more than a novelistic style and the extent to which it was associated with the United States. "Some would have it an age of Sensation / If the age one of Sense may not be— / The word's not *Old* England's creation, / But New England's over the sea."²⁶ The poem goes on to give a laundry list of American stereotypes that resonate with the unnatural excitement of the sensational: high pressure, dizzying social mobility, fast-changing laws, the mass appetite for vulgar thrills. England might now have its sensational excesses, the piece concludes, but only because it has been "poisoned" by the United States.

An article in Dickens's periodical, *All the Year Round,* echoed this sentiment soon after. Entitled "American Sensations," it described the enthusiasms of US audiences as extreme, advanced versions of the changing cultural atmosphere in England. *All the Year Round*'s New York correspondent claimed that American sensations—from the hype surrounding the French acrobat Charles Blondin to the urban rallies of Abraham Lincoln's first presidential campaign—were "epidemic," and familiar. "We at home have our insanities," the article explained, "but I think the Americans run madder, and suffer oftener."²⁷ The United States had no unique claim on the styles of sensation culture, as the careers of Braddon and Collins showed. But the new nation was seen as especially addicted to sensational attractions, consumerist media, and popular fashions. Whether one agreed with sensation's critics that the form reflected dangerous indulgence or with the fans of sensation who viewed it as liberation from dull moralism and dry literature, the style seemed tied to America's presence on the world stage.

GREATNESS

Others saw American literature destined for greatness. Like sensation, the idea of the great American novel had been mentioned from time to time before the Civil War but would not become a major cultural touchstone until the latter half of the nineteenth century. This literary ideal brought the project of national consolidation into dialogue with the professionalization of both authorship and criticism. But it was also very much a creature of the mass market for print, in which the phrase quickly became hackneyed. In 1880, New York's *Puck* magazine placed "Writing the Great American Novel" at number three on their list of "Certain Dangerous Tendencies in American Life." "Every new novel is advertised as the great American novel," *Puck* complained, "either directly or suggestively."²⁸ The more critics such as Howells, John DeForest, and Thomas Wentworth Higginson did to make the great novel a goal of serious literary endeavor, the more book marketing did to make it seem ridiculous.

Although the great American novel was never a clearly defined concept, attempts to discuss it shed light on the discourse of the not-so-great. As Lawrence Buell notes in his remarkable history of the idea, *Dream of the Great American Novel*, the definitive role of regionalism in the nineteenth-century United States meant that writing an American novel would have to be a feat of *unification*. The great American novel "must be a novel of national life," one critic wrote, "that is, it must be based entirely or partly on national ideas." According to an 1892 review, the great American novel would present the entirety of the nation's citizens in "expressive epitome."[29] But this literary work that would somehow reveal a nation larger than the sum of its parts never seemed to arrive. "Instead of a national novel," another review complained, "we now have a rapidly accumulating series of regional novels." The great American writer should instead be "grasping all the accumulated details and blending them into a harmonious whole."[30]

Most agreed that writing the great unifying novel would require a broad knowledge of national geography, social groups, and attitudes, a kind of near-omniscience that was coded masculine with varying degrees of subtlety. "Who will the novelist be?" an 1898 article in the *Philistine* asked. "Let us discuss him as a man, for he is more likely to be of that gender." This author would need to have "the right faith," the article contends, but also the right knowledge: "He will know [America's] back trails as well as its highways. He will know its trees, its rocks and its gullies. . . . And more than anything else, he will know its people."[31] It made sense that the great American novelist would be thoroughly familiar with the wide variety of terrain and social breadth he was to unify. And this expectation gave the discussion of American greatness a certain bias, both toward masculine figures of authority and toward a fantasy of comprehensive knowledge. The great American novel would be an unquestionably intellectual text.

The project of great national novel writing elevated the individual in two ways, first calling for an author whose individual perspective would contain multitudes, and then imagining a narrative that would epitomize the American through representative characters. In the nineteenth century, then, discussions of literary greatness went hand-in-hand with a powerfully individualist ethos. When Higginson described what the "New World's

New Book" might look like, he voiced a common idea about the difference between European and American society: "democracy has just as distinct a place in society, and, above all, in the realm of literature. The touchstone there applied is just the same, and it consists in the essential dignity and value of the individual man."[32] It stood most often as a given that the great American novel would not only be a tribute to a political body but also a celebration of the sovereign individual.

According to one 1896 article in the *Dial*, the great American novel must be "a concrete and vital presentation of certain individual lives as they are lived, or conceivably might be lived, at the present day. Such a novel is under bonds to be an epic of individualism, for democracy, if it means anything, means *la carrier ouverte aux talens*, means the fullest opportunity for the development of the individual."[33] These notions of the ideal author as a comprehensive intelligence and the individual character as representative of national types can be found in the literary nationalism that surrounded novelists in other countries—Charles Dickens, Victor Hugo, and Alexandre Dumas, for instance. But the exaggeration is worth noting. American responses to novels were formed against a backdrop of expectations about the individual that seemed extreme to the point of being unrealistic. And these expectations would shape the states of self-division in the face of literature that cool audiences would explore.

The anticipation of the great American novel might seem unrelated to the culture of sensation, but they shared an estimation of American literature. Proponents of sensationalism freely admitted that mainstream culture had little value beyond entertainment. Those seeking out the great American novel decried the current state of American writing. Although sensationalists flaunted their low expectations for literature's social worth and the discourse of the great American novel had the highest hopes, both agreed that American culture had not yet achieved much world-historical importance. As Buell suggests, noting that the national communities most infatuated with the "Great Novel" in the nineteenth century were the United States and Australia, the concept was very much a postcolonial dream, an artifact of the "cultural legitimation anxiety" felt in England's satellite states.[34] Ideas about literary greatness and its absence, in other words, were intricately bound up with perceptions of Americanness.

YANKEE PERSPECTIVES: FROM CUTE TO COOL

The contradictory mix of cultural insecurity and hyperbolic confidence that shaped discussions of sensation and literary greatness in the United States also informed ideas about the not-so-great. In American comedy, the embodiment of these mixed feelings was the bumbling Yankee, at once ridiculous and remarkably capable of getting his way. The so-called cute Yankee appeared throughout early and mid-nineteenth-century print culture, often in short newspaper articles meant as comic relief. Essentially cheats, cute Yankees were odd folk heroes. They stole whiskey, sold phony goods, and forged wills in their favor. Some versions of the character were also extraordinarily dense: one 1846 cute Yankee story from a Connecticut newspaper, for instance, described a man who refused to hand over his ticket for a boat ride, thinking that the boat operator was trying to steal it: "the old fellow being a regular and cute Yankee, was not easily gulled," the story concluded.[35]

Why the culture-wide celebration of the stupid and the unethical? An article in the *Knickerbocker* magazine asked that very question in 1845. Entitled "The Morality of 'Cuteness,'" the piece interrogated the "open or thinly-disguised approbation" that had come to surround the cute Yankee in the popular imagination. Why, it asked, do we insist on applauding petty swindlers in the ostensible "land of steady habits?"[36] In the place of an answer, the article related its own cute Yankee tale, in which a would-be con man gets conned himself. I would argue that the question is more answerable than this piece suggests. What makes the cute Yankee so puzzling is that he reflects the allure of low expectations. Hardly a romanticized outlaw, the selfish, wily, and often dense Yankee embodied the idea that America didn't need to create great individuals to be a great nation. What is being romanticized here is not antiauthoritarianism or even self-fashioning, but something more like being exempt from the imperative to be a well-formed person. As one article on an especially brazen "cute Yankee quack" selling fake medicine in England put it, "such assurance is almost sublime."[37] There is something nearly awe-inspiring about lacking greatness and getting away with it.

Laughing at a national inclination for slippery ethics is ugly business at any time, but, as Walt Whitman noted, it was a particularly awful affectation in the era of slavery. Outraged at Boston's compliance in returning escaped slave Anthony Burns to Virginia in 1854, Whitman responded with "A

Boston Ballad," which concluded with a strong rejection of Yankee morality: "Stick your hands in your pockets, Jonathan—you are a made man from this day; / You are mighty cute—and here is one of your bargains." The poem takes issue not only with Boston's guilt in upholding the system of slavery but also with the common equation of American cuteness with immorality small-time enough to be a joke. But Whitman was one of few who objected to the term's significance. The postwar stage traditions of *Uncle Tom's Cabin*, for example, attest to its ongoing approbation in American popular culture. From the Civil War period onward, it became standard practice for touring companies to add a cute Yankee character to the story, as if no American best seller could be without this "typical" American figure. As chapter 1 discusses, the conspicuously shady cute Yankee helped give concrete form to ideas about the novel's own supposedly questionable quality.

The tradition of cuteness in *Uncle Tom's Cabin* offers a glimpse into the subtle shift in which the cute Yankee of the nineteenth century became the cool Yankee of the early twentieth. *Cute* and *cool* shared a sense of low expectations, but *cool* would shift the focus away from self-interested calculation to the self-presentation of style. Writing in 1902 about one of the most well-known Yankee characters from the postbellum *Uncle Tom's Cabin* plays, theater critic Henry Austin Clapp remembered him as a "cool, shrewd Yankee," "interpolated chiefly for purposes of farcical mirth."[38] *Cool* does not appear anywhere in the play Clapp is discussing, Henry Conway's 1852 adaptation. The script instead refers to the Yankee as "cute and calculatin'." Clapp's reference was part of a slight semantic shift that illustrates a broader change in the way this American stock character was seen as representative.

Cool entered the popular vocabulary as a sign of resistance to outward pressure. The children's literature of the late nineteenth century is filled with cool Yankee stagecoach drivers and gunners, figures that meet danger with preparedness and skill.[39] By the turn of the century, though, the term had become the go-to word for the mix of misunderstanding and selfishness that cute had represented earlier. The shift was significant. Where cuteness had everything to do with what you could steal from others, coolness was more about styles of asserting what others couldn't take from you. A cool servant might respond to a request for breakfast by saying no thanks, "I ain't very hungry this mornin'." A couple eloping in plain sight of their parents were married in a "cool way."[40] These varieties of coolness were not explicitly connected to the culture of novel reading, but I would suggest that a lot of the chatter surrounding best-selling fiction can be understood as attempts to perform what reading in a "cool way" might look like. Indeed, the stubborn resistance to one's environment that coolness named was ideally suited to a culture in which greatness had not yet arrived. Playing up forms of detachment and partial participation represented a kind of safe bet, a willingness to believe that the most widely read books could convey hugely significant meaning, without giving them too much credit. In a context of deep cultural insecurity, popular reading promoted the idea that it was American to be cool.

BEFORE "GENRE"

Today we have a term for novels not expected to be great: *genre fiction*. The ongoing discussions of the value of genre fiction—and, indeed, what constitutes a genre novel in the first place—have highlighted the huge amount of social significance that takes place beyond the pale of elite, high art, and literary fiction: Janice Radway's claims for the romance novels as "a form of individual resistance" to isolation and "emotional depletion," for instance; or Fredric Jameson's reading of contemporary sci-fi as a vivid repository of utopian feeling.[41] Some critics argue that we have not fully grasped the merit of certain genre writers, such as Agatha Christie, Philip K. Dick, and Stephen King. Others ask about the meaning of blurred boundaries (Why are more and more grownups reading young adult fiction?). But our basic understanding of genre novels remains relatively straightforward. Genre fiction does not have to be great to be successful; instead, it needs to meet the somewhat predictable expectations of one subsection of the reading public.

The acts of reading that the following chapters explore predate the fragmentation of audiences into consumers of genre. As many cultural historians have argued, this meant that categories of "high" and "low" were not well articulated for most of the nineteenth century. Scholarship on the rise of realism and the emergence of the art novel has shown how high hopes about fiction gained increasing clarity and influence as the century progressed. But it is important to note that the low expectations that would become solidified in part through concepts of genre fiction were equally unclear in the era of *Uncle Tom's Cabin*, Dickens's massively popular novels, *Ben-Hur*, and *Trilby*. We might understand sensationalism as the first major genre fiction category, an attempt to name a form that was less than literary because it aspired to no purpose beyond catering to predictable appetites. But the blockbusters that *Guilty Pleasures* discusses weren't perceived as sensation novels. Ambivalence about them did not boil down to uncertainty about what a subset of American readers enjoyed but uncertainty about what nearly *everyone* seemed to like.

In other words, although I am discussing a kind of fiction that was in some ways poised in between the pandering of sensationalism and the lofty flight of the great American novel, these works functioned in a far different way than the middlebrow culture that would emerge in the twentieth century. As both Radway and Amy Blair have argued, the twentieth-century middlebrow was primarily a site of aspiration: the many readers who enrolled in the Book of the Month Club or bought mass-marketed guides to literature seem to have been looking for ways to better themselves, to become more knowledgeable, more cultured, or more socially mobile.[42] It was crucial to formations of the middlebrow that they were seen as widely available and accessible, but middlebrow consumers were seeking out texts more intellectually or aesthetically relevant than the common ground of mass culture. Nineteenth-century popular reading reflected a different type of entryway: not a door to a more intelligent future but a window into a highly questionable American common ground.

This meant that both the majestic auras and the low expectations that shaped popular literary culture easily slid into conceptions of national community. And even if Benjamin's ideas about the nineteenth century as a crucial stage in a communal awakening from a shared nightmare seem a bit far-fetched, it's clear that this loosely connected improvisational space informed by majesty, approachability, weakened modes of authority, and national ideals offered innovative ways to question the status quo. Perhaps, in any period, there is no place like mainstream consumption for challenging the assumptions that govern mainstream narratives. And, if we understand art with mass appeal as a site of compromise in which, as Fredric Jameson puts it, ideological content always shares space with a utopian dimension, it makes sense that popular response has the potential to elaborate on the relationship between normativity and an ideal communal life. Understood this way, the dialogues considered here can be read as a kind of ongoing negotiation, channeling discontent with the compromises made to appeal to mass audiences.

Again, though, I want to keep open the possibility that the sensibility I am describing here is a special American product from the Benjaminian century. At one point in *The Arcades Project*, Benjamin cites a passage from Karl Marx's *Eighteenth Brumaire* which claims that the "feverish, youthful movement" of commerce and production in America "has left neither time nor opportunity for abolishing the old spirit world." Benjamin then writes, a bit cryptically, "It is remarkable that Marx invokes the world of spirits to help explain the American republic."[43] This was the kind of juxtaposition between the most modern, individualistic, and commercial cultural activity and vaguely arcane spiritualism on which Benjamin based his analysis of modern life. And it reflects a confusion of awe and disdain for American progress shared by many besides Marx in the nineteenth century. The sphere of popular reading and its avenues of response were ideally suited for engaging this confusion.

CHAPTER 1

Uncle Tom's Cabin and the Unprivileged Public Sphere

In one of the most frequently cited recollections of *Uncle Tom's Cabin*, Henry James describes Stowe's novel as a kind of omnipresence in 1850s New York. As he remembers, the story seemed "much less a book than a state of vision, feeling, and of consciousness," a field in which "we lived and moved." Much of what James writes about *Uncle Tom's Cabin* anticipates twentieth-century critiques of mass culture as mind control. New Yorkers didn't "read and appraise" the novel, he claims, but instead "walked and talked and laughed, and cried . . . in a manner of which Mrs. Stowe was the irresistible cause." The more James remembers about *Uncle Tom's Cabin*, however, the less authoritative Stowe's text seems to have been. He goes on to suggest that the "amount of life" in the novel might be measured by the degree to which it is "taken up and carried further, carried even violently furthest" by its audience. Theater crowds flock to the show "in order *not* to be beguiled."[1] James's memory bears out an irony of mass circulation: the greater a narrative's appeal, the more appealing it is to be seen avoiding its pull.

This chapter explores the long tradition of ambivalent reaction to *Uncle Tom's Cabin*, showing how the cultural life of Stowe's text and its countless spin-offs helped define a sensibility of detachment. Charged with racial politics and ethical urgency in ways that distinguish it from later best sellers, *Uncle Tom's Cabin* nonetheless set the stage for novel reception to come. Seeing this requires keeping in mind how many things *Uncle Tom's Cabin* did at once: rallying support for abolition, drawing fire from proslavery voices, showcasing a truly national cultural reach, and promoting ideals of whiteness and womanhood that would stay prevalent long after the Civil War. The many-layered response to *Uncle Tom's Cabin* reflected this unique complexity. But it also registered how Stowe's text laid bare a contradiction shared by many other Victorian narratives. Making huge claims for a novel's power to change the social world and circulating as widely as it did, *Uncle Tom's Cabin* came to signify the tension between grand ideals and humble formats that shaped the meaning of popular reading throughout the nineteenth century.

This tension between form and format inspired responses to *Uncle Tom's Cabin* that didn't align with the extremes of praise and blame which surrounded the novel then and continue to surround it today. We now have a broad body of scholarship on the proslavery reaction, including the subgenre of "anti-Tom" literature that attempted to counter Stowe's abolitionist message. On the other side, there is plenty of evidence that *Uncle Tom's Cabin* deeply moved and convinced a wide range of readers, as cultural historians who praise the novel's relatively bold antislavery and feminist ethics often point out. Other twentieth-century critics have suggested new ways of thinking about *Uncle Tom's Cabin* as a pernicious text—most notably James Baldwin, who argued that Stowe's narrative sidesteps realism in favor of racist caricature and white self-congratulation, and Ann Douglas, who took *Uncle Tom's Cabin* to task for embodying consumer culture's celebration of superficial feeling.[2] The long social life of *Uncle Tom's Cabin* has been defined, in part, by very strong and very contentious judgments.

But just as much of the response surrounding *Uncle Tom's Cabin* was spoken in weaker terms, as ambivalent readers reacted with a vocabulary of uncertainty. These readers peppered criticism of *Uncle Tom's Cabin* with phrases like "despite its flaws," "though comeliness of form was lacking," and "artistic—if the word can stand the strain." The critique articulated by these hesitant voices was not a rejection of Stowe's text but a questioning of what it meant that valuable moral sentiment seemed to travel most widely in an artistically dubious novel, and later in its outlandish stage adaptations. This question became especially pressing in the postwar decades, as its stage versions became increasingly absurd—a fact emphasized over and over by its many parodies. While Stowe's writing struck some as lacking in proper authorial control, the explosion of stage versions literally demonstrated what it looks like when a popular story takes on a life of its own in the United States. Those observing this explosion voiced a wide-ranging critique of the intertwined ideals of American progress and the elevation of individual feeling.

This chapter does not present an overview of *Uncle Tom's Cabin*'s transformation from a trenchant serial novel in 1851's *National Era* to a massive, diffuse phenomenon of spin-offs, merchandising, and, above all, repetition by the end of the century. This story has been told thoroughly by Harry Birdoff, Jane Tompkins, Sarah Meer, Eric Lott, Barbara Hochman, Lauren Berlant, and David Reynolds. Neither does it recount the shifts in technological production and mass literacy that, as Trish Loughran and Claire Parfait have detailed, paved the way for *Uncle Tom's Cabin*'s unprecedented popularity. Instead, the following focuses on a sensibility that scholarship on Stowe's novel has tended to overlook by reading across three sites that expressed uncertainties about *Uncle Tom's Cabin* "mania:" early newspaper and magazine criticism; *Agnes of Sorrento* (1862), a novel Stowe wrote after witnessing nearly a decade of mixed reaction to *Uncle Tom's Cabin;* and postbellum parodies of the novel's many stage adaptations, from the pages of the humor magazine *Puck* to Langston Hughes's defiant "Colonel Tom's Cabin." In very different ways, these sources express the feeling that *Uncle Tom's Cabin*'s extreme faith in privileged individuals does little to represent the truth about the American populace.

At the center of these reactions to *Uncle Tom's Cabin* was little Eva, Stowe's iconic image of the white redeemer. Countless racist renditions of *Uncle Tom's Cabin* would turn the novel's black characters into minstrel caricatures, implying in the process that African Americans were less worthy of sympathy than Stowe had proclaimed. The long tradition of revising Eva contested Stowe's faith in the power of sympathy itself. Since Eva was the moral center of *Uncle Tom's Cabin*, rethinking her character became a way of engaging with questions not only about racial equality but also about the potential of sentimental ethics more broadly conceived. Writing at the end of a long stage career, Cordelia Howard, one of the first actresses to play Eva on stage, lamented that *Uncle Tom's Cabin* had become "the butt of all the critics' ridicule," losing the "grandeur" that it once conveyed.[3] The loss of grandeur to which Howard refers can certainly be seen in the trajectory of the character she helped make famous, who is so often singled out for mockery and violent parody. But the many attempts to ridicule little Eva attest to the difficulty critics and everyday readers alike had in writing her off entirely.

Recalling the popular uncertainty about *Uncle Tom's Cabin* foregrounds three points about cool readership to which the following chapters will return. First, the attitude cut across erudite criticism and more popular discourses of humor: one would have been as likely to encounter ambivalence about *Uncle Tom's Cabin* in a Henry James essay as in a stridently lowbrow comic magazine. Second, the response to Stowe's novel portrayed uncertainty about national community as a typically American point of view. And third, cool reading turned an especially skeptical eye on the privileging of individual subjects, an attribute that placed it at odds with the individualism so central to Victorian novels themselves. Helping to imagine an American community unattached to the graciousness of any privileged individual perspective, the reaction to *Uncle Tom's Cabin* laid the groundwork for a kind of critical consciousness that would appear again and again as audiences engaged with the period's best-selling fiction.

Following Eva's changing fate over the nineteenth century offers insight into the ways cool audiences pushed the novel's exploration of race and redemption toward reflection on consumption and community. And this shift makes sense when we consider the special relationship that *Uncle Tom's Cabin* seemed to have with the emerging consumerist culture that surrounded and included it. It might be a bit extreme to say, as Ann Douglas does, that Eva's saccharine goodness anticipated the shallow self-congratulation that would characterize so much twentieth-century mass culture. But it is certainly true that Stowe's faith in easily accessible fiction as a catalyst for social change helped *Uncle Tom's Cabin* reflect a rosy view of the mass marketplace. Ultimately, the reassessment of Eva as an exemplary individual was hard to distinguish from the critique of the popular novel as an exemplary market object. In Lauren Berlant's words, *Uncle Tom's Cabin* was a "beacon" within commercial culture, a symbol of "the power of a commodity to shock its consumers into a contemporary crisis of knowledge and national power."[4] Stowe's novel was about the corruption of a democracy that allowed slavery to exist, but it would come to represent a different subject as well: the potentially transformative force of a consumer-driven mass culture.

In the postwar decades, audiences reversed the terms. Particularly as it became common to note how the theater industry had distorted *Uncle Tom's Cabin*, the text came to signify not the commodity's power to transform the social world but consumers' power to turn political momentum into the inertia of entertainment. Somewhat ironically, just when *Uncle Tom's Cabin* could seem to have directly changed the nation—calling for the end of slavery that did, in fact, take place—as a long-running cultural presence, the story became a symbol of a disappointing status quo. It was in the context of this shift that the revision of Stowe's imagery of redemption took on its most critical edge. The clearer it became that *Uncle Tom's Cabin* was played out, the less audiences could take its faith in the power of sympathetic individuals at face value.

The uncertainties about *Uncle Tom's Cabin* this chapter discusses were not voiced by harsh critics as much as by readers unable to accept its sentimental ethics without reservation. One of the first and most conflicted of these voices was Stowe herself, who explored her rising doubts about sentimental heroines in a text not often considered alongside *Uncle Tom's Cabin*: her novel, *Agnes of Sorrento*. The connection between these two texts has been obscured in part by the convoluted timing of Stowe's post–*Uncle Tom's Cabin* literary production. The nonfictional *A Key to Uncle Tom's Cabin* (1853) and the follow-up novel *Dred: A Tale of the Great Dismal Swamp* (1856) directly answer criticisms of Stowe's 1851 bestseller, *A Key* providing a range of sources confirming the plausibility of her fictional portrayal of slavery and *Dred* depicting an insurrectionary black hero in stark contrast to the nonviolent Uncle Tom. She also published a European travelogue, *Sunny Memories of Foreign Lands* (1854), reissued a collection of pre–*Uncle Tom's Cabin* short stories and poems, *The Mayflower*, in 1855 (originally published in 1843), and published a novel she had begun writing just after she finished *Uncle Tom's Cabin*, *The Pearl of Orr's Island* (1862).[5] The second novel she published in 1862, *Agnes of Sorrento*, deserves special attention, as it was the first narrative she wrote in its entirety after witnessing the surprising and contentious early years of *Uncle Tom's Cabin*'s life in American culture.

Shaped by this context, *Agnes of Sorrento* is an extended exploration of sentimentalism as an unstable and unreliable social form. Although the novel departs from the setting of American slavery that Stowe had struggled with in *Uncle Tom's Cabin*, *The Key*, and *Dred*—set instead in fourteenth-century Italy—*Agnes* presents the most complex treatment of sentimentality that her works have to offer. Notably for the purposes of this chapter, the novel approaches sentiment as a problem of reception, depicting a priest who tries to reach his sinful congregation by describing others' suffering only to find that his audience *enjoys* the imagery of pain. Portraying the appeal to mass feeling as a risky venture, *Agnes* anticipates the coolness that would come to surround *Uncle Tom's Cabin* later in the nineteenth century. The novel also shares with later critics and parodists the desire for an updated version of *Uncle Tom's Cabin*'s little Eva. *Agnes* reimagines Eva through the eponymous heroine, a figure of inspiration and redemption who stands out less for her sensitivity to others' suffering (as Eva does) and more for her compulsion to inflict pain on herself. *Agnes of Sorrento* is thus the first of many para-texts of *Uncle Tom's Cabin* that will imagine Eva withstanding extended ordeals of abuse.

I would argue that the violence surrounding Eva reflects a larger ambivalence about American mass culture that *Uncle Tom's Cabin* played a major role in making visible. Over the course of the nineteenth century, Stowe's heroine became a sign of an increasingly doubtful fantasy, as the adaptation of *Uncle Tom's Cabin*—but also the growing prominence of consumerist genres like sensationalism and spectacular theater—made it difficult if not impossible to believe that a popular commodity might change the world. Against this backdrop, responses to *Uncle Tom's Cabin* took up and questioned the redemptive promise of sentimental consumption and individuality rooted in domestic space. As Lori Merish has shown, sentimental novels did much to link ideals of femininity with the acquisition and care of commodities in the home, a crossing between literary content and market expansion that helped make a healthy love for lithographs, carpets, and furniture part of what it meant to be a "true woman."[6] The imagery of cool response tied sentimentality to consumerism in a different way, less invested in the familiarity of the home. Ambivalent readers of *Uncle Tom's Cabin* expressed the suspicion that for a commodity to "shock its consumers into a contemporary crisis," it would have to be a stranger thing than Stowe's novel.

Where Stowe had asked what the United States might look like if its citizens followed their hearts instead of their heads, the response to *Uncle Tom's Cabin* shied away from faith in individual feeling. Stowe's famous appeal to the "men and women of the North" to counter the cold calculations of politicians and clergymen with the simplicity of sympathy was a powerfully accessible political statement. But this hope only made sense by exalting the actions of individuals uncorrupted by the world around them: the peaceful resistance of Uncle Tom, for instance, or the purity of little Eva. If popular novels were allowed to set the limits of their reception, this fixation on the selves exempted from the violent pull of their surroundings would strongly support the long view—a running theme in the historiography of the novel—that the genre both reflected and enabled the ascendency of modern individualism. But no novel as popular and controversial as *Uncle Tom's Cabin* is allowed to have a meaning this fixed.

EARLY REVIEWS

In many initial reviews, *Uncle Tom's Cabin* sounds more like a gift from God than a well-written book. According to one *National Era* review, this "providential" novel "was a necessity of the age, and *had* to be written, and we are grateful to God that he put the writing of it into the hands of one who has interwoven Evangelical influences with every page of its narrative."[7] Abolitionist critics certainly had doubts. Many, for instance, questioned Stowe's support for the colonization efforts that involved sending ex-slaves to Africa and the Caribbean. But, on the whole, these politically passionate readers were lavish with their praise. "[*Uncle Tom's Cabin*] is, in its line, the wonder of wonders," *Frederick Douglass' Paper* exclaimed. "Thank God for this little space wherein one vivifying ray may enter!"[8] *Uncle Tom's Cabin* inspired strong language; the most positive takes on the novel were as hyperbolic as the most hateful.

And the hateful reviews took harsh judgment to the extreme. Proslavery responses denounced Stowe and her book from many angles at once. One eleven-page diatribe in the *Southern Literary Messenger,* for instance, countered the idea of Stowe as God's instrument with the image of Stowe as an irretrievably fallen woman. The anonymous critic compared her to a "termagant" and a "foul-mouthed hag," claiming that Stowe had lost her natural right to protection by speaking out against slavery: "If she deliberately steps beyond the hallowed precints [sic]—the enchanted circle—which encompass her as with the halo of divinity, she has wantonly forfeited her privilege of immunity as she has irretrievable [sic] lost our regard, and the harshness which she may provoke is invited by her own folly and impropriety."[9]

There were many more lukewarm voices. Not so much struggling with Stowe's politics, these strove to understand what it meant to be moved by an object while also viewing it as insufficiently made—particularly when that object seemed somehow imbued with an aura of spiritual power. From early on, this questioning took up the antithesis of thought and feeling that played such a major role in Stowe's novel itself: many critics echoed the anti-intellectualism of *Uncle Tom's Cabin* as they applauded the general impulse behind the text while also describing it as aesthetically unsound. Thus an 1852 review originally printed in Boston's *Morning Post* called *Uncle Tom's Cabin* "one of the most remarkable literary productions of the time," a work "stamped on every page by genius," while describing it as a "gross exaggeration" of slavery's evils, "unduly crowded" with tragic incidents.[10] The best way to appreciate *Uncle Tom's Cabin,* the article suggests, is to leave questions of its accuracy aside and focus instead on identifying with the general feeling it expressed.

How one felt about novelistic accuracy could determine how one understood little Eva. Being unconcerned with realistic detail helps the *Morning Post* critic celebrate Stowe's sacrificial heroine as a beautiful moral symbol. The reviewer compares Eva to Charles Dickens's figures of innocence, purity, and premature death and defends Stowe's version as an admirable—though improbable—ideal individual: "Eva, indeed, is not to be criticized. She stands with Little Nell and Little Paul—unnatural, it may be, as a child of man, but a creation of exquisite beauty, tenderness, intelligence and affection—an embodiment, in baby form, of all that is highest, holiest, and best in human nature."[11] Eva here reflects a crucial tension in *Uncle Tom's Cabin,* which depicts an imminent and complex social crisis redeemed by an innocence that is hard to view as real. As this reviewer points out, Stowe's imaginary solution to America's ongoing injustice works by exalting the individual to a degree that seems glaringly fictional.

Other reviewers accused Stowe of simply preaching to the choir. Trying to understand what they saw as *Uncle Tom's Cabin*'s undeserved popularity, these voices ascribed its success to abolitionists' demand for impassioned accounts of slavery. The "multitudinous success of Uncle Tom" amounts to "a phenomenon that nothing in the previous history of books can explain," one critic writing for New York's *Literary World* argued. The piece explained that the phenomenon took shape because of "the enthusiasm in behalf of the cause in support of which it has been written." But according to this review, Stowe worked with an unfair advantage: "This negro sympathy, moreover, is kept in a state of unnatural and unwholesome excitement by means familiar to organized agitation. This state is one of smouldering [sic] enthusiasm, a fire never allowed to go out and ready to blaze forth into a spreading flame of fanaticism upon the smallest stir or lightest breath of excitement. The appearance of Uncle Tom aroused this antislavery enthusiasm and called into play all its intense energy."[12]

Unnatural characters, *unnatural* excitement: wariness of *Uncle Tom's Cabin* reflected uneasiness about mass readership's disorderly emotions. The remarkable thing is the extent to which this uncertainty about the American public dovetailed with national pride. As the *Literary World* review continues, its tone shifts from alarm to self-satisfaction: "Thousands have read Uncle Tom, to whom we are sure Shakespeare is but a name, the outside title of a closed book, and the 'Vicar of Wakefield' an unknown thing. The popular success, proclaimed by few tens of thousands, more or less, of Dickens and Bulwer, are but whispers in the public ear, faintly heard, in comparison with the trumpet blast of the fame of Uncle Tom, blown loudly, far and wide, by the voices of the million." This print-cultural phenomenon could only happen, this critic asserts, on the cutting edge of literacy and leisure, a "land of twenty-five millions of people, with occasions for literary enjoyment beyond any other people under the sun."[13] Torn between uncertainty about the quality of Uncle Tom's Cabin and excitement about the Americanness of its popularity, reviews like this signaled the national-cultural ambivalence that would come to define the novel's long life.

As Parfait's publishing history of Uncle Tom's Cabin suggests, the book's huge social reach inspired not only pride in the assumed leisure of its readership but also wonder at the variety of formats and social settings in which the text could be seen circulating. Citing a contemporary review from the Liberator, Parfait highlights how the book seemed to be everywhere: "Let it be circulated far and wide, till it shall have penetrated 'every log-house beyond the mountains,' and been perused by every individual who can read . . . until it becomes irresistible, giving freedom to all in bonds, and peace and reconciliation to the whole land."[14] In its most sanguine reviews, Uncle Tom's Cabin was for everyone, "from the child six years old to the aged veteran whose sight is not yet wholly extinct." For this imagined audience on the fringe of literary circulation, ideals of inclusiveness and emotional harmony overshadow any considerations of taste and connoisseurship. What makes Uncle Tom's Cabin especially inspiring here is that it is a novel for those who don't typically appreciate literature.

Whatever the assessment of its literary worth at home, Uncle Tom's Cabin was unquestionably representing American culture on an international stage. But what makes the nationalist pride in the sheer demand for Stowe's novel characteristically American—and cool—is the depth to which patriotic feeling was intertwined with low opinions of the novel's quality. One Putnam's Monthly magazine review throws this tension into especially stark relief. Responding to English critic Sydney Smith's famous disdainful remark about American literature, the article suggests that US culture has arrived: "Who reads an American book, did you inquire, Mr. Smith? Why, your comfortable presence should have been preserved in the world a year or two longer, that you might have asked, as you would have done, 'who does not?'"[15] This is rhetoric of cultural arrival, but also a celebration of quantity instead of quality.

The *Putnam's* reviewer makes no claim for *Uncle Tom's Cabin*'s merit, instead attributing its success to new capacities of production and demand that the text made especially plain: "A dozen years ago, *Uncle Tom* would have been a comparative failure . . . Such a phenomenon as its present popularity could have happened only in the present wondrous age." This depended on the modern machinery of "steam-presses," "steam-ships," "iron roads," and "electric telegraphs," but "beyond all," the review concludes, "it required readers to consume books, and these have never before been so numerous."[16] Even as *Uncle Tom's Cabin* called attention to those suffering under the slave system, then, its circulation made the bustling world of consumption especially conspicuous. In large part because the controversy over slavery attracted a gigantic readership, Stowe's novel would never simply be about slavery. The politically charged narrative brought to the foreground not only the national crisis but also new abilities to cater to popular demand that were changing the face of national and transatlantic cultures.

The sense of spirit effusing the work helped early reviewers reconcile *Uncle Tom's Cabin*'s mass appeal and supposed literary deficiencies with optimism about its social value. *Literary World* could state in the same review that "Uncle Tom bids fair yet to number its millions of copies and to be immortal from quantity, not quality," but also praise the "pathetic interest that warms the heart of the reader and fills his eyes with tears." Likewise, the *Putnam's Monthly* critic so admiring of the "miraculous" consumer infrastructure that made Stowe's success possible also characterized *Uncle Tom's Cabin* as morally strong and artistically weak: "There are not . . . any of the delicacies of language which impart so great a charm to the writings of Irving and Hawthorne, nor any descriptions of scenery such as abound in the romances of Cooper, nor any thing like the bewildering sensuousness of *Typee* Melville; but there are broader, deeper, higher and holier sympathies than can be found in our other romances, finer delineations of character, a wider scope of observation, a more purely American spirit, and a more vigorous narrative faculty."

Like Ann Douglas would a century later, *Putnam's* places Stowe in a category of inferior aesthetic value relative to her male contemporaries, but the 1850s review sees crucial social significance in this sphere of lesser quality. Again, this delineation was national as well as gendered. Stowe's text not only stood out as containing "higher and holier sympathies" than novels authored by men, but also expressed something "more purely American." These early responses, then, reveal a national self-consciousness that is often missing from accounts of nineteenth-century popular reading and consumer culture alike. Rather than unquestioning acceptance, the dominant tone in *Uncle Tom's Cabin* reviews was a critical ambivalence, as quick to question Stowe's novel as a work of art as to proclaim its status as a sign of national relevance. It was precisely because the novel found such a broad readership that it was not consumed passively but rather interrogated as an object that might or might not reveal new information about the national community that devoured it.

This is a very different attitude than the escapism that Douglas would read into *Uncle Tom's Cabin* in her analysis of the novel's association with mass consumption. In *The Feminization of American Culture*, Douglas links Stowe's novel to an ethos of uncritical consumerism. And the reader she imagines for *Uncle Tom's Cabin* represents a kind of ultimate complacency: "Little Eva's most ardent admirers, the active middle-class Protestant women whose supposedly limited intelligences liberal piety was in part designed to flatter."[17] The voices of the contemporary reviews are more akin to James's detached theater crowd than to these imaginary devotees of the easily consumable cultural object. This is not to claim that racism, moral weakness, avoidance, hypocrisy, and superficiality did not play as big a role in the *Uncle Tom's Cabin* phenomenon as its harshest critics have suggested. But to understand the revisions and reimagining of Stowe's narrative that were to come, it is necessary to see how the early reviews portrayed *Uncle Tom's Cabin* as both representative and problematic: as essentially American, spiritually relevant, and undeniably flawed. For every ardent admirer of little Eva, there was a reader who viewed her critically. And while this cool reception would inspire a wide range of voices to revise, question, and build upon *Uncle Tom's Cabin*, the first major reimagining of Eva came from Stowe herself, in *Agnes of Sorrento*, her story of sentimentality and its discontents. In the strange plot of this follow-up novel, we can see Stowe taking part in the skepticism that surrounded her antislavery text as she backed away from its implied faith in both the idealized individual and the mass reading public.

FROM EVA TO AGNES

Writing to her editor Gamaliel Bailey shortly after beginning work on *Uncle Tom's Cabin*, Stowe compared her authorship to a "simple" image of painting: "My vocation is simply that of a painter, and my object will be to hold up in the most lifelike and graphic manner possible Slavery, its reverses, changes, and the negro character."[18] The idea that writers simply needed to circulate the facts of slavery in order to convince the public of its evil was by then an abolitionist commonplace. By the time Stowe began writing *Uncle Tom's Cabin* in 1851, nonfiction works by authors such as William Wells Brown, William Lloyd Garrison, Theodore Weld, and Lydia Maria Child had created a subgenre of literature that presented to the public, as Weld put it, "American slavery as it is."[19] Stowe's innovation was to translate this straightforward theory of reading—one need only learn the facts to be convinced—into idealism about fiction. Part of *Uncle Tom's Cabin*'s originality was to combine this deadly serious approach to circulation with a genre many were in the habit of taking lightly.

It is no surprise, then, that Stowe spends a good deal of time in *Uncle Tom's Cabin* depicting the truth's overwhelming power to convince. The subplot of Senator Bird presents this vividly, as a northerner willing to compromise with southern demands has a complete change of heart when brought face-to-face with a runaway mother and child. Stowe describes Senator Bird's conversion in supernatural terms: "The magic of the real presence of distress,—the imploring human eye, the frail, trembling human hand, the despairing appeal of helpless agony,—these he had never tried. He had never thought that a fugitive might be a hapless mother, a defenceless [sic] child,—like that one which was now wearing his lost boy's little well-known cap."[20] The senator's story illustrates Stowe's belief in a public sphere made morally accountable by the connection between those in power and the kinds of sympathy nurtured by life at home. Seen this way, social change becomes simply a matter of spreading the word about injustice.

At first, Stowe's hopefulness about politicians extended to her readership more generally. The epilogue of *Uncle Tom's Cabin* put this open-ended optimism in clear terms. Addressing "Christian men and women of the North," the epilogue urges these relatively privileged figures to honor their natural instincts: "There is one thing that every individual can do,—they can see to it that *they feel right*. An atmosphere of sympathetic influence encircles every human being; and the man or woman who *feels* strongly, healthily and justly, on the great interests of humanity, is a constant benefactor to the human race" (404). Stowe's ideal of social change implies a theory of fiction. By humanizing the victims of slavery for its audience, a novel like *Uncle Tom's Cabin* might bring about, or at least accelerate, redemption through collective feeling. As we will see, this ideal was so central to Stowe's narrative that it would be hard for even the most cynical revisers of *Uncle Tom's Cabin* to ignore it completely.

Ultimately, though, the idealism of *Uncle Tom's Cabin* was extremely vague; indeed, as Berlant argues, this vagueness was a tremendously significant part of sentimentality's mass appeal. Marking a space of critique and emotional solidarity that lay somewhere just outside of politics as concrete practice, sentimentality spoke to those who felt cut off from and disillusioned by the public sphere precisely by *not* engaging with the political process. Berlant calls this world in between public and private "juxtapolitical," and her discussion of its unique constellation of consumption, privilege, and suffering should be required reading for anyone interested in the ongoing politics of popular culture. As she argues, the fantasy of commodities such as sentimental novels changing the world relies largely on the sympathies of those in social positions close enough to influence those in power but far enough away to feel let down by politics as usual.[21] By this logic, the suffering of the most disadvantaged is given voice by figures that mediate between the most privileged and the least. In *Uncle Tom's Cabin,* the central image of this mediating function is little Eva, who at once feels the pain of Tom, Topsy, and their fellow slaves and exposes it to her slave-owning parents.

The popular reaction to *Uncle Tom's Cabin* would take issue with the way Eva represents this relatively privileged position as especially undeniable. Where a morally sound character like Senator Bird can be convinced of slavery's evil by the "real presence" of suffering, the most hardened figures in the novel need Eva. Her powers of persuasion inspire her father, southern apologist Augustine St. Clare, to pledge the freedom of his slaves (though too late to save Tom, Eliza, and Harry from being sold). Eva's kindness to Topsy offers Miss Ophelia a model of affectionate care that transforms the relationship between the flinty New Englander and the orphaned ex-slave. After her death, Eva's influence even extends to the most unredeemable character in the novel, the slave-driver Simon Legree. Her impact parallels within the narrative Stowe's overarching approach to fiction itself, which she presents as a force of moral truth that will render it impossible to remain on the fence about slavery.

Legree's moment of conscience once again figures moral persuasion as a kind of magic, when one of the many locks of hair that Eva had distributed on her deathbed appears to come to life. "There dropped . . . a long shining curl of fair hair—hair which, like a living thing, twined itself round Legree's fingers. 'Damnation!' he screamed, in sudden passion, stamping on the floor, and pulling furiously at the hair, as if it burned him" (338). Stowe explains that this encounter causes Legree to feel a fleeting pang of remorse about his "hard" heart, reminding him of the mother's love that had been the sole nurturing presence in his otherwise brutal life. Piecing together a loose network of women's influence placing pressure on the slavery system, this scene presents the kind of juxtapolitics that Berlant sees as crucial to sentimentality. I would argue that it also reflects the broader faith in the novel-as-commodity that defined Stowe's abolitionist text. It is a short leap from the image of this lock of hair—an object that extends Eva's influence as it circulates—to the fantasy of a book radiating moral persuasion far from its origin in a feminized, domestic space.

In other words, *Uncle Tom's Cabin* expressed a remarkable amount of trust in its white readers and the market for fiction. And while many did respond to Stowe's novel just as she had hoped, with outrage and renewed antislavery conviction, many did not. As *Agnes of Sorrento* begins to suggest, the figure of little Eva took on special significance as a symbol of this gap between ideal and real. Precisely because Eva represented such high hopes about privileged observers, distortions and revisions of the character channeled discomfort with this idealization of individuals next to those in power. Alongside and often intertwined with the misogyny and casual racism that contemporary critiques of *Uncle Tom's Cabin* entailed, then, cool reactions struggled to express a different feeling: the desire to question the social role of privileged perspectives. This sensibility was less invested in imagining white sympathy than in seeing privileged characters brought down to earth by feeling pains of their own.

Agnes tells the story of its eponymous heroine, a poor and virtuous girl who starts out selling oranges in the Sorrento marketplace and ends up as a figure of religious inspiration in a world where corruption has tainted the official Catholic church. Like *Uncle Tom's Cabin*, *Agnes* has a lot to say about the sanctity of domestic space over and against public life and religious institutions: a good deal of the plot involves a double correction in which Agnes's piety convinces a jaded nobleman, Augustino Sarelli, not to turn his back on the church, while Sarelli in turn persuades Agnes to marry him instead of joining a convent as she had planned. It is hard to miss the parallel between Eva and Agnes, both young, guileless girls able to correct the hearts of those in power. But the context of Catholic Italy allows Stowe to develop this role in a manner more attuned to the possibility that sentimentality might miss its mark.

In the world of *Agnes*, sentimentality's simple message of sympathy for others is extremely hard to get across, a fact made clear by the subplot of Agnes's priest, Padre Francesco. A "reformed libertine," Francesco is obsessed with reforming his congregants in turn. And his failure is nowhere more obvious than when he attempts to convert the sinful crowd using imagery of others in pain. This fire and brimstone approach falls short because the audience reflects a mix of sadism and personal weakness: "[Francesco] had been shocked and discouraged to find how utterly vain had been his most intense efforts to stem the course of sin by presenting . . . images of terror: how hard natures had listened to them with only a coarse and carnal appetite, which seemed to increase their hardness and brutality; and how timid ones had been withered by them."[22] The priest's frustration could just as easily belong to the author of *Uncle Tom's Cabin*, disturbed by her mass audience's capacity for coldness.

After all, although Stowe tried to ignore the outpouring of harsh criticism her novel received, it was impossible to avoid it entirely. "It is a melancholy but unavoidable result of such great encounters of principle," she wrote in 1854, "that they tend to degenerate into sectional and personal bitterness."[23] There were many examples of "personal bitterness": William Gilmore Simms's claim that Stowe hid a cloven foot beneath her petticoat, for instance, or the mocking of her authorship in early parodies like the stage show "Uncle Tom's Cabin as It Is," or G. M. Flanders's proslavery narrative *The Ebony Idol* (1860). As Stowe commented amidst the backlash, "When 'Uncle Tom' came out first there was such a universal praising of it that I began to think 'Woe unto you when all men speak well of you.' I have been quite relieved of my fears on that score; if there is any blessing in all manner of evil said falsely against one I am likely to have it."[24]

Agnes gives its audience far less credit than *Uncle Tom's Cabin* had. And this imaginative distance shapes the very different emotional worlds of the narratives' two redeemer-heroines. Where Eva's impact on others relies on the absolute simplicity with which she views the suffering around her, Agnes is a figure of intense and troubling self-division. Indecisive about whether to pursue her love interest or her faith, she also stands out for her desire to cause herself physical injury. Agnes's self-mutilation begins after she confesses her feelings for Sarelli to Padre Francesco, who blames the girl's sinful nature for leading her away from the church. "From that day," Stowe explains, "Agnes wore upon her heart one of those sharp instruments of torture which in those times were supposed to be a means of inward grace,—a cross with seven steel points for the seven sorrows of mercy" (279).

This exterior sign of inner conflict allows Agnes to reach the "popular heart" of the multitude (102). She succeeds where Francesco fails precisely because she represents a less coherent subject—a torn individual. The story ends with several chapters describing a pilgrimage to Rome on which Agnes becomes a kind of popular religious figure. Along the way, an encounter with a notoriously fallen woman suggests the importance of her penance to her appeal with the people. When the woman, Giulietta, sees the instrument of torture that Agnes wears, she exclaims in disbelief, "Oh, Agnes, what *are* you doing to yourself?" But Giulietta is inwardly moved: "In her heart, Giulietta had somewhat of secret reverence for such austerities," Stowe writes, explaining that "people who live in the senses more than in the world of reflection feel the force of such outward appeals" (341–42).

Popular reception becomes an increasingly prominent theme as Agnes makes her way to the urban crowds of Rome. On the outskirts of the city, she impresses a group of morally questionable onlookers with her appearance of devotion. But this is no Eva-esque conversion scene; the audience has too few redemptive qualities: "The fact that any or all of the actors might before night rob or stab or lie quite as freely as if had not occurred," might, she admits, justify doubts about the value of this brief moment of connection, but "for our own part, we hold it better to have even transient upliftings . . . than never to have any at all" (358). As this crowd scene suggests, *Agnes* and *Uncle Tom's Cabin* are separated not only by different settings but also by a shifting sensibility. No longer grounded with the faith in popular audience that defined *Uncle Tom's Cabin*, *Agnes* inquires into how sentimentality might be adapted to address a more resistant mass. In moving from Eva to Agnes, Stowe explores an alternate model of moral persuasion, one that is notably loosened from the ideals of domestic purity and self-coherence.

Although Stowe sets *Agnes* further away from the contemporary American scene than any novel she would write before or after, it takes up questions of audience response that were becoming more and more relevant in the mass cultural marketplace. The final major scene offers an especially vivid example, as Agnes becomes the ultimate ambivalent reader of Rome's morally suspect public culture. Attending a crowded Palm Sunday procession—a "pantomime of shifting scenic effects" and "strange variety"—Agnes at first feels uneasy about the sensuality of the religious gathering, which Stowe refers to as the "satire of the contrast" between the "worldly pomp and splendor" and the suffering of Christ it commemorates. It seems to threaten Agnes's self-composure, "as if earth had been ransacked and human invention taxed to express the ultimatum of all that could dazzle and bewilder" (382–83). It is not hard to imagine Eva recoiling from this scene of urban hedonism; Agnes, on the other hand, meets the spectacle at least partially on its own terms.

Watching the street parade, Agnes "seemed to burn and brighten like an altar coal, her figure appeared to dilate, her eyes grew deeper and shone with a starry light, and the color of her cheeks flushed up with a vivid glow,—nor was she aware how often eyes were turned upon her, nor how murmurs of admiration followed all her absorbed, unconscious movements" (385). This scene echoes the logic of Agnes's rapport with Giulietta and the small gathering outside of Rome, which depends on Agnes's ability to represent two contradictory attitudes at once. On the one hand, she seems to reflect a distance from the ordinary that is awe-inspiring; on the other hand, she seems to be more deeply entangled than any other character in the sensuality that shapes common experience. If the former marks Agnes's similarity to Eva, the latter signifies her affinity with her disappointing audience. In this world apart from *Uncle Tom's Cabin,* feelings are just as powerful but far less reliable. *Agnes* explores an emotional world it would be a mistake to invest in too completely.

In offering *Agnes* as a revision and a kind of worldly penance for the angelic little Eva, Stowe is not far off from the more raucous and exuberant responses to *Uncle Tom's Cabin* that began almost immediately after her book was published. As Stowe's narrative circulated through a skeptical public, uncertainty about its idealism became a central aspect of the novel's cultural life. It is an irony of *Uncle Tom's Cabin* that its post-emancipation revisions—that is, the novel's presence after its political goal had ostensibly been accomplished—only highlighted the disparity between its faith in the white public and the reality of American mass audiences. This distance was visible to the many critics and parodists who (like Stowe) observed the movement of her best seller through the 1850s public sphere. Expanding on the ambivalence of the early reviews, cool response to *Uncle Tom's Cabin* after the Civil War zeroed in on the phenomenon as both archetypically American and flimsily produced. And in ways that revisit the thematic concerns of *Agnes of Sorrento,* this cool response paid special attention to the idealization of little Eva.

POSTBELLUM EVAS

By the turn of the twentieth century, it was common to view *Uncle Tom's Cabin* as a narrative compromised by a long tradition of shoddy performances. As Cordelia Howard recalled, dramatizations of Stowe's novel started out with dignity but soon became more burlesque than respectable theater. Under copyright law that gave authors no control of theatrical reproduction, no mode of response shaped the impact of *Uncle Tom's Cabin* more than its reverberations on stage. Stowe had seen this writing on the wall. When asked to write an Uncle Tom play in the 1850s, "she rejected the idea as 'wholly impracticable' and 'dangerous,' saying that even a thoroughly moral play would 'make the public hungry for less exalted fare, and soon there would be five bad plays to one good.'"[25] After years of adding minstrel performances, live animals, and special effects to Stowe's narrative, the ubiquity of touring companies that played *Uncle Tom's Cabin*—known as "Tommers"—became a running joke.

Much of this humor pointed out the gap between Stowe's sentimental vision and the reality of daily life. A 1907 cartoon from *Puck* magazine, for example, imagines an alternate social world in a Tommer Christmas party. Uncle Tom has a drink with Simon Legree, Topsy shoots craps with Marie St. Clare, Eliza feeds the bloodhounds that will chase her across the frozen Ohio River: this "behind the curtain" image shows diverse figures bonding over the carnal appetites they share. And the greediest is Eva, who in this one moment is smoking, drinking, and carousing with a fellow actor. The set piece just behind her, depicting the scene in which she ascends to heaven, underlines the distance from Stowe's fictional world.

Awareness that *Uncle Tom's Cabin* was stretched thin cut against the lofty rhetoric that often accompanied the novel after emancipation. Stowe would famously claim in her preface to the 1878 edition that "God wrote" *Uncle Tom's Cabin,* and this sense of the novel's divine origins was, at times, reinforced by the belief in its supposed political efficacy. The anecdote that Abraham Lincoln greeted Stowe as the "little woman who wrote the book that started this Great War" appears to be apocryphal, but its wide circulation as truth suggests the extent to which *Uncle Tom's Cabin* could be seen as a novel that worked. The outpouring of high praise that *Uncle Tom's Cabin* received on the occasion of Stowe's death in 1896 illustrates the extent to which reverent views of the novel stayed current. *Uncle Tom's Cabin* was given a place of honor that same year at the World's Columbian Exposition in Chicago, an event accompanied by effusive memorials from journalists, critics, and African American dignitaries like Frederick Douglass.[26]

This meant not only that irreverence about the story stood out; more significantly, it meant that attitudes toward *Uncle Tom's Cabin* came to be defined by a conspicuous ambivalence. The *New York Times* critic who wrote in 1901 that "Little Eva has been a joke so many years" couldn't ignore the fact that readers continued to revere the spiritual "power" of Stowe's novel half a century after its initial publication.[27] Uncertainties about the phenomenon opened up more space for cool response. One remarkable 1878 piece, again in the *New York Times,* offers an example. The short, sarcastic article presents a rare glimpse into the casting of African American performers for a lavish production of *Uncle Tom's Cabin.* The casting call, held in a curiosity shop at Twenty-second Street and Broadway, was for a particularly outlandish production put on by Jarrett and Palmer, the impresarios who had made themselves synonymous with over-the-top spectacle in the late 1860s by producing *The Black Crook*. The article begins by mocking the newspaper advertisement that announced the auditions. With "excellence of composition and smoothness of flow," it reports, the ad proclaims "the approaching reproduction by Jarrett & Palmer of the unique, ornate, magnificent, and triumphant work of genius, 'Uncle Tom's Cabin,' the colossus of the stage, and the wonder of the nineteenth century."[28]

The anonymous *Times* reporter neither shares this exaggerated enthusiasm nor expects his readers to. To him, *Uncle Tom's Cabin* seems untimely

"Between Performances. The Uncle Tommers' Christmas Dinner on the Road." *Puck* magazine, December 4, 1907. (Courtesy of the Library of Congress)

and worn out: "poor old Uncle Tom doesn't get much of a chance to rest in his grave," the article observes, "even though all the Uncle Toms have gone out of the Eva and St. Clare business and joined the Freedmen's Bureau." The wry article picks up on the wariness of the singers and actors as well. One African American man approaches cautiously, looking "suspiciously" up and down Broadway, and quickly rushes in the door only after "seeing none of his friends in sight." Another, described as "smarter than the rest," remarks under his breath as he exits that "this would be the fourth time 'the most magnificent spectacle ever produced in New York' had been brought out this month." The hollowness of Jarrett and Palmer's grandiose claims seems clearly evident to the embarrassed actors and the curious journalist alike, who make sure to show their emotional distance from the play.

The theatrical conventions that attached themselves to *Uncle Tom's Cabin* helped make this attitude the norm. Massive casts, minstrel numbers, live animals, and the doubling of characters (having two actors play a single role simultaneously—an innovation that seems to have been developed as an attraction for Tom shows) turned what might have been a somber play into a many-layered spectacle. By the 1880s, no Tom show could survive without promising stagecraft that resembled a circus. As one typical poster advertised, the play would feature gimmicks like "2 Famous Topsys, 2 Marks, the Lawyer, 2 Educated Donkeys, Jack and Jill. 6 Mammoth Trained Siberian Bloodhounds." Another 1880s Tommer ad made the link between its performance and Barnumesque showmanship even more explicit: "The most Colossal Production Ever Made of This All American Drama. The Barnum of them all!"[29] Just as Stowe had feared, the widespread retelling of her narrative on stage turned eagerly and unapologetically away from moral gravity toward light entertainment.

The shift resonated through the dramatizations' content as well as their stagecraft, most noticeably in the cool Yankee characters added to Stowe's narrative by its first major adapters, George Aiken and H. J. Conway, and embellished throughout the later nineteenth century. As Eric Lott points out, early on these two competing versions reflected the tension between anti-southern feeling in the North and hopes for sectional compromise, the abolitionist press embracing Aiken's (which stuck more closely to Stowe's novel) and voices of compromise tending to favor Conway's (when P. T. Barnum brought it to his American Museum, he promised the play did "nothing extenuate nor set down aught in malice").[30] Indeed, Lott sees the

Yankee additions to the Aiken and Conway versions—Aiken's Gumption Cute and Conway's Penetrate Partyside—as compromising figures themselves, watering down Stowe's "intrusive and pointedly abrasive" voice in the name of complacency about slavery. The Partyside of Conway's text offers particularly compelling evidence for this reading by playing both sides. A northern character visiting the South to gather evidence for a book on social customs, he is a vocal opponent of slavery, but he also spends a good deal of the play making racist jokes.

While the effort at comic relief embodied in Partyside and Cute certainly took on significant sectional meaning in the 1850s, it also served a different purpose in the broader life of *Uncle Tom's Cabin*. Linking imagery of typical Americanness with both the ridiculous and the disappointing, these new characters echoed the idea that in order to represent the American mass, it helps to be a deeply questionable individual. Both Cute and Partyside are nothing if not pathetic: Cute has failed as a teacher, spiritualist, and plantation overseer and in the play ends up failing to woo Ophelia and then undertaking a scheme to raise money by posing as a war veteran. Partyside similarly loses much to speculation and punctuates his antislavery arguments by reaching for a drink and exclaiming, "Let's liquor!" As Cute's name suggests, both figures were meant to be stock American characters. In Aiken's play, Ophelia scorns Cute as a cute Yankee. In the Conway version, Partyside refers to his home state of Connecticut as having a "cute and calculatin' population."

If the cute characters lack acuteness, they do have a kind of bumbling goodness. A tableau in Aiken's play depicts Cute standing over Simon Legree after a series of happenstances lead him to knock the slave driver down. Addressing the audience at the conclusion of Conway's version, in which Uncle Tom lives and is given a plot of land for himself and his family, Partyside has the final word: "Why then [our] best wishes will attend our Uncle Tom to his cabin, and their hopes that his life may be happy though it be life among the lowly." While these additions to Stowe's text cater to a popular demand for comic relief, they also put a different spin on her moralism. Unlike Eva, these forces of good are distinguished by no special purity of feeling or intention. They represent a cultural cohesion and moral value that does not rely on social distinction. Aiken demonstrates this vividly in an exchange between Cute and Topsy, the wild, uneducated orphan who reflects the absolute lack of social standing in Stowe's novel. When Cute proposes putting her on display like "Barnum" did the "wooly horse," Topsy highlights his low status by swatting him away with a broom.

The reference to Barnum suggests that Cute is a creature of the popular style the showman represented, the humbug of thinly veiled appeals to the public's ability to spot a hoax. American audiences had been rolling their eyes at Barnum for years, but the distance between being skeptical about his fake natural wonders and having doubts about *Uncle Tom's Cabin* is significant. Where Barnum appealed to a broad appetite for knowledge and novelty, Stowe had proposed to change the world. As Lott claims, "*Uncle Tom's Cabin* was revolutionary in its effortless and near-immediate replication everywhere; rousing for its politics but apprehended as pop-culture iconography, the story so transcended the usual media of culture that it put an uncanny new spin on one's *relation* to the culture."[31] The antislavery message of *Uncle Tom's Cabin* ensured that this new spin carried moral meaning, even if that meaning wasn't always clear. To remain unconvinced by Stowe's narrative, in other words, hinted at an alternate vision of social change, or at the very least the possibility that its potential might be open-ended. Cute and Partyside fit into popular versions of *Uncle Tom's Cabin* by embodying the question of identification that the broader phenomenon raised: How to relate to a sphere of consumption (or a character) of deeply uncertain value?

The rift between the narrative's moralism and the humor and spectacle of its later incarnations was a central theme of postbellum reviews. But the air of skepticism continued to share space with claims about the play's essential Americanness. "This, be it understood, is a moral production," one *Spirit of the Times* reporter wrote of *Uncle Tom's Cabin* at New York's Niblo's theater. "Ten real live bloodhounds, a real live donkey, and reserved seat in the parquette [*sic*] for fifty cents are among its moral qualifications." The review continues with mock seriousness, "There is no play which we can more heartily recommend for a Fourth of July lesson . . . every American citizen ought to be compelled by law to sit through Uncle Tom at least twice."[32] The tone here is hard to describe. We might call it vaguely optimistic and self-deprecating, upbeat in appreciating the overlap of hollowness and social interconnection. The most interesting thing about this relatively complex attitude is that the reviewer takes its clarity for granted.

While this kind of national self-deprecation became common in reviewing *Uncle Tom's Cabin*'s continuing presence on the contemporary stage, discussions of the novel itself began treating it as a thing of the past. As

Hochman shows in her study of *Uncle Tom's Cabin*'s publishing history, postwar commentators often placed "the enthusiasm that greeted *Uncle Tom's Cabin* in the somewhat misty past of 'older readers,'" while later print versions were often prefaced with the acknowledgment that, as the Eaton and Mains edition put it, "the great emancipation question of a few decades ago" no longer held "all the old interest" for modern readers.[33] But even when regarded as a kind of historical relic, the novel could suggest the pathos evoked by Cute and Partyside: the basic worthiness of a bumbling American culture. As the *Atlantic Monthly* described the phenomenon in 1879, Stowe's text still repays attention as a "great American novel" despite its "fearful lapses," "false colors of character," and "errors of taste." And as a reminder of slavery's place in recent history, it makes an unseemly present-day culture of "political corruption and decay" seem more acceptable. "We may be a fraud," the *Atlantic* concludes, "but we are no longer an open lie."[34] Both as a reminder of the past and as a contrast to the present, *Uncle Tom's Cabin* made visible the value of the substandard.

To many male novelists in the process of articulating the serious, professional literary terrain of realism, the substandard, amateurish *Uncle Tom's Cabin* was a source of envy as well as disdain. The pages of the magazines that promoted the late nineteenth-century movement are filled with backhanded praise for Stowe's work. Along these lines, in an 1887 essay, Thomas Wentworth Higginson admired the international reach of *Uncle Tom's Cabin* while suggesting that the novel would soon be forgotten. In 1895, William Dean Howells recalled being enthralled by *Uncle Tom's Cabin* as a boy. "With certain obvious lapses in art, and with an art that is at its best very simple, and perhaps primitive, the book is still a work of art," Howells assured. But he is unable to explain its appeal: "I could not say why this was so. Why does the young man's fancy, when it lightly turns to thoughts of love, turn this way and not that? There seems no more reason for one than for the other."[35] Like James, Howells does not mention slavery in his recollection of reading Stowe's novel (especially strange since Howells grew up in an abolitionist household in eastern Ohio, a major center of antislavery resistance), emphasizing the growth of individual aesthetic taste over and against social conscience. Portraying his interest in Stowe's novel as essentially random, Howells sidesteps the complex ways in which *Uncle Tom's Cabin* represented both questionable quality and moral force at once.

An earlier article by John William DeForest, another influential proponent of literary realism, took a different backhanded angle. In DeForest's analysis, *Uncle Tom's Cabin* was the "nearest approach" yet to the "great American novel" precisely for depicting the national tragedy of slavery with such a realistic eye—with two very notable exceptions. "There were very noticeable faults in the story," he wrote, echoing the commonplace language of *Uncle Tom's Cabin* as a flawed text, "there was a very faulty plot; there was (if idealism be a fault) a black man painted whiter than angels, and a girl such as girls are to be, perhaps, but are not yet."[36] DeForest was not only voicing the realist distaste for idealism here, but also the more diffuse—and less intellectual—popular incredulity toward the most idealistic moments at the heart of *Uncle Tom's Cabin*. Ultimately, though, this incredulity would be expressed more vividly by less erudite voices.

The late parodies of *Uncle Tom's Cabin* show this particularly well in the way they treat (and mistreat) Eva. In a way that echoes *Agnes of Sorrento* and anticipates *The Feminization of American Culture,* the comic traditions surrounding *Uncle Tom's Cabin* reflect a desire to humble the white redeemer of Stowe's novel that seems excessive even in the context of parody. One surviving 1903 play text, for instance, depicts the ordeal of "Little Eva, who finds it wearing on the constitution to die so often," a character to be played by a large, "grotesque" man in a wig and tutu. A gambler and a smoker, Eva takes up the running joke of the fallen angel; but this version of the white redeemer has to withstand more humiliation than others. During her death scene, it becomes clear that she is too heavy to be hauled up to heaven on the stage ropes, which leads to her struggling for a while in midair. Eva yells at Uncle Tom and Simon "Degree," the two characters holding the ropes, as Topsy holds out a pan of "red fire" underneath her feet. Finally, Tom and Degree give out and Eva falls to the stage, collapsing on top of Tom.[37]

In this turn-of-the-century parody, Tom sums up the aggression toward little Eva by saying on her deathbed, "that's all right Miss Eva, it's a pleasure to see you die—no trouble at all." The line turns Stowe's vision of redemption on its head by suggesting how easily Eva's death scene can provide repetitive, superficial enjoyment, making it a commodity fit for a consumerist public sphere. Parodies of Eva stress this undermining theme by making Eva herself an arch consumer: a drinker, a smoker, or, in the 1929 comic film, *Eva the Fifth,* simply crazy for candy. This screen version hinges on the jealousy of a stage performer who had played Eva before being replaced by a younger actress. For revenge, the older actress gives the younger so many sweets that she eats until she literally throws up on stage. In exploring Eva's iterations in popular culture, these jokes become repetitive themselves. Again and again, they depict the angelic Eva as not just flawed but grotesque.

This grotesque Eva takes part in conventions from the minstrel stage that shape the parodies' depictions of the novel's black characters. As if to highlight this racial slipperiness, 1920s productions with names like *Topsy and Eva* and *Little Eva's Temptation* paired the angelic white girl and the "impish" Topsy as partners in mischief. Where Eva inspires Topsy to behave better in *Uncle Tom's Cabin,* the parodies present Eva as the bad influence, convincing Topsy to steal, lie, and chase after men. *Little Eva's Temptation* is especially focused on undermining the religious overtones of the white redeemer. At one point, when Ophelia asks Eva how much progress she has made on her catechism, Eva replies, "Oh, I'm way beyond redemption." The final scene mocks her death in *Uncle Tom's Cabin.* Eva faints after having Uncle Tom steal a chicken and convincing Topsy to sneak out with her to "go after the boys." Her father, thinking she is dead, wails, "Sweetest Eva: The gates are closed after thee." When she soon wakes up, he sees that she was only playing dead to avoid a 'lickin'."

This Eva is said to be "part angel," but the comic exchange that follows makes it clear that this version of Eva cares nothing about being angelic:

> *St. Clare:* If you are bad like this you'll never go to Heaven
> *Eva:* Oh I don't care Papa, 'cause I want to go with you.
> *St. Clare:* You'll never climb great stairs.
> *Eva:* Huh! I never intended to, I'm going to take the elevator.
> *St. Clare:* You'll never sing pretty songs.
> *Eva:* Oh yes I will. I can sing "Nobody knows what a yellow headed Mamma can do."
> *St. Clare:* You'll never have wings.
> *Eva:* Well, I'll have two things—a great big long tail with a spear on the end.[38]

What is being rejected in the reversal of Eva's ascent is not only Stowe's sweeping optimism about privileged observers but also the broader ascendency of the individual that Eva represents. From the self-mutilation of *Agnes* to the profane Evas of the late parodies, reactions to *Uncle Tom's Cabin* imagine Eva undergoing a range of compulsive behaviors that rewrite her as a symbol of self-division. The "part angel" character that chooses hell in *Little Eva's Temptation* is, in this way at least, not far off from little Agnes, whose aggression toward herself reflects the tension between her spiritual and worldly aspirations. Though taking place sixty years apart, both of these revisions evoke the feeling that *Uncle Tom's Cabin* places far too much value in the purity and sanctity of selfhood.

Coolness toward *Uncle Tom's Cabin* is undeniably a story of political loss. As the minstrelsy and buffoonery that crowds the parodies attests, the uncertainty about sentimentality that defined ambivalence toward *Uncle Tom's Cabin* did little to engage with the American racial and gender politics that Stowe had attempted to explode. More than that, the responses to Stowe's novel and its offshoots around the turn of the twentieth century exuded a giddy stupidity about the ongoing plight of African Americans under Jim Crow and women's continuing disenfranchisement. But this is not the whole story. The attitudes of detachment and uncertainty that accompanied *Uncle Tom's Cabin*—and contemporary best sellers like *Ben-Hur, A Tale of Two Cities,* and *Trilby*—developed a popular vocabulary of critique that took aim at certain images and not others. This language was political in the sense that it painted a picture of the American public as a site of missed connections, misplaced idealism, and failed ascents. And it was culturally meaningful to the extent that it conspicuously took place outside of the intellectual sphere of literary criticism and the sentimentalized zone of domestic space.

This is not to say that cool reading couldn't, at times, take on more specific critical significance. As illustrated by one final example, Langston Hughes's 1930s skit "Colonel Tom's Cabin," ambivalence held the potential to challenge a popular novel's ongoing social significance in clear terms. A short piece, which Hughes wrote to run before longer plays at the Harlem Suitcase Theater, "Colonel Tom's Cabin" was meant for an audience highly attuned to American racial politics. But it draws heavily on the less engaged tradition of *Uncle Tom's Cabin* parodies. Hughes's Eva, in particular, is an epitome of the grotesque consumer. "Only Little Eva is abnormal," the stage directions explain. "She is an overgrown adult in child's clothes, frills and ribbons. Also, alas, she is colored, with blond curls." Tom and "Sinclair" argue about politics in the opening scene (to the plantation owner's chagrin, Tom plans to vote for Roosevelt), while Eva whines in the background about wanting to go to drinking and dancing at the Cotton Club.

Hughes's piece not only heightens the sense of Eva's abnormality, it also raises the stakes of the negative feelings surrounding the character. Before leaving the plantation for Chicago, Colonel Tom calls Eva over to do something he'd "been wanting to do ever since the Civil War": "smack Eva down." Where earlier revisions of Eva depict her undergoing various forms of penance and punishment, Hughes's version reads more like an exorcism. It is significant that the symbolic subject expelled here is not the figure of white southern political power—the plantation owner, who is standing right there as well—but the little girl who stands for the cultural authority of the privileged white individual. The brief theatrical interlude refocuses the comic convention that had become part of the *Uncle Tom's Cabin* phenomenon. Eva's ascent into heaven had been ridiculed for decades; Hughes uses this stock joke to present an image of black cultural force. As Tom walks off stage, Sinclair underlines this power by calling out, "you have broken her wings for good!"[39] On the one hand, this image of finality shows how little Hughes wants to do with the content of *Uncle Tom's Cabin*. On the other hand, his parody revisits the hope that runs through the ambivalent tradition of the novel's cool response: that the right retelling might allow a more inclusive public to "feel right."

CHAPTER 2

Ben-Hur
Spectacles of Belief

Fearing that its studio logo sequence might clash with the nativity scene that opens *Ben-Hur,* MGM cut out the audio track that traditionally accompanied its image of a roaring lion. The eerily quiet reel that fronts the 1959 film embodies an awkwardness that had dogged *Ben-Hur* from its first appearance, in 1880, as a religious novel that doubled as an epic adventure story. Retelling the gospel narrative alongside a parallel plot made memorable by a battle at sea and a fast-paced chariot race, Lew Wallace's Christian thriller blurred the boundary between devotion and entertainment like no other nineteenth-century text. MGM's nod to solemnity echoed the caution with which Wallace himself guarded the stage adaptation of his best-selling novel. After reluctantly licensing a *Ben Hur* performance to American impresarios Klaw and Erlanger in 1899—on the condition they would limit the live representation of Christ to a silent, glowing light—Wallace wrote that he had always feared "whoever should undertake the production dramatically would fail to treat it in the proper spirit of reverence. This is one of the reasons why I have heretofore declined to allow it to go on the stage."[1]

The story of *Ben-Hur* is in part a story of taking liberties with a religious text. But the *Ben-Hur* phenomenon didn't just stand out for pushing sacred boundaries; this chapter argues that the Christian epic's prominent place in the culture of popular reading had much to do with how it also disrupted notions of the profane. Amid the volumes of skepticism and sarcasm that came to surround *Ben-Hur,* it became common to claim that one would have to be extremely naïve to view the novel or the play as a truly religious experience. As one critic put it, "the thousands of well-meaning people who still need some excuse to go to the playhouse" might take refuge in the story's Christianity, but "we—the ungodly ones—realized, first of all, that we were watching a 'spectacle' the like of which has never been seen in New York before."² Something about *Ben-Hur*, however, made it uncomfortable to be in the know. For many of the "ungodly" ones, the imagined experiences of more reverent audience members inspired feelings of nostalgia, fascination, and even envy.

Where the ambivalent response to *Uncle Tom's Cabin* voiced discomfort with the privileged, white redeemer, reactions to *Ben-Hur* took a different approach to social leveling. In the context of religious entertainment, discussing the novel became an occasion for questioning the value of critical intelligence, not the power of sympathy. As one extraordinarily ambivalent critic wrote in 1905, "perhaps there is genuine regret in the fact that one cannot always be fifteen years old and retain that age's impression of the lasting greatness of *Ben-Hur*."³ It seems as if this critic can't decide between insulting popular taste and making a subtle point about his or her own contradictory feelings. Ambiguities like this come up often in discussions of *Ben-Hur*'s religious fans as well. "As a sop to Christian sentiment," a reporter for *Life* magazine noted in 1899, the producers of *Ben-Hur* on stage advertise the "'reverent spirit' in which the piece is presented." In the face of this disingenuous pandering, the reporter concludes, Christian viewers will need to develop a taste for profanation to enjoy the play: "It is for each believer to decide for himself to what extent he is willing to let his desire to witness a theatrical spectacle prevail over his respect for his religion."⁴ Part condescension, part exploration of mixed feelings, cool responses to *Ben-Hur* often revolved around imagining what it would be like to read the novel or see the play with different eyes.

This fascination with viewing *Ben-Hur* from different perspectives—and, in particular, *less* critical, *less* authoritative perspectives—reflected the generic instability at the heart of the novel. There could not be one representative experience of *Ben-Hur* because the text itself was several things at once. It joined earlier novels such as Joseph Ingraham's *The Prince of the House of David* (1859) and Ernest Renan's *The Life of Jesus* (1863) in the project of contextualizing Christianity's emergence in Judaic traditions and against Roman imperial power. But, as Gregory Jackson argues, *Ben-Hur* also fell into a category of religious novels meant to bolster faith, not just educate. What Jackson calls the nineteenth-century "homiletic novel"—works like Elizabeth Stuart Phelps's *The Gates Ajar* (1868) and Charles Sheldon's *In His Steps* (1896)—"engaged religious readers in narrative enactments aimed at merging fictive settings with readers' everyday lives . . . to facilitate private devotion, strengthen moral autonomy, and foster social engagement through particular acts of reading."[5] Wallace's own discussions about *Ben-Hur* portrayed it as a homiletic work. He described writing the novel as a personal conversion experience and hoped that it would have a similar effect on others.[6]

In at least one famous case, it did. Soon after the book's initial publication, President James Garfield—an acquaintance of Wallace's from their time in the Union Army—sent Wallace a letter that would become a staple of *Ben-Hur* advertising. "Dear General," Garfield wrote, "I have this morning finished reading 'Ben-Hur,' and I must thank you for the pleasure it has given me. The theme was difficult; but you handled it with great delicacy and power . . . With this beautiful and reverent book you have lightened the burden of my daily life."[7] Garfield's testimony helped solidify *Ben-Hur*'s reputation as religious literature that *worked* and encouraged Harper and Brothers to print the costly "Garfield" edition of the novel, which one critic described as "probably the most elaborately illustrated book ever issued in this country."[8] Confidence in *Ben-Hur*'s appeal to Christian audiences was apparently still high in 1908, when Sears, Roebuck and Company placed what was then the largest print order in American history, commissioning one million copies from Harper. It is unlikely that the mail-order giant would place such a bet without anticipating huge sales among devout readers.

On the other hand, there seems to have been just as much confidence in the narrative's religious illegitimacy. Many critics of the book chalked up its remarkable popularity to the sensationalism of its adventure scenes. In 1901, for instance, an article going over the huge sales figures of *Ben-Hur* attributed its success to "the interest in the chariot race and other exciting passages."[9] Once Klaw and Erlanger invested record-breaking amounts in the scenery for the stage version, which became notorious for its sinking ship and live chariot race effects, *Ben-Hur*'s status as a sensation piece was beyond doubt. The text having such a confused identity to begin with, it was easy to imagine its readers and viewers as split subjects, whether torn between religious devotion and the appetite for entertainment, between the desire to deepen one's knowledge about the Bible as history and the visceral experience of conversion, or between the authority of critical distance and the pleasure of absolute immersion in the plot. Many agreed that *Ben-Hur* asked its audience to be of at least two minds at once.

But there was a kind of coherence in *Ben-Hur*'s mixed bag of genres: biblical history, homiletic narrative, and adventure story. The common thread was the lack of greatness. "The charge used to be made," one critic wrote in a 1919 article for *Outlook*, "that American fiction was either the child of the Sunday-school story or of the dime novel—or of both."[10] *Ben-Hur* had clear ties to both these sources of literary embarrassment, and indeed the *Outlook* article went on to name Wallace's epic novel and *Uncle Tom's Cabin* as prime examples of best sellers that supported these charges against American popular culture. From any vantage point, in other words, it would have been hard not to see *Ben-Hur* as drawing a line in the sand between popular enthusiasm and informed, critical judgment. "The consensus of New York critical opinion appears to be that . . . reviewers do not seem to think it possesses any engrossing merits," the *Chicago Tribune* reported, "and it is evident that the acting at the first night's performance failed to impress them as a body."[11] This condescension extended to the novel as well. As a *Bookman* article on Wallace's death noted, "such intelligent criticism as was directed toward him was almost invariably disparaging, and yet utterly futile have been and still are all attempts to eradicate in the minds of tens of thousands of American readers the stubborn belief that *Ben-Hur* is one of the very greatest novels that the world has produced."[12]

What made this interesting was not the relatively obvious point that popular taste differed from critical consensus, but the vague aura of legitimacy that *Ben-Hur*'s biblical subject matter conferred on its mass consumption. Alongside the many jokes about the disingenuousness of its religious message, others floated the idea that, although the novel was not "great," it was "permeated with the beatific spirit of the New Testament"; although it was lacking in "elegance," it had the power to "convert"; or, at the very least, the phenomenon would be thought-provoking.[13] As one *New York Times* critic wrote in advance of the play's opening night, "the announcement of the scene of the Mount of Olives . . . and the indication of the Divine presence by a shaft of light, suggests that the play may invite much 'discussion.'"[14] Like more purely sensational novels, such as *Lady Audley's Secret*, and shows such as *The Black Crook*, *Ben-Hur* was largely seen as unworthy of serious critical attention. But the biblical epic charged this unworthiness with implications of spiritual import.

To understand the excitement and the ambivalence surrounding *Ben-Hur*, it helps to consider Walter Benjamin's description of "profane illumination," a concept that appears in his essay on the French surrealist movement. Because Benjamin viewed organized religion as a corruption of revolutionary impulses—the overwhelming appeal of social transformation and the reverence for de-individualized modes of being—he viewed experiences that took shape with religious intensity but outside of traditional spheres of observance as especially significant. The surrealist literature and visual art of André Breton, Louis Aragon, Philippe Soupault, and others gave him a vivid example of this displaced religiosity, taking a reverent attitude toward conspicuously unsacred things: intoxication, dreams, and seemingly random juxtapositions of common objects. Ultimately, Benjamin would describe surrealism as a highly questionable artistic movement. But he nonetheless claimed it as a window into a profane illumination that would bring about "the true creative overcoming of religious illumination" by aesthetic means.

Although far less theorized, something like this fascination with the margins of religious experience informed the response to *Ben-Hur*. And driving this interest was the major role that the theme of religious outsiderhood played in the novel itself. When Wallace recalled his motivations for writing the Christian epic, he claimed that he was first driven by a sense of intellectual curiosity about the period and later by the ecstatic feeling that, through the act of writing, he was becoming more devoted to God. But the book's many long digressions on the role of mass entertainment in the Roman empire suggest an additional motive: exploring the ethics of popular taste. Like *Agnes of Sorrento*, *Ben-Hur* treats Rome as a case study of crowd-pleasing events, processions, and performances. It was fitting, then, that the most famous scene from Wallace's novel—the chariot race thrilling the Roman populace—would become an iconic image of mass attraction in American popular culture. Both *Ben-Hur* and its reaction reflected an awareness that crowds like to read about crowds, that mass consumption is often driven by a self-reflexive desire to question and understand what drives the mass public.

THE NEARLY CHRISTIAN CROWD

By the end of *Ben-Hur*, many central and marginal characters have been converted by witnessing Christ's crucifixion, but for most of the novel the savior is an absent presence, introduced into the plot in few and far between moments, through secondhand accounts and rumors. More than a book about the dawn of Christianity, it is a story of religious *expectancy*. The central narrative of Judah Ben-Hur explores this state as his motivation shifts from revenge (as the story begins, he is unjustly accused of treason against Rome and enslaved while his mother and sister are banished to a leper colony), to leading an army that will prepare for Jesus's rule by overthrowing Rome, to dedicating himself to an otherworldly, spiritual kingdom of God. Plotting what Wallace depicts as a conversion from Jewish to Christian modes of religious experience, the central thread of Ben-Hur's story stresses that the acceptance of Christian salvation was prepared for by partially misguided belief.

As Wallace tells it, this focus on the dawning of religious sense was an effect of his wanting to write an impossible novel. Initially, he had written a scene of the Magi visiting Christ at his birth, and he planned to end the book with the crucifixion, but Wallace felt it wouldn't be appropriate to write a work of fiction filling in the unknowns of Jesus's life. After struggling to solve the problem, he recalled, "at last I decided to use the blank to show the religious and political condition of the world at the time of the coming. . . . The commitment to the galley, the sea-fight, the chariot-race and its preceding orgies were Roman phases; just as the love marking the Hur family, the steady pursuit of vengeance by the son, and his easy conversion by Simonides to the alluring idea of the Messiah to rule like Caesar, were Jewish."[15] Wallace's need to fill in the blank would lead him to develop two of the most iconic action sequences of nineteenth-century popular culture, but it also opened up space for him to consider what it meant to be just on the verge of religious awakening.

Wallace's interest in sensational entertainment and his fascination with this state of spiritual readiness come together in his portrayal of Roman pastimes and Roman crowds. In ways that anticipate American responses to *Ben-Hur*'s own thrill scenes, the passages he calls the "preceding orgies" meant to convey the characteristic attitudes of the Roman populace explore the connection between the psychology of entertainment and the experience of religious feeling. The tension between Wallace's harsh judgment of Roman morality and his desire to depict people on the cusp of salvation makes things interesting. He describes the Roman crowd as a remnant of belief: "reverence as a quality of the Roman mind was fast breaking down, or, rather, it was becoming unfashionable. The old religion had nearly ceased to be a faith; at most it was a mere habit of thought and expression."[16] This space in between two religions—old and new—is disappointing but filled with possibility.

Like *Agnes of Sorrento*, *Ben-Hur* treats Rome as an occasion for considering issues of taste that resonated with American popular culture. Consider, for instance, the parallel between Wallace's above description of the Roman mind and the *New York Times'* take on Klaw and Erlanger's stage adaptation of *Ben-Hur* and what is missing from its modern audience: "The scene on the Mount of Olives might at least have been spared. But reverence for sacred things is much rarer than it used to be."[17] Wallace's hesitance to license his novel for the stage suggests that he was well aware that popular American forms might encourage irreverence similar to the kind he projected onto Rome. And, at least in hindsight, his attitude toward this lack of respect was severe. As he would later write to a friend about *Ben-Hur*, the disgracefulness of religious outsiders was the book's unspoken central theme: "it would not do to say plainly that such was the object—viz., that mankind in its organization and ideas of all sorts was so debased as to be past salvation except by direct interposition of the Almighty. That idea gave me coherence and opportunity to rest in labor. *It made the book possible.*"[18]

Ben-Hur actually depicts the coming of salvation quite differently, putting much more stock in the states of uncertainty, ambivalence, and communal awareness that build up to the final revelation. A key to this complex attitude is the way Wallace has his central character represent not only Judaic piety but also Roman devotion to spectacle and pleasure seeking. Because Ben-Hur was freed from slavery, adopted and educated by a wealthy Roman general, he comes to represent a mixture of Jewish roots and Roman habits. And this combination of temperaments is crucial to his ultimate conversion to Christianity. The transformation begins to take shape in an unlikely place. In the extended "Grove of Daphne" sequence, Wallace sets up both the chariot race and the religious awakening in the sprawling, pagan pleasure grounds he describes as the epitome of the "extravagance and dissoluteness of the age," which flowed from East to West like a "demoralizing river" (168).

Ben-Hur wanders into the Grove of Daphne after meeting with his father's ex-slave, Simonides, a figure who will become crucial to the novel's revenge plot. The bustling grove is the stuff of spectacle: the "unmixed sensualism" that appeals to the "mass" (204). "Words may not be used to tell of the voluptuousness of the dance," Wallace writes, and he goes on to describe the grove as filled with music, lavish chariots, and fashionable display (195). In a way that Wallace first attributes to Ben-Hur's exhaustion, the hero finds himself drawn gradually to the atmospheric attractions. "By the time [Ben-Hur] reached Heracleia, a suburban village intermediate the city and the Grove, he was somewhat spent with exercise, and began to be susceptible of entertainment. Once a pair of goats led by a beautiful woman, woman and goats alike brilliant with ribbons and flowers, attracted attention" (194). In keeping with Wallace's judgment of Roman decadence, he depicts openness to these charms as a form of weakness.

The more Wallace explains Ben-Hur's enchantment with the grove, though, the murkier his motivation becomes. Just after Ben-Hur admires the procession of goats and woman, Wallace addresses the reader directly: "The goodness of the reader is again besought in favor of an explanation. A certain facility of accommodation in the matter of religion comes to us after much intercourse with people of a different faith; gradually we attain the truth that every creed is illustrated by good men who are entitled to our respect" (197). Under this umbrella of tolerance, the reader learns, Ben-Hur "was yet a Jew. In his view, nevertheless, it was not an impiety to look for the beautiful in the Grove of Daphne" (197). *Ben-Hur* has shifted from describing its hero's vulnerability to spectacle as a kind of moral failing to sketching the outlines of profane religious feeling. Indeed, Wallace goes as far as calling the Grove of Daphne an introduction to the force of love that Christianity will reconcile with the rule of law. "The law of the place was love," Wallace writes, "but love without law" (203). The profane Roman spectacle has gone from signifying an absolutely fallen state to standing for a crucial faculty of readiness.

This is so-so religion, not-great religion: the word Wallace settles on in his increasingly puzzling description of Roman grandeur is *adequate*. "What adequate mysteries were hidden behind an introduction so marvelous!" he exclaims about the pagan grove (202). And while this vague conception is at first individualized in Ben-Hur's realization plot, the notion of near or partial religion spills over into the novel's consideration of collective consciousness when Wallace depicts the Roman chariot races. The reader is introduced to the crowd's mentality through Ben-Hur's experience of fellow feeling as he watches a race alongside thousands of other spectators. "There was nothing to compare with the gatherings at Jerusalem in celebration of the Passover; yet when he sat under the purple velaria of the Circus Maximus one of three hundred and fifty thousand spectators, he must have been visited by the thought that possibly there might be some branches of the family of man worthy of divine consideration, if not mercy, though they were of the uncircumcised—some, by their sorrows, and, yet worse, by their hopelessness in the midst of sorrows, fitted for brotherhood in the promises of his countrymen" (267).

Where Wallace typically relates Ben-Hur's inner experience through free indirect discourse, here he opts for supposition. He assumes Ben-Hur "must" feel this way, as if the character here stands less for any specific life story than for the natural reaction anyone would have as part of a mass audience. In other words, Wallace describes the experience of popular entertainment as a prelude to religious awakening that is available to any of the hundreds of thousands standing in the crowd, despite its being assembled in the name of profane pleasures. And Wallace seems intent, too, on making sure the reader imagines him- or herself in this place. "Let the reader try to fancy it!" he enjoins in the climactic chariot race scene. "The divine last touch in perfecting the beautiful is animation. Can we accept the saying, then these latter days, so tame in pastime and dull in sports, have scarcely anything to compare to the spectacle offered by the six contestants" (360). With deep indecisiveness, the novel has moved from the discussion of Roman pastimes as "depravity" to the claim that they represent a touch of divinity painfully absent from 1880s America.

The very scene Wallace is describing will, of course, do much to dazzle the contemporary popular culture he calls "tame in pastime." And this self-fulfilling quality of *Ben-Hur* reflects a productive generic crossing. In both the novel and the play, the sense of impending salvation opens up space for combining the driving assumption of sensationalism—the crowd can never have enough spectacle—with the more socially and morally conscious language of religious literature. It is impossible to say how much Wallace considered the tension between his condemnation of popular amusements and his near-reverent treatment of them as he wrote *Ben-Hur*. His confused and contradictory spectacle scenes suggest that he was comfortable leaving ideas about the divinity of entertainment unresolved. It is clear, however, that his audience responded to the space he indicated between the sacred and the profane by taking up the central question *Ben-Hur* implied: To what extent can events outside of religious practice be charged with valid spiritual force?

As audiences took this question out of Wallace's hands and into their own, this curiosity about the profane became linked with curiosity about the amateur. Questions about whether irreligious things could have religious importance dovetailed with questions about whether not-great novels could communicate something majestic. By the late 1890s, it was well understood that, though *Ben-Hur* continued to move readers and theater audiences nationwide, the phenomenon would not win much critical praise. *Ben-Hur*'s popularity, one commentator would note, "was a success in which the reviewer took no part. His approval or disapproval of the book no one seems to have heeded, but long afterwards, when his criticism had vanished into the spaces into which so much that is said soon disappears, there rose a tide whose source was innumerable rivulets of personal opinion."[19] Klaw and Erlanger's stage adaptation was discussed in similar ways. "As a play the reviewers do not seem to think it possesses any engrossing merits," the *Chicago Daily Tribune* would proclaim.[20] Several contemporary articles mentioned the play being "hissed" and the novel critically disparaged in London.[21]

With the line so clearly drawn between critical and public opinion, *Ben-Hur* became a sounding board for ideas about unprivileged perspectives. And this is one reason that responses to the novel and play develop a near obsession with the experiences of less-than-ideal viewers—adventure-loving boys and unsophisticated adults. The biblical aspect helped turn this fascination with nonelite perspectives into something more than plain condescension. As one reviewer wrote in 1907, "General Wallace's novel has won a popular rather than a critical success; but a novel that can grip the hearts of a whole people becomes, by that very fact, a literary portent of the first order."[22] A people's book rather than a critic's book, *Ben-Hur* seemed capable of signifying something fundamental in the shared experience of the "whole" American people. And while what this something was never became entirely clear, the discussion focused attention on the idea that a novel didn't have to be "one of the great novels of English literature" to deliver a grandiose message.[23] In other words, divine energy might show up in unlikely places.

If this is profanation, it is softer than the forms through which the concept is often understood. Critical discussions of the profane have tended to associate it with the radically antisocial and the renegade, which doesn't quite line up with the mainstream world of popular reading. When Julia Kristeva praises modernist literature's exploration of abjection, or Benjamin traces the "cult of evil" that extends from Arthur Rimbaud through the surrealists, or Georgio Agamben contemplates the "inexplicable" actions portrayed in Fyodor Dostoyevsky's *The Idiot* as versions of self-profanation, they link the concept of the profane with iconoclastic art and its analogue in communal life: the unmistakable, rebellious defiance of social norms.[24] The *Ben-Hur* phenomenon presents the act of profaning—refusing in public to recognize the boundary between mundane and sacred things—in a different light. The response to Wallace's novel was a far cry from the antisocial impudence that Rimbaud, for instance, channeled in his writing (proclaiming his attraction to "idolatry, and love of sacrilege; oh! All sorts of vice, anger, lechery—terrific stuff, lechery; lying above all, and laziness").[25] But the more subtle and comedic blurring of the boundary between sacred and profane that took shape in the reaction to *Ben-Hur* pressed valuable questions nonetheless.

Call it "profanation lite." Not the brazen act of sacrilege but the culture-wide attraction to Christian imagery out of ritual contexts: appearing in a novel that wasn't great, represented in a performance that stood out for pandering to the appetite for sensationalism. Crucial to the public's reaction, I would argue, was the way critical uncertainty about the novel and the play charged the phenomenon with a lack of authority. This was a reconsideration of the Christian narrative written not by a prophet, a preacher, or even a scholar but by an amateur. Discussions of Wallace's authorship are revealing here, as they often return to the claim that he is not an especially talented artist, that anyone could have written *Ben-Hur*. Indeed, Wallace himself would insist that he possessed no special talent. What he did was open up the topic of religious experience on the margins of Christianity and then refuse to be authoritative about it.

LEW WALLACE, NOT-SO-GREAT AMERICAN AUTHOR

The premise of one 1893 *New York Times* interview with Wallace begins to suggest the lack of gravity with which he was viewed. The reporter has apparently run into Wallace by chance at a Manhattan newsstand, the randomness of the occasion mirrored by the casual nature of the exchange. The article's headline sets a glib tone: "Philosophy between Puffs: Gen. Lew Wallace Smokes a Cigar and Chats Pleasantly." Everything is taken lightly in this short piece, which makes it fitting that we first see Wallace in the act of cool reading: "At the newsstand Gen. Wallace balanced on one foot, resting the toe of the other lightly on the floor. With one hand he held his cigar to his lips, while he took short puffs, and with the other hand he picked up a yellow-covered novel and began turning its pages carelessly."[26] From the start, Wallace is held up as a symbol of reading, writing, and philosophizing with a kind of languid partial attention.

"The author of 'Ben Hur' looked cool," the article claims. And its detailed description of Wallace's look warrants attention, as it hints at the term's movement in the late nineteenth century from designating matters of temperature to signifying more abstract notions of individuality and style. It was a hot day, and his "waistcoat was unbuttoned and the coat was unwrinkled, crisp, and fresh. On his head was a Panama hat of rather uncertain though comfortable style." Part of his coolness is certainly the fact that his waistcoat hangs unbuttoned, but the oddity of his comfortable hat—unique enough to be uncertain—seems to play a role, too. So does the self-gratification and lack of total engagement in the ensuing conversation that his puffing on a cigar represents. Just as the article's headline depicts his philosophizing going hand-in-hand with his smoking, the piece refers incessantly to his constant puffing. This has nothing to do with regulating his temperature, but much to do with managing his image as a carefree writer—even though famous for tackling a subject that warrants the utmost care.

Wallace goes on to assert that there is nothing special about any author, including himself, claiming that "every one ought to write a book." And then, in a passage literally punctuated by pulls from his cigar, Wallace presents a remarkable image, which half seriously suggests a connection between American amateurism and divine force. "If some angel of the Lord (puff, puff) could fly through this land (puff) and gather up (puff) the manuscripts of what were intended (puff, puff, puff) to be books, (puff;) . . . I imagine that the great pyramid of Egypt (puff, puff,) would be a small thing (puff, puff,) compared with this pile of manuscript, (puff.) Valuable thoughts, too, (puff,) in many cases." This would be a strange monument, a pile of unfinished novels gathered together by God, only some of which would contain "valuable thoughts." But the image is an apt representation of how religious reverence, condescension, and ideals of social leveling could intermingle in late nineteenth-century popular literary culture.

Wallace was not the only one to suggest that anyone could do his job. An 1891 *Nassau Literary Magazine* review, for instance, made this case quite plainly. "In judging an author's writings," it argued, "we must distinguish sharply between the inherent interest they possess and the fascination given them by the writer's genius. . . . The tale of Ben Hur, from its very picturesqueness, would be of interest, whether told by Lew Wallace or a canal driver."[27] Echoing a criticism often leveled at *Uncle Tom's Cabin*, this claim that *Ben-Hur*'s appeal reflected the interest of the subject rather than the method of treatment left little room for revering the author. This perspective on *Ben-Hur* reversed the terms of "great American novel" discourse. Where the great American novel would showcase a single, comprehensive view of the nation, the not-so-great work instead implied that any of the multitudinous perspectives that make up the national community might be as valuable as the next. Precisely because *Ben-Hur* was not viewed as a great work of literature, it took on the capacity to represent the United States as a site of extraordinary, untapped potentiality.

This leveling attitude might be understood as a form of pluralism, echoing the ideal that every voice has an equal, positive value. But the web of sarcasm and coolness that was spun around *Ben-Hur* suggests a less upbeat idea: that all American voices and perspectives are equally *unworthy*. Where the claim could be made that a presumably uneducated and unpracticed "canal driver" might have written *Ben-Hur*, it was also common to joke about how little sophistication and genuine religious reverence the novel and play required of their audiences.[28] A satirical piece in *Life* magazine, which imagined an "after-theatre symposium" among contemporary characters come to life—Ben-Hur, Sapho [sic], Petronius, Sherlock Holmes, and Hamlet's father's ghost—made this joke bluntly. After Hamlet's father's ghost complains that New Yorkers won't come to see him and his son, Ben-Hur and Petronius, a character from *Quo Vadis* (a novel of biblical-era Rome that rode *Ben-Hur*'s coattails to moderate success in the 1890s), discuss their plays' strong ticket sales.

In this satire, Ben-Hur is the unwitting beneficiary of bad taste. After Petronius explains to a character from a fairly successful "wholesome, natural play" that she was "kept alive for the most part by out-of-town people," Ben-Hur asks Petronius why he is so skeptical about fashionable audiences. "What are you objecting for, Petronius? New Yorkers come to see you." Petronius sets Ben-Hur straight on the subject of popular appeal: "They don't come to see me, nor you either, on account of our art. It's only because we're flavored with a little sacrilegious religion, that the same people who would crowd a tent to see a two-headed calf, rush to behold our chariot races and dancing-girls and spectacular scenes. They don't care for dramatic art, and wouldn't know it if they saw it."[29] If *Ben-Hur* reflects a national public, in other words, it is a profoundly profane and disappointing one.

This judgment was perhaps inevitable for a show like *Ben-Hur*, which was heavily promoted as a wonder of special effects. A *New York Times* critic, writing in 1899, suggested that there are "a few mature playgoers" who might not be won over by the dazzling sea fight and chariot race scenes. "To the great majority of spectators who see this new production," the article argued, "the two big mechanical scenes . . . will irresistibly appeal."[30] Klaw and Erlanger promoted the play as an unprecedentedly expensive spectacle, and behind the scenes access for journalists led to a series of articles focusing on the performance's impressive logistics. As the *Overland Monthly* declared, "nothing like this has ever been previously known in theatrical business. . . . The production cost $71,000 before the opening night. It employs 350 people."[31] The realism of the chariot race, which featured two teams of live horses running on a treadmill, became the focal point of the behind the scenes coverage.

One of the most richly descriptive accounts of *Ben-Hur*'s effects appeared in *St. Nicholas,* an illustrated magazine for children, in 1900. The kids' venue indicates the association between sensational spectacle and unsophisticated perspectives that shaped the reaction to *Ben-Hur*, but the article also begins to show how the play's sensationalism inspired a kind of reverence in its own right. The journalist, Benjamin Smith, claims that the live chariot race scene, "if not as exciting as that described in the book, is nevertheless very interesting to the children, big and little, who watch it from the auditorium."[32] Where in Wallace's novel the racing scene reveals the divine animation that shapes the Roman crowd, the scene here shows how childlike the entire crowd can become. The American audience is united by a common lack of mature judgment in the face of expensive special effects.

In an elated way, Smith describes his experience viewing the scene from just offstage. The audience watches the chariot race in profile, but the journalist gets to stand directly in front of the charging horses, "whose noses we can almost touch." The excitement he feels is so intense that it defies description. "To describe the effect of this extraordinary spectacle—the sensations that crowd themselves into that brief interval—so that the reader will grasp it, is impossible.... I will only say that it is something to stir the blood with a most unwonted thrill, and to haunt the memory." Coverage like this helped solidify *Ben-Hur*'s reputation as a sensation play that delivered as promised. And with sensationalism playing such a leading role, suddenly the American audience of *Ben-Hur* became hard to distinguish from the pre-Christian, pleasure-seeking crowds that Wallace had described in the novel. As Smith put it, the average viewer of the chariot race scene "shouts as loudly as the Jews and Bedouins who, when the scene changes, crowd from the wings and surround the victor."[33]

Ben-Hur's reputation as a crowd-pleaser continued to grow as the play toured the United States and Europe. By the time it was revived in the 1900s, doubts about its religiosity needed no introduction. "'Ben-Hur' is with us again," one critic announced, "best of the religious melodramas.... The object all sublime of the religious melodrama is well known. It is to entice to the theatre the tens of millions in our still puritanical Nation [*sic*] who regard the delights of the theatre as illicit, but who are only too glad of the fleshpots if they can be presented in sanctified and holy guise."[34] A few Christians protested the mix of religion and spectacle; according to *Billboard* magazine, for example, many people tore up their tickets to the play in 1903 after hearing one especially effective anti-*Ben-Hur* sermon in Atlanta.[35] A *London Times* review from the previous year claimed that "any capable hack playwright could have put together a better setting . . . and we should be spared the unedifying mixture of religious elements with that particular kind of melodrama."[36]

For the most part, however, people treated *Ben-Hur*'s questionable religion as a joke. Like the responses to *Uncle Tom's Cabin*, reactions to *Ben-Hur* became increasingly biting as the decades of its popularity rolled on. In 1923, the year that Samuel Goldwyn and Louis B. Mayer bought the rights to produce a movie version of the epic, the *New York Times* channeled this sarcasm in a mock history lesson that bears quoting at length. "The possibilities of a play (American style) were first illustrated by 'Ben-Hur,' for it perfected dramatic and fathered 'movie' spectacle, formed the theatre's right wing in echelon with the Church, got the parsons to acting, put its signs in the sky and its name on every lip, linked business and the theatre, developed 'circusing' and national propaganda, and finally became an institution that fully

12,000,000 Americans attended as a solemn duty. Whew! *Some* twenty-two years of history!"[37] The *Times* is describing a cultural object at once typically American, dubious, and forcefully appealing.

This retrospective on *Ben-Hur* also invokes a cool Yankee figure, in the form of an Illinois man who had made a killing on *Ben-Hur* ticket sales. He is asked if the success of the play wasn't "wonderful." "'Wonderful?' repeated the Yankee millionaire, who long presided as his own treasurer and ticket taker at the Court Square Theatre, 'Waal, I dunno. When that feller Erlanger put a hoss race, a ballet dance and the Divine Spirit all intew one show, seems like what hez happened wuz jes' about th' most nachural thing in the world!"[38] One would have to be less than sophisticated and somewhat thoughtless, the drawl suggests, to view the phenomenon as natural. More critical observers would presumably see through the ruse of piety, but this reviewer seems much more aligned with the Yankee than any more analytical point of view, as the article continues to discuss *Ben-Hur*'s popularity and its thrilling spectacular scenes. In fact, the piece spends a lot of time focusing on how the American art form bridged gaps among audience members with varying levels of sophistication.

"The 'Ben-Hur' audience was unlike any other audience in the country," the *Times* asserted. "Deacons and deaconesses from backwoods hamlets; professors and parsons, their families and disciples from mid-continent seats of culture; the educated, the self-educated, the thrill-hungry, music lovers, dance devotees. 'Rubes' and small-town sports . . . all this motley throng were there." Even though the play's depiction of sacred symbols is a source of sarcasm in the article, it helps the reviewer explain the positive connections made among its motley audience members, "all of them united by the flavor of culture and romance and pietistic tradition." If there was something mildly profane about the play's mixture of big business and Christianity, according to this account there was also something vaguely unifying about it. Tellingly, whatever this flavor was, it needed no refined intellect or taste to be detected. In order to take in this American cultural experience, one would need to check good taste and critical judgment at the door.

Reactions to *Ben-Hur*, then, explored the potential value of bad taste—or at least the suspension of better judgment. Satirists and serious critics alike made it a commonplace to identify the appeal of the book and the play with unsophisticated perspectives. A comic poem in *Puck* magazine, for instance, relates the difficulties a wealthy woman, Mrs. Jones, has in finding a reliable servant. She has to fire a long procession of types, from "the plump and pleasing Milesian" to the "Swede all skin and bones," but finally tracks down a woman whose favorite novel signifies her fitness to serve: "Her manners were simply perfect: she attended the proper church; / And when Mrs. Jones found that she read 'Ben-Hur,' she knew 't was the end of her search."[39] To Mrs. Jones, it seems, the quaint religious devotion implied by *Ben-Hur* is an ideal fit for the low end of social hierarchy.

But *Puck*'s joke hinges on revaluing the *Ben-Hur* fan. While Mrs. Jones is congratulating herself on finding the perfect servant, her son ends up marrying the new employee. The drawing of the scene in which the newlyweds tell Mrs. Jones that they are married reinforces the reversal of values that this satirical poem celebrates. Mrs. Jones throws up her hands in dismay, and her new daughter-in-law sits with a smirk that shows her cool self-possession. In the end, it is left unclear whether enjoying *Ben-Hur* signifies a lack of sophistication or a kind of irreverent knowledge or canniness. The generational differences that shape the *Puck* satire are significant, suggesting that traditional associations with religious reading material no longer hold true. Mrs. Jones can't see what her son sees because she doesn't understand that *Ben-Hur* reflects a new kind of Christian media, which does not necessarily correspond with the piety and humility that might help a servant accept her social position.

Other depictions of *Ben-Hur* readers and viewers focused more intently on the lived experience of reading the novel or witnessing the play. Echoing the critic who lamented the fact that he no longer could read the novel as a boy does, these depictions tended to voice states of ambivalence about the supposedly lesser perspectives that the phenomenon seemed to address. One *Washington Post* article about the play's flailing success in England sketched out a theory of childish viewership to explain what the ideal audience for such a religious drama would look like. "We do not doubt that there have been times when such dramatic productions had a good effect," the article claimed. As an example of "good" Christian theater, it suggests the "Passion Play . . . enacted by simple peasants, in an obscure corner of the world," a play that "possibly strengthened the faith of the ignorant people who witnessed it."[40] In this analysis, the representation of biblical narratives on stage requires an ignorant audience to be worthwhile.

This was not the case with *Ben-Hur*, the article continues, due to the "influx of tourists" that "undoubtedly cheapened the character of the representation" and "more than that [the] shrewd managers [who] saw a good business venture in the production of the spectacle in large cities." The missing piece was a childish audience. As the *Post* concluded, "to childish, imaginative minds the stage effects and individualities of actors may not appear. But to the average theatergoer they are obtrusive, and, in a play of so sacred a character, offensive."[41] This article places the line between the sacred and the profane within observers themselves. What is clearly culture-industry sacrilege to an adult might be transformative for an ignorant or childish viewer. This could be read as either a condemnation of the play or an acknowledgment that, as Smith writing in *St. Nicholas* put it, *Ben-Hur* must be understood to address the "big" child in each member of its audience.

In other words, only a perspective that falls short of mature judgment can truly appreciate *Ben-Hur*. And if these imagined audience members seemed absent in London, they were certainly there in the United States. As one article about the life of a "country spinster" from Lake Seneca, New York, suggests, *Ben-Hur* was seen as the archetypical novel of choice by rural Americans at the turn of the century. After taking the reader through the ins and outs of her daily life, the spinster, "Aunt Jane," notes that recently she has begun to read "story books." "We used to think them wicked, but they're not wicked at all—only silly—they're all alike."[42] All but *Ben-Hur*: "Still, there are times when I have nothing else to do, and then I like to take up a book. I got so excited over 'Ben Hur' that I was all of a tremble when I was reading."[43] A parallel to the unsophisticated child that critics imagined encountering *Ben-Hur* with an intense immediacy, this country character illustrates how the simplicity of religious feeling can make popular novel reading a truly powerful experience.

It is worth asking whether or not the middle ground between religious legitimacy and its opposite allowed *Ben-Hur* to become the advertising phenomenon it ended up being in the United States. The list of products endorsed by the novel's name—and, invariably, the image of the chariot race scene—is remarkable even within a commercial history in which novels like *Uncle Tom's Cabin* and novelists like Dickens routinely appeared in ad media. As one observer recalled, "the 'Ben-Hur' chariot race horses worked from 1905 on for underwear, candy, cigarettes, autos, movies, what you will—the heavens were free."[44] A current-day eBay search yields a far longer list of

Ben-Hur merchandise from the nineteenth and early twentieth centuries, including buggy blankets, clocks, ketchup, freezers, sleds, curlers, tents, flour, and whiskey.[45] I would suggest that the joke, "the heavens were free," captures the air of profanation that this frenzy of merchandising expressed, the feeling that the line between sacred and worldly space had been blurred in some small way. Not too reverent to seem out of place on a hair curler or underwear but still linked closely enough with Christianity to give these objects an air of respectability, *Ben-Hur* was an ideal sign for an emerging consumerist marketplace.

Wherever it appeared, *Ben-Hur* stood out for being seen as both typically American and unapologetically profane. The phenomenon went beyond associating the United States with the amateur and the not-so-great; it implied a deeper connection between national culture and a loosened boundary between sacred and worldly experience. This might not have reflected the intense profane illumination that Benjamin imagined revolutionizing lived experience, wrenching religious feeling out of its traditional forms. But it did help define a somewhat positive attitude about irreverence toward sacred things. The novel's long social life addressed an audience analogous to the Roman crowds it portrayed, together on the margins of proper religious feeling and practice. Morally speaking, this was not a great place to be. In terms of popular culture, however, no way of viewing national community could do more to invest questionable devotion with a sense of possibility and significance. For Wallace's Roman audience, the intensities of the chariot race are the closest they get to experiencing the divine. In a somewhat similar way, contemporary American popular culture viewed through the lens of cool might be at once absolutely inadequate and uniquely meaningful.

This was, of course, hardly a consensus belief. The caution with which Wallace, Klaw and Erlanger, and ultimately MGM tiptoed around *Ben-Hur* shows how aware they were about crossing a boundary between religious gravity and popular culture that many held sacred. Indeed, one of the reasons that there were far fewer parodies of *Ben-Hur* than of *Uncle Tom's Cabin* was that Klaw and Erlanger aggressively pursued not only copyright infringement but also comic revisions they deemed harmful to the play's public image. The records of one 1903 injunction case suggest, though, that the producers were more interested in protecting their investment than in sheltering their viewers' sensibilities. We are not often privy to authors' or producers' doubts about their audiences, but a moment in Mark Klaw's testimony in a case heard before the US Circuit Court in northern Illinois offers a rare glimpse.

Klaw is being cross-examined by the attorney representing William Cleveland, a Chicago impresario who had produced a parody entitled "Her Bun." Referring to *Ben-Hur*, the attorney asks: "You spoke of the class of people that attended this play. What would you say Mr. Klaw with regard to the intelligence of the class of people that attended the play, were they as a rule people of high grade intelligence?" Klaw attempts to evade the question: "We got all kinds of patrons for all parts of the theatre were full. We certainly got the best and the mediocre too." But when the attorney presses him, he finally admits that the mediocre were the actual target audience. "What would you say," Klaw is asked, "in your opinion, as to the class of people the play would most likely appeal to?" And he responds, "I should say that it would appeal to the religious element. That is to say not the most intelligent."[46] This is a striking statement from a producer who still owns the rights to the play and will later produce it again. But the relative ease with which Klaw describes the religiously devoted audience members of *Ben-Hur* as lacking intelligence indicates just how widely understood was the contradiction that the show was *inspiring* and it *wasn't great*.

The script of Cleveland's parody hasn't survived, but the court record does include a reprinted character list that illustrates how the revision played on the doubts about the American public embedded in *Ben-Hur*. The parody seems to have retold *Ben-Hur* as a tale of Chicago immigrant culture, including "Romans from Little Italy," a "South State Street Brunette," a "Belle of the Cicero Tracks" named "Irish," and a supporting cast of "Egyptians, Greeks, Turks, Arabs, Mongolians, Japs, Hindoos," and "Hobos." Where the original *Ben-Hur* takes place on the margins of religious respectability, this parody focuses on the margins of American ethnic identity. Its character descriptions suggest that the production would reproduce its own form of social hierarchy, presenting Italians and Irish figures in leading roles over and against the undistinguished otherness of darker-skinned extras. It turns the original narrative's interest in religious experience into an occasion for drawing lines in social space.

But one detail cuts against the grain of this social demarcation, in a way related to the questions that *Ben-Hur* raised about mass taste. The description of the final scene indicates that Wallace's Roman crowd has been replaced by an all-black audience: "Great and thrilling Chariot Race, Grand Panorama of Colored Spectators." Since Cleveland's theater specialized in minstrelsy as well as vaudeville, this was likely to have been either a painted backdrop of racist caricatures or a live panorama of actors in blackface. As with much of minstrelsy's material, it is difficult to gauge the degree to which simple ridicule and the anxiety of preserving whiteness shared space with more complex forms of identification. But the playbill's description of the scene—it claims that the chariot race "will haunt you in your dreams"—suggests that its author had at least a dim appreciation of its potentially unsettling force. Given the uncertainty about what it meant to enjoy *Ben-Hur*, this grand panorama was not imagining black figures in a questionable space reserved for them alone but placing them in a questionable space that all Americans seemed to share.

As these first two chapters have shown, cool reactions to the two most widely read novels of the American nineteenth century—*Uncle Tom's Cabin* and *Ben-Hur*—produced waves of imagery that deemed mixed feelings and amateur efforts more American than either sentimental purity or intellectual clarity. Popular attitudes toward these books implied a creative approach to reading: if best-selling novels could have profound effects while lacking greatness, it made sense to be only partially attached. The next two chapters explore how this positive view of American partial attachment was reinforced by narratives of transatlantic circulation, both through the reception of British best sellers in America and through narratives of Americans traveling abroad. As American readers made fun of British celebrities like Charles Dickens, and as both British and American authors imagined Yankees bumbling through England, popular literary culture continued to promote the sense that cool reading was a characteristically American endeavor.

CHAPTER 3

British Authorship, American Advertising

A long British tradition depicts American audiences as vulgar. In one infamous example, Frances Trollope noted in her 1832 travelogue the incessant spitting, "mixed smells of onions and whiskey," and strange postures that made the American crowd more memorable than the play: "The bearing and attitudes of the men are perfectly indescribable; the heels thrown higher than the head, the entire rear of the person presented to the audience, the whole length supported on the benches, are among the varieties that these exquisite posture-masters exhibit. The noises, too, were perpetual, and of the most unpleasant kind."[1] Charles Dickens expanded on the idea that US audiences lack sophistication in his 1842 *American Notes*. Framed by his crusade for international copyright protection, his descriptions of American crowds imagine them not only violating his literary property but also literally tearing his body to pieces. Twenty years later, Matthew Arnold would link the American appetite for news with its cultural hopelessness, calling it "likely" that the "home of newspapers and politics . . . is without general intelligence."[2]

This chapter shifts the focus from the religiously inflected reception of American novels to the alternately hostile and adoring American consumption of popular British texts. While shifting from the sacred to the secular, however, the underlying dynamic is similar. In reception contexts shaped by attitudes of coolness, consumption of popular novels conspicuously blurred the line between the revered and the unrefined. As Peter Stallybrass and Allon White explored in their landmark study, *The Politics and Poetics of Transgression*, the long history of authorship is filled with clashes between "the symbolic extremities of the exalted and the base."[3] Stallybrass and White traced a lineage of English writers—Ben Jonson, John Dryden, Jonathan Swift, Alexander Pope, and William Wordsworth—who worked to define authorship as an exalted personal act, elevated above the more communal and unrefined interactions epitomized by the marketplace. *The Politics and Poetics of Transgression* added a new dimension to the often made argument that the stories novels tended to tell in the eighteenth and nineteenth centuries idealized individualism to a maniacal degree. It stressed that the ideal of exalted individualism was promoted not only through narrative content but also through constructs of authorship itself.

If authorship carries connotations of selfhood set apart from the everyday, we might say that any act of cool reading is an affront to this imaginary boundary. But in the context of transatlantic literary circulation—shaped by assumptions about British cultural superiority and the crudeness of American audiences—this violation of the exalted figure of authorship took on a unique urgency. Focusing on the American treatment of two British celebrity writers, Charles Dickens and George du Maurier, this chapter looks through the archives of popular reading for moments that turn the tables on critical voices that would dismiss American crowds, siding with unsophistication over and against the pretense of English greatness. Like any celebrity bashing, coolness toward Dickens and Du Maurier was loaded with contradictory feelings of adoration and aggression. And it would make sense to read this tension as a fairly simple expression of the cultural insecurity that permeated the American nineteenth century. The preoccupations that surface again and again in the ambivalent reception of British novelists, however, moved beyond simple nationalist envy; the popular response gestured toward a broader critique of the individualist ideology implied by contemporary notions of authorship.

One sign that the appeal of contesting and revising British authors cannot be reduced to national pride is the fact that both Dickens and Du Maurier found a strange thrill in the symbolic violence of their American receptions. Their transatlantic fame is worth comparing not only because they were the two most widely read British authors in the nineteenth-century United States, but also because their novels reveal a similar fascination with the idea that American audiences might somehow counter, compromise, or even destroy the authoritative individuality they put into play as celebrity novelists. Along these lines, the phobic imagery with which Dickens described his transatlantic readership in *American Notes* returns in his late work with an entirely different tone, signifying the possibility of creative social transformation. Similarly, after experiencing the "Trilbymania" that his second novel set off in 1890s America, Du Maurier writes a follow-up novel that portrays American literary fame as a kind of pleasant and productive demonic possession. These writers *loved* the notion that unsophisticated America might not allow them the last, authoritative word.

We could chalk this up to the appeal of otherness. In Stallybrass and White's analysis (which echoes a loosely Hegelian assumption that runs through much of literary studies) forms of identity based on exaltedness—on excluding a term seen as lower—always seem to harbor unconscious attraction to the "low."[4] The poet in the ivory tower secretly longs for the disorderly marketplace. The interiorized, bourgeois subject dreams about figures that trouble the boundaries of domestic space, from servants to rodents. In transatlantic contexts, this mode of reading resonates strongly with Paul Giles's scholarship on the transgressive aspects of British-American literary relations. Amid the national formations taking shape from the eighteenth through the twentieth centuries, Giles argues, the United States and England served as "others" for one another. British writers uncomfortable with the constructs and exclusions that define Englishness could always invoke America as an alternative social space, and Americans drew on England to critique social arrangements at home. In Giles's words, the two "separate political identities . . . can be seen as intertwined with a play of opposites, a series of reciprocal attractions and repulsions between opposing national situations."[5]

But the models of troubling otherness put forward by Stallybrass, White, and Giles fall short of capturing the period- and nation-specific qualities of late nineteenth-century American culture. The examples in this chapter show that, somewhat like the medieval marketplace as described by Stallybrass and White, US consumer culture served as a foil for exalted authorship, its socially mixed, communal nature contrasting ideals of individualized, elevated creativity. Where medieval markets were face-to-face, unmistakably embodied affairs, though, nineteenth-century consumerism took shape first and foremost as a media spectacle. Parodists, in particular, took note. American revisionists imagined Dickens's characters strolling through Manhattan streets filled with mysterious, provocative posters. Others depicted Du Maurier's archvillain Svengali hypnotized by American advertising. These rewriters drew on the genre difference between the novel and the ad as a way of marking national distinction, poking fun at British authors' pretensions while also depicting the expressivity of commerce as a kind of new

American supplement to the novel. Not until nineteenth-century cityscapes overflowed with advertising media could this alternative form put so much pressure on constructions of authorship and genre.

The often noted tendency of American audiences to be irreverent and vulgar appealed in this moment, at least in part, because it pushed toward questions about the novel's uncertain place in an increasingly consumerist culture. Cool responses to Dickens and Du Maurier drew on ad media as a way to critique their popular novels' overinvestment in the individual as the primary source of social value. For the two British authors, engaging with—and fantasizing about—the hostilities of American audiences offered fresh ways of imagining how to write a wholly different kind of novel, a preoccupation especially palpable in Dickens's last finished work, *Our Mutual Friend* (1865). Even more than best-selling American works like *Uncle Tom's Cabin* and *Ben-Hur,* advertising was conspicuously *not* a grand, imposing form of expression. Not only did ad media address an unsophisticated audience for the sole purpose of profit, it also plastered American cities with speech attributed to nobody in particular. As Michel Foucault suggests in his now classic essay on authorship, "an anonymous text posted on a wall probably has an editor—but not an author."[6] While the response to Dickens and Du Maurier certainly dealt with national difference, it also engaged with questions about genre that grew out of the American scene.

What made this scene American was not just the presence of flamboyant advertising; anyone walking through contemporary London or Paris would find the same thing. But only American popular culture would embrace the low form of advertising as a representation of national identity. As *Frank Leslie's* would write with pride at the turn of the twentieth century, "there is no country in the world where advertising has become such an art or forms so essential a part of business as in the United States."[7] Profiles of Barnum's creative advertising techniques heralded his Yankee ingenuity. Throughout the nineteenth century, the ad was portrayed as a characteristically American form of creativity: "It has been said," one observer repeated in 1880, "that the American people are the most original in the world in the invention of new styles of advertising."[8] The notion that commercial culture reflected something unique about the United States resonated with criticism of the nation's vulgarity, but it also became a source of defiant pride.

This underlying attitude set the stage for American audiences to explore commercial culture's gestures toward critiques of authorship. As Jennifer

Wicke claims in her study of advertising and fiction, the simultaneous rise of the novel to cultural prominence and birth of mass-mediated advertising over the course of the nineteenth century meant that these two forms crossed paths in many contexts.[9] Dickens's and Du Maurier's American reception added an aggressive touch to the comparison of art and modern commerce, contrasting the anonymous creativity of advertising with British novels in ways that resonate with Foucault's desire to know what fiction might look like if loosened from the concept of the author. Foucault admits that his call for "a form of culture in which fiction would not be limited by the figure of the author" is a mode of "pure romanticism." But his ideal of "the free circulation, the free manipulation, the free composition, decomposition, and recomposition of fiction" is worth keeping in mind as we turn to American distortions of British narratives.[10] If nothing else, this ideal helps describe a kind of romanticism that thrives in popular discourse because it can be vividly expressed through acts of irreverence and deliberate misreading.

SENSATION ADS, THE AMERICAN DICKENS, AND DICKENS'S AMERICA

One of the most striking appropriations of Dickens's work in America consisted of a single word printed in giant red lettering on the side of a building near Manhattan's City Hall Park in 1863. The word—*Blood!*—would have been a familiar piece of graffiti to the thousands of New Yorkers who had read Dickens's hugely popular *A Tale of Two Cities*, which had debuted in *Harper's Weekly* magazine four years before. In that novel's opening scene, an anonymous Parisian revolutionary writes this menacing message on a wall in red after an angry mob loots a store and smashes wine bottles in the street. The transformation of wine into blood sets the stage for Dickens's extremely crowd-phobic narrative. It serves as a grotesque inversion of the Christ-like sacrifice it will take to counter this animosity toward property owners and the powers that protect them.

In Civil War–era New York, marked by the class-conscious and racist violence of the Manhattan draft riots, the message of "Blood!" on the side of a building might seem to play a similar role to the foreboding graffiti in Dickens's novel. In *A Tale of Two Cities*, this scrawled message is at once a warning and a call to arms, announcing a revolutionary breaking point and the violence to come. But in its New York setting, this citation of Dickens was not meant to instill fear. In fact, the opposite is true: the "Blood!" sign is an example of the form of promotion that came to be known as sensation advertising, a kind of marketing that reflected the emphasis on mass pleasure and conspicuous consumerism the term *sensation* signified in the transatlantic 1860s. Whoever imposed this message on the passersby at City Hall Park would have known that the context in which it was placed would dramatically alter the revolutionary slogan's significance.

Ironically enough, the record of the giant red "Blood!" comes down to us from a French tourist who missed its resonance with Dickens's retelling of 1789, but who paid close attention to the carnivalesque character of American commerce. In a typical New York scene, according to Ernest Duvergier de Hauranne's *A Frenchman in Lincoln's America*, "there isn't enough room for the advertisements as they overflow onto the street, on the edge of the sidewalks, between the gutter and the feet of the passersby. A little while ago I read the sinister word 'Blood!' written in red letters, the meaning of which no one yet knows. Last year, in the same place, the astonished public read for six months the mysterious word 'Sozo-don't!' and for six months the author of the enigma persisted in keeping the word a mystery."[11]

The author—or, as Foucault would prefer, the editor—of "Sozo-don't," it turns out, was a toothpaste company by the same name, a brand that launched one of the biggest sensation campaigns of the 1860s. As an 1863 *New York Ledger* article shows, this kind of mystery advertising had become highly visible by this time. The piece describes the placards on the fence around City Hall Park, citing a number of ads that deliberately obscure their meaning: "'Why will ye die?' says a pictured quack with a pill box in his hand, the words being enclosed in what appears to be a bladder issuing from his mouth. 'Stop and think!' exclaims a sensation poster in letters a foot long—as if there was any time to stop and think in New York during business hours. 'Autoperipatetikos!' says one slip of paper three yards long—but gives you no explanation of the awful word. 'Zampilaerostation,' says another, leaving you equally in the dark."[12] De Huaranne has come across Dickens's "Blood!," then, in a spot well known for its sensation ads, messages that aim to create brand familiarity by leaving the public to wonder at their vague significance—but messages that, for all their mystery, were instantly recognizable as advertising.

These cryptic ads dovetailed with the broader shift in sensibility that *sensational* began to signal in the 1860s, not only by attempting to grab the eye but also by aiming to create excitement above and beyond what the actual products they marketed would warrant. While fans of sensationalism celebrated novels and theatrical displays that overexcited the audience despite their lack of moral or sublime value, the mystery messages in New York and other American cities attempted to bring a similarly irresistible attractiveness to advertising: to turn the everyday process of informing the customer into a source of mass enthusiasm in its own right. One final example illustrates this process at work. In an 1860 sensation campaign that seems to have been particularly successful, the dime novel pioneers Beadle and Company caught the public eye with the ads for their second book, *Seth Jones*. As author Edward Ellis later recalled, *Seth Jones* became a hit because of the "ingenious way in which it was advertised":

> All of a sudden all over the country there broke out a rush of posters, dodgers, and painted inscriptions demanding to know "Who is Seth Jones?" Everywhere you went this query met you. It glared at you in staring letters on the sidewalks. It came fluttering in to you on little dodgers thrust by the handful into the Broadway stages . . . In the country the trees, the rocks and the sides and roofs of barns all clamored with stentorian demands to know who Seth Jones was. It got to be a catchword and a joke of the day. The theatres and the traveling shows took it up and billed announcements that the identity of the mysterious Seth would be revealed . . . then it was that a new rush of decorations broke out all over the country. This was in the form of big and little posters bearing a lithographic portrait of a stalwart, heroic-looking hunter. . . . And above or below this imposing figure in large type were the words: "I am Seth Jones."[13]

To move from an advertisement to a "catchword and a joke of the day" was to cross the line between selling a product and entertaining a crowd. Sensation ads thus earned the name "sensational" by working in similar ways to sensational fiction and drama, playing with advertising's form of address to highlight the attractiveness of identifying with the public that consumerism makes visible.

Citing one of Dickens's most crowd-averse scenes in this context was a revisionary act that, brief as it is, sheds light on the ways in which American readers leveraged consumerist culture to critique his authorial voice.

Whatever the ad was meant to sell has been lost to the archive, but we can still see that part of the gesture's meaning was its conspicuous refusal to share Dickens's anxieties about the French mob. The cry of "Blood!" only makes sense in its New York context if it is drained of its negative connotations, made available as yet another object for public fun. And while this gesture was hardly as aggressive as the revolutionary graffiti Dickens imagined on the Parisian wall, it did convey a form of dissent. To reject Dickens's fears about the passions and monstrosities that threaten political security is to cast doubt on his depiction of social stability as a means of keeping this threat at bay. The New York graffiti rebuffs Dickens's authority by turning away from the forms of sociality his novel holds up as sacred.

This gesture would have been particularly noticeable because *A Tale of Two Cities* worshipped social stability to such an absurd degree. Indeed, Dickens's antirevolutionary novel offers strong support for Nancy Armstrong's claim that the Victorian novel idealized bourgeois selfhood, property ownership, and nationhood ad absurdum.[14] Dickens's American readers would have remembered the portrayal of English domesticity embodied in Lucie Manette, at the center of *A Tale of Two Cities*'s happy ending. Where the revolutionary Madame Defarge monstrously records death sentences in her knitting, Lucie oozes social constancy, "winding the golden thread which bound her husband, and her father, and herself, and her old directress and companion, in a life of quiet bliss."[15] Invoking Dickens's monstrous mob under the signs of pleasurable social excitement and consumerist fun, the "Blood!" ad resists the conservative construct he builds around home and homeland. In doing so, the ad cites Dickens to imply a more collectively fulfilling culture than his novel could portray.

This ad was in keeping with a more general distrust of Dickens that shaped his American reception despite his gigantic popularity. The backlash that surrounded Dickens after his first trip to the United States has been well documented. Although American readers would continue to devour his books, Dickens ruffled many feathers by first advocating the widely unpopular cause of international copyright and then publishing an account of his national tour that many Americans viewed as condescending. As Meredith McGill relates in her study of anti-copyright sentiment in the nineteenth-century United States, Dickens's travel through 1840s America left him feeling attacked by both his fans and the American press. While journalists described his advocacy for copyright as mercenary greediness, his letters home reveal his surprise at the aggression with which his transatlantic audience adored him. Disembarking from his steamboat in New York, he was mobbed by "some twenty or thirty people, screwing small dabs of fur out of the back of [his] costly great coat." He is hesitant to visit a barber shop "lest the barber (bribed by admirers) should clip it all off for presents."[16] Dickens seemed to fear that the American crowd might take liberties with his physical body as well as his body of work.

Dickens's subsequent travelogue, *American Notes,* channeled some of his distaste for the new nation in criticism of its manners, politics, and culture which American readers would not soon forget. In 1850, Dickens attempted to clarify his attitude toward the United States for his offended fans by adding a new preface to *American Notes* that emphasized his objection to slavery over his other complaints: "Prejudiced, I am not, and never have been, otherwise than in favor of the United States. I have many friends in America, I feel a grateful interest in the country, I hope and believe it will successfully work out a problem of the highest importance to the whole human race. To represent me as viewing AMERICA with ill-nature, coldness, or animosity, is merely to do a very foolish thing: which is always a very easy one."[17] Downplaying the text's dismissiveness of American manners ("there is no conversation, no laughter, no cheerfulness, no sociality, except in spitting"), American politics ("cowardly attacks upon opponents, with scurrilous newspapers for shields, and hired pens for daggers"), and American attitudes (an ethos of "universal distrust" parading as "superior shrewdness and independence"), Dickens tried to make peace with his American readers.[18]

But two decades after *American Notes* first appeared, when Dickens visited the United States for the second time, bitter memory of his travelogue continued to shape American perceptions. Responses to his 1867 US tour reveal not only the ongoing tension between Dickens and his transatlantic audience but also the ever-increasing prominence of consumerist culture and advertising media that provided the backdrop to his trip. One journalist for the *New York Observer,* for instance, cautioned against treating Dickens too cordially by suggesting that the celebrity author was not worthy of an American sensation ad: "Some years ago," the article claimed, "the walls were placarded 'Gungel is coming!' Go where you would, in city or surrounding country, the great capitals stared you in the face, GUNGEL IS COMING! It proved to be to the advance announcement of some musical performer, whose agents were thus working up a sensation to prepare a way for his advent."[19]

Comparing American newspapers' excitement about Dickens's second trip to the advance work for "Gungel," the *Observer* called for more restraint, arguing that Dickens's national pretensions don't warrant the mass enthusiasm represented by the sensation ad. The article predicts that Dickens will "easily pick up thousands of dollars during his travels, and make as much more out of the books which he will write in ridicule of his American friends when he returns to his native land." And while the *Observer* has no objection to "his turning an honest penny by showing himself," it questions the integrity of the American audience that eagerly anticipates his arrival: "It is against the toadyism of the press and the people, already developing, that we are constrained to enter an earnest protest." It is great that Dickens is coming, the article suggests, but let's reserve judgment, hold part of ourselves back from full assent (in other words: *keep our cool*).

As *Putnam's Magazine* reported in 1868, Americans met Dickens with plenty of adulation. "A welcome awaits Dickens wherever he may go in the United States," the article announced. "With as many readers of his books here as in his native land, the great English author holds in subjection by the power of his genius, hundreds of thousands of American citizens, who are eager to acknowledge personally their allegiance."[20] But alongside this language of submission, and this worshipful attitude toward personal genius, other American voices sounded more like the *Observer* had hoped: a bit less starstruck, somewhat more ambivalent. An article entitled "Charles Dickens and His Worshipers," for example, claimed the following year, "It is absurd to pay homage to [Dickens] as if he were the first of men; and, indeed, there is a point at which homage to any man becomes degrading alike to the giver and the receiver."[21] The *Putnam's* journalist wished that Americans would take a step back from hero worship.

In line with this hope, many parodies of Dickens's works embodied detached coolness. One example, *Dolby and Father*—the title a play on Dickens's *Dombey and Son*—portrayed a main character visited by a ghost reminiscent of *A Christmas Carol*. After describing Dolby's personal transformation, the narrator concludes by promising not to be like Dickens: "we wish it distinctly understood, that we never intend to write an appendix to this work announcing a change in any of our opinions, even if Mr. Dolby . . . should allow us to visit their home, listen patiently to our stories, and send us away richer than we came." The parody wraps up with a couplet on charity and repentance that fits its fictional story of ghostly visitation and the remorse of Dolby. But the reference to Dickens's revision of *American Notes* allows the conclusion to take on a second meaning. In the eyes of this American parody, it is not only Dolby but also Dickens who needs forgiveness.[22]

A later parody pokes fun at Dickens's sentimentality by comparing its appeal to the advertisements on a Brooklyn train. The opening of *Puck* magazine's "Thanksgiving Story," written "After the Manner of Dickens," introduces the reader to a newsboy "weary and numb with the cold." We then see a wealthy, well-fed man riding home from Thanksgiving dinner with his daughter's family. He will soon end up being conned by the newsboy, and the piece depicts his gullible nature by first showing how easily he is taken in by advertising. "Since the oyster-stuffing had been seasoned exactly to his taste," the parody relates, "he felt kindly toward all the world. He even had half a mind to follow the disinterested suggestion to 'Use Celluloid Soap'; had he been a woman, he would have bought a jar of 'Pompadour Balm' at once; and, even though he was that political freak known as a 'Prohibitionist,' he hardly felt a wish to smash the sign calling attention to 'Old Bird and Nunnery Sweet Jam Whiskeys.' When he had read all this commercial literature in the car, and had lazily wondered why the drink in question was so named, it was time to get out."[23]

The newsboy then convinces the man to give him a silver dollar to help his family, and just as the man walks away, the boy buys and eats two ice cream cones as he works up more fake tears for his next victim. The happy man has made the same mistake with the newsboy that he does with advertising: he reads a "disinterested" and truthful nature into urban, commercial modes of address. The fact that this naïve attitude can be traced to his enjoyment of a Thanksgiving meal at the home of "his married daughter and her family" links his misunderstanding to the kinds of domestic ideals that Dickens and many of his fellow Victorian novelists were fond of promoting. The parody implies that a worldview grounded in the individualized happiness of domestic space can't do justice to the life of a modern, commercialized city. *Puck* takes a detached look at Dickens by associating his manner with the conned man's false sense of personal well-being. And, in the spirit of cool reading, opposition to the finality of Dickens's texts goes hand-in-hand with doubting the value of domestically rooted selfhood.

What begins to appear in these revisions of Dickens is a sense that advertising and consumerist culture run counter to the drift of mainstream novels, that commercial literature and popular novels are somehow at odds.

To bring *A Tale of Two Cities* into the context of sensation advertising is to cast doubt on its conservatism. To read the ads in a subway car through the glow of a happy Thanksgiving with family is to miss the point entirely. And in light of these ideologically loaded scenes of reception, it is significant that Dickens's own late works develop a fascination with texts like advertising signs that circulate anonymously in urban space, as well as modes of creativity that might limit or weaken his role as the final authority on the meaning of his own writing. By placing Dickens's 1860s fiction alongside his American reception, I don't mean to suggest that he knew of, or cared about, specific transatlantic rewritings of his novels. Rather, I want to point out that Dickens and his cool readers were engaged in different versions of the same activity, as they both drew on consumer culture to question the value of the Victorian novel's most favored terms: the happy individual, and the home and homeland that supposedly made this happiness possible.

Where Dickens's readers explored this conceptual space by refusing him the last word, for Dickens this involved considering the limits of his authorial influence. The imagery of language floating freely through urban settings that returns again and again in his late novels—particularly in his last completed work, *Our Mutual Friend*, a novel obsessed with unattributed speech—helps Dickens express a desire he often mentions in his letters around this time, that the form of the novel might operate less like a delivery system for one person's point of view and more like a collaboration with his audience. In his late career, Dickens was in search of what he would call a novel "written in company." And in light of his commercially minded American reception, it is significant that Dickens begins to explore this deconstruction of authorship in a collection of stories that he announced with a sensation advertisement of his own in 1860s London.

Dickens's ads promoted the 1862 Christmas edition of his periodical, *All the Year Round*, which featured a collection of stories written by Dickens and several others entitled *Somebody's Luggage*. In a sense, Dickens was making an American choice here. This was not the first such mystery campaign in London, but in the discourse of transatlantic popular culture, these types of ads were still seen as suspiciously un-British. *All the Year Round* ran stories on "American sensations" throughout the decade; another London periodical, *Once a Week*, would report around this time that "in America . . . the sensation advertisement runs to absolute riot."[24] When Dickens decided to build interest in his story collection with the ad campaign that one contemporary observer described as "the perplexing line, 'Somebody's Luggage,' which for many days has been a standing enigma to the readers of our advertisement columns," he was experimenting with a form that had been notably shaped and developed by American commercial culture.[25]

First promoted with an anonymous ad, *Somebody's Luggage* portrays an author who has disappeared. In what begins as a story of lost possessions, a waiter at a public inn opens an unclaimed suitcase to find a stash of short fiction handwritten on paper stuffed into various articles of clothing. Dickens's table of contents dissects the absent traveler's things, with titles like "His Boots," "His Paper Parcel," "His Black Bag." This small violation evokes a more graphic dismemberment: "He had put no Heading to any of his writings," the narrator exclaims. "Alas! Was he likely to have a heading without a Head, and where was *his* Head when he took such things into it!"[26] The image compares the author's absence at the scene of reception to the literal loss of his head, his inability to oversee the ordering of his text with his physical destruction.

Dickens continues to develop this theme of the absent author in "His Brown Paper Parcel," a contribution to the Christmas number that sheds light on his interest in commercial modes of address. Another tale of textual dispossession, "His Brown Paper Parcel" tells the story of Tom, a London sidewalk chalk artist who avoids publicity, allowing others to pretend, for a fee, that his work is theirs. "You have seen my works over and over again," the mystery artist informs the reader, "and you have been curious about me, and you think you have seen me" (138). In 1860s London, chalking was a widely used method of advertising; but Tom employs this medium to present a strange jumble of begging and nonsense: "An honest man is the noblest work of God. 1 2 3 4 5 6 7 8 9 0. £ s. d. Employment in an office is humbly requested. Honour the Queen. Hunger is a 0 9 8 7 6 5 4 3 2 1 sharp thorn. Chip chop, cherry chop, fol de rol de ri do. Astronomy and mathematics. I do this to support my family" (143).

Tom's ambivalence about taking credit for his crowd-pleasing work leaves him violently inclined toward those who do. After watching Tom's reaction to one of the phony artists, a friend exclaims, "Why you looked as if you would have his blood." "I am sensible that I did," Tom admits, "I know I did" (146). Later on, another friend notices his anger, and Tom explains to her how much he would like to bloody the imposter's nose (154). Staging the tension between anonymity and the visibility of authorship in this way,

Dickens emphasizes the problematic nature of literature as property: not the legal issue of who has the right to reproduce aesthetic works (Tom allows he has no "copyright" in his chalking), but the deeper question of how a creative act might or might not belong to a single person. Arranged by a figure who refuses to be recognized, the chalking itself is a collage of fragmented aphorisms, song lyrics, and other expressions that conspicuously belong to no one—a format and a form that calls attention to the free-floating, public nature of its expressiveness.

There is a kind of thematic continuity, then, between the sensational style with which Dickens advertised *Somebody's Luggage* and the stories he writes for the volume. Playing with the disruptive aspects of anonymity, both the ads and the tales evoke a world shaped by the disappearance of authors, where crowds puzzle together over a message about a mysterious lost possession, a waiter works to arrange and publish a stranger's texts, and an artist fantasizes about attacking those who take credit for creative acts that seem to elude notions of ownership. In the final installment of *Somebody's Luggage*, the author returns to the inn and is pleased to learn his work is now in print; but his brief appearance underscores how much time Dickens has spent meditating on his absence, on rifling through his belongings, and even on his beheading. While his first American trip revealed his paranoia about audiences violating his personal space, by the 1860s Dickens was entertaining this as a kind of pleasant fantasy.

Why the shift? Dickens's interest in commercial culture and anonymous text seems to have helped him express discomfort with the fixity of print that, critics have noted, came to surround his reading tours through both the United States and England toward the end of his life. Throughout the 1860s, Dickens would pursue his desire for live contact with his audience through the reading tours that defined his late career, from his first public appearance for profit in 1858 to his death in 1870. David Payne argues persuasively that there was something quasi-penitential about the celebrity author's performance schedule, which came to resemble a religiously inspired drama of self-mortification. Ascribing Dickens's self-sacrificial fantasies to his uncertainty about his novels' social roles, Payne claims that Dickens's willingness to surrender his health for face-to-face interaction with British and American audiences reflects a kind of deep guilt about the failure of his novels to realize his overriding aesthetic ambition: to imbue modern industrial society with transcendent value.[27]

In resolving Dickens's desire to "tear himself to pieces" on stage into a conflict between Christian traditions and modern progress, though, this reading glosses over how central the notion of collective authorship had become in Dickens's late work. Writing to a friend after an exhilarating performance of *The Frozen Deep*, a play he coauthored with Wilkie Collins and starred in throughout the '50s, Dickens related that he had "never seen audiences so affected," depicting the crowd response as a form of shared creativity. He claimed that he found "a strange feeling out of [*The Frozen Deep*] . . . like writing a book in company. A satisfaction of a most singular kind, which has no exact parallel in my life."[28] Soon he confided to Collins, "I have never known a moment's peace or content, since the last night of the Frozen Deep. . . . In this condition, though nothing can alter or soften it, I have a turning notion that the mere physical effort and change of the Readings would be good, as another means of bearing it—I suppose it is the penalty I pay for having written all these red-backed books upon my shelves."[29] The penitence Dickens expresses here is less related to his perceived distance from a Christian God than to the wish that he could write in "company," in collaboration with his readers.

This distinction between divine communion and communal self-realization is definitive for *Our Mutual Friend*, a work that many critics misread as an exemplary nightmare of modernity. As J. Hillis Miller claims, *Our Mutual Friend*'s preoccupation with the circulation of mass print and the relentless commercialization of every aspect of life—its depiction of a cityscape in which everything from orphans to bones to garbage becomes commodified—locates the 1865 novel on the "threshold of the twentieth century."[30] Miller views this market-saturated, impersonal society as horrifyingly empty: Dickens's cityscape offers "no transcendence"; only human powers hold sway and "no one can escape his given place."[31] "The only possible escape from this world," he argues, "would be some kind of fissure, a rupture of the closed circuit between man and the world which would allow the nonhuman world to show through. Only then could man see the world as it was before everything was transformed into value or use. But this is apparently impossible."[32]

Our Mutual Friend's fascination with modern commerce, and its morbid interest in corpses, skeletons, and mutilated bodies, certainly offers reason for understanding the text as dystopian fantasy. In this vein, more recent interpretations by Mary Poovey and Catherine Gallagher suggest that the text expresses uneasiness about the breakdown of traditional value systems and finds reassurance in projecting these fears elsewhere—onto a racialized idea of colonial otherness, in Poovey's reading, or a feminized notion of weakness, according to Gallagher.[33] These interpretations go a long way in showing how Dickens's novel subtly promotes racism and sexism it elsewhere seems to disavow. But in portraying *Our Mutual Friend* as a sounding board for anxieties of modernity, they leave one of the novel's most persistently strange aspects by the wayside: despite its horrific imagery of dispossession and mutilation in the modern marketplace, of murderous plots and the extreme poverty of London's slums, *Our Mutual Friend* represents a world in which there is staggeringly little to worry about.

Unlike the monstrous mob of *A Tale of Two Cities,* which it takes the Christ-like sacrifice of Sydney Carton to hold at bay, the villains of *Our Mutual Friend* are laughably unthreatening. The unsuccessful murderer Bradley Headstone and the failed schemer Rogue Riderhood end up killing one another, while the bumbling extortionists Silas Wegg and Fascination Fledgeby are taken out with little effort by the two characters who might seem to need the most protection.[34] Wegg is eventually tossed in a garbage heap by the mentally challenged Sloppy (770), and the physically disabled Jenny Wren peppers and plasters Fledgeby (703). Two major subplots depict dilemmas of cross-class romance that require elaborate but relatively painless solutions: John Harmon is able to marry Bella Wilfer not because his father ordered him to but out of love; the money-hungry Bella marries John with no knowledge of his wealth. Eugene Wrayburn's friends convince him to marry working-class Lizzie Hexam in the face of his family's disapproval. There is no transcendence in *Our Mutual Friend* because nobody particularly needs it, since the forces of evil are weak and the complications arising from London's heterogeneous social scene easily evaded.

The optimistic modernity of *Our Mutual Friend* is characterized again and again by texts that are refashioned by their readers, the corollary to the absence or at least abeyance of authors the novel explores. The subheadings of its opening sections hint at the theme, calling attention to themselves, like the street art in *Somebody's Luggage,* as common sayings chopped up and put to new use: "The Cup and the Lip," "Birds of a Feather." Much of the sprawling plot depends upon similar acts of appropriation, many of these portraying characters dealing innovatively with forms of mass print.

Sophronia Lammle and Twemlow send secret messages with a picture book (411); Sloppy entertains his adopted family by acting out the police gazette (198); Mr. Boffin teaches Bella a lesson by feigning an obsession with misers' biographies (460–65); Bella displays her independent approach to housekeeping by smacking a cookbook against a table as if to punish it (666). Dickens's novel persistently thematizes mass cultural consumption as a site of creative reworking, paralleling the maneuverability its characters find within a modern marketplace that at first glance seems to degrade social life beyond repair.

Our Mutual Friend, in other words, hinges on a desire that takes many forms in the transatlantic 1860s, portraying a consumerist print culture not as a social dead end but a new horizon of collective participation, driven by the productive energy of mass audiences. Whether expressed in the sensation advertisements of "Blood!" and "Somebody's Luggage," or Dickens's own preoccupation with sharing the act of authorship, this desire reflects an increasing self-consciousness about the pervasiveness and the pleasures of the transatlantic mass media. Philosophically minded readers of *Our Mutual Friend* have long noted its obsession with social interactions based on collaboration and improvisation.[35] In suggesting a context in which this theme takes shape, I want to emphasize both its origin in the crossing of media forms and its implicit critique of the novel as a conservative force.

As this celebration of resistant reading became visible in the space between consumerism and popular narratives, it offered a new way to imagine pushing the boundaries of literary culture. This meant questioning the boundaries of nationhood and property ownership as well. In sharp contrast to *A Tale of Two Cities*, only the most hopeless characters in *Our Mutual Friend* hold on uncritically to the anchors of Britishness, domesticity, and ownership: the ridiculously patriotic Podsnap claims that every country other than England is a "mistake"; and the would-be extortionist Fledgeby has an awkward respect for preordained plots and textual ownership: "I consider it very fortunate that Fate has written in the book of—in the book which is its own property—that I should go to the opera for the first time under the memorable circumstances of going with Miss Podsnap" (264). While enthusiasm for American culture is nowhere on the surface of *Our Mutual Friend*, this exemplary sample of Dickens's penitential late work is strongly invested in letting go of Britishness as a mark of social value. And this antinationalist subtext makes the moments in which *Our Mutual Friend* echoes *American Notes* seem especially noteworthy, particularly since the United States was on his mind as he was writing the novel.

In 1862, while Dickens was working on *Our Mutual Friend*, he published a short piece in *All the Year Round* reconsidering his 1840s American travelogue. At the height of the Civil War, with the nation's future hanging in extreme uncertainty, Dickens recounted the backlash against his criticism of the United States, reprinted some of *American Notes*'s discussion of distrust and the malicious press, and asked his readers to judge for themselves whether any or all of his observations appeared to be valid twenty years later.[36] *American Notes*, then, was at least somewhat on his mind when he invented the minor character, Gruff and Glum, a one-legged sailor who takes center stage as a participating audience member in *Our Mutual Friend*'s elopement scene. Like the Americans Dickens encountered in 1842, whose sole form of sociality is spitting their tobacco juice, Gruff and Glum has "no object in life but tobacco," making him vividly disengaged from his surroundings: "most events acted on him simply as tobacco-stoppers," Dickens writes, "pressing down and condensing the quids within him" (649–50). Self-centered and uninterested, Gruff and Glum is a worst-case scenario for anyone hoping to entertain a crowd.

But Gruff and Glum comes alive as the small, secretive wedding party makes their way into the church. He glides as if on "wings," and his expressive acts become an integral part of the scene: "It was a pleasant sight ... to see this salt old Gruff and Glum, waving his shovel hat at Bella, while his thin white hair flowed free" (652). As if to emphasize the link between this odd character and Dickens's attitudes toward an unsophisticated mass populace, the officiating clergyman recruits Gruff and Glum to play the role of the "People" in the ceremony, "the Minister speaking, as directed by the Rubric, to the People, selectly represented in the present instance by G. and G. above mentioned" (650). In a novel so invested in moments that defy the fixity of rubrics, we are meant to see Gruff and Glum's addition to the ceremony as a creative break in business as usual. The hopeless stranger's transformation into both a crucial partner in the wedding and a representative of the people suggests a rosy view of popular participation over and against the marriage plot's self-contained conclusion for two.

This faith in transpersonal, cooperative creativity as opposed to individual expression has another avatar in the skeleton that seems to come alive in Mr. Venus's store—another aspect of *Our Mutual Friend*'s joyful modernity that it is easy to misread as gothic horror. The patchwork skeleton makes a single body out of many, with "one leg Belgian, one leg English, and the pickings of eight other people in it" (85). When this assortment moves uncannily in the candlelight—"winking and blinking with both eyes" and "no eyes"—it reflects the hope that forms of life in excess of individual identity might become as visible as the commodities lining the shop windows of London (563). But it also revisits a scene from *American Notes*. Among the many tourist attractions that Dickens's visited on 1842 was the Five Points barroom in which the celebrated African American dancer William Henry "Juba" Lane performed. There, after Juba and his fellow dancers rise from the dark corners of the bar as if "every obscene grave were giving up their dead," his strangely body-defying movements anticipate the skeleton in Venus's shop: "dancing with two left legs, two right legs, two wooden legs, two wire legs, two spring legs—all sorts of legs and no legs—what is it to him?" (101–2).

As McGill emphasizes, American culture could be the stuff of Dickens's nightmares. "The spectacle of Dickens's lack of control over the circulation of his texts in America causes him to fantasize about a mode of relation to his writing and his readers that was never wholly within his grasp," she suggests.[37] McGill locates an anxiety of modern dispossession in the phobic crowd scenes of *American Notes,* as Dickens portrays his transatlantic audience tearing apart both his clothing and his body. The enthusiastic tone of the Juba passage, however, suggests that even in the 1840s, Dickens found the idea of public performance as a kind of self-destruction at least somewhat attractive. The vocabulary of death and physical disorder that *American Notes* weaves around the racially marked exoticism of Juba's dancing playfully invokes the threat of self-loss Dickens's American trip elsewhere causes him to take very seriously. It is fitting, then, that this scene returns as Dickens works to imagine a collective and creative life that would disrupt the rigidities of private identity.

The exhilaration of this attempt to think beyond the structures of the novel easily becomes obscured out of context. One of the ironies of *Our Mutual Friend* is that while Dickens dreamed about modern appropriation, the most prominent literary borrowing of his novel treats its imagery of shared creativity as a source of horror. To T. S. Eliot, a line from *Our Mutual Friend*—"He do the police in different voices"—seemed an apt working title for *The Wasteland*, his epic of social emptiness in modern London. But this phrase is taken from one of the most memorable scenes of shared pleasure and care in *Our Mutual Friend*. "He" is Sloppy, the unkempt orphan who will later figure the triumph of the lowly as he throws Silas Wegg in the trash. In the scene Eliot cites, Sloppy is refashioning a text, dramatizing the police gazette for his impoverished caretaker, Mrs. Higden, and the roomful of needy children she supports. "You mightn't think it," Mrs. Higden says, "but Sloppy is a beautiful reader of a newspaper. He do the police in different voices" (198). Mrs. Higden's ungrammatical speech frames this as a scene of misunderstanding, but this not-so-great reading is productive. Sloppy's reproduction de-authorizes the text, turning a record of policing London's poorest neighborhoods into a source of enjoyment for some of the city's poorest inhabitants.

For a reaction more attuned to Dickens's novel than Eliot's act of appropriation, we might turn instead to the American humorist Orpheus C. Kerr (pseudonym of Robert Henry Newell). His 1870 parody of Dickens's unfinished final work, *The Mystery of Edwin Drood*, claims that American culture has become so commercialized that it now reflects a society "without normal body."[38] Taking this rootlessness lightly, Kerr imagines an American version of *Edwin Drood* in which its main characters play with dead bodies for fun. On a drunken whim, they descend into a "pauper graveyard" to "do a few skeletons," by which they mean performing with them as props, in different voices—just as Sloppy does with the police gazette.[39] In this striking moment of narrative revision, Kerr borrows Dickens's fascination with uncanny forms of resurrection to imagine a marginal, anonymous crowd coming to life on the fringe of his novels.

Before arriving at the graveyard, though, Kerr's characters misread one of the most pervasive sensation advertisements in 1860s America, a mysterious ad for Drake's Plantation Bitters that simply says "ST—1860—X." Stumped by the message, they suppose it is a cryptic symbol for the "experiences" unfolding inside the tenement house on which it is printed. This moment of creative misreading forges a connection between the staged exuberance of commercial culture and the unfamiliar, crowded interior of the tenement. It links the threat of social disorder and foreignness that this alternative domestic space represents with the disrupting forces of anonymity and pleasure the advertisement invokes. The less seriously Kerr takes Dickens, it seems, the closer he comes to the serious concerns that shape Dickens's late works, as they will define Du Maurier's at the turn of the century. Designed to sell in a marketplace keyed to enjoyment, Kerr's parody channels the utopian wish that runs through the cool reading of Dickens: that a life beyond the "normal body" of home, homeland, and the boundaries of individuality might be best imagined by thinking outside of popular novels.

TRILBYMANIA: ANTIREALISM

The outlines of Dickens's American response returned in the 1890s mania for George du Maurier's *Trilby,* a British novel that not only sold better in the United States than at home but also was transformed by its American admirers into a mega-phenomenon of merchandising and revision. Like *Uncle Tom's Cabin* and *Ben-Hur* before it, *Trilby* exploded into American cultural consciousness through book sales and a variety of adaptations, parodies, and commercial items, from hats to ice cream. But *Trilby* arrived with the extra baggage of national difference. Du Maurier's novel tells the tale of three young British artists spending time in Parisian "Bohemia," where they meet an alluring girl, Trilby, and the narrative's villain, Svengali. A figure of ethnic otherness, the Eastern European Svengali, a Jew, eventually forces Trilby to marry him and work as a celebrity opera singer after he discovers that hypnosis brings out her hidden talent as a vocalist.

The popular craze that became known as Trilbymania has been discussed in detail but most often in ways that reduce American reactions to pure fandom and leave unexplored how the public response conveyed differential and even antagonistic relationships to Du Maurier's novel. To begin with, the simple fact that America went crazy for *Trilby* cut against the spirit of the text, which warned readers with its tale of bohemian body snatching: *don't get carried away*. Before becoming an author, Du Maurier had enjoyed a successful career as a caricaturist for London's *Punch* magazine, where one of his preferred targets was the fashionable ideal of art for art's sake promoted by contemporaries such as Oscar Wilde and James McNeill Whistler. His hit novel furthered his critique of aesthetic abandon. *Trilby*'s eponymous heroine, an attractive art model known for posing nude, represents a Parisian culture that leaves the line between sexuality and artistic pleasures far too hazy. The hypnotist Svengali suggests the dispossessing power of aesthetics. And the overly passionate British artist, Little Billee, who falls in love with Trilby and dies a premature death, serves as a cautionary tale for those interested in artistic pursuits.

Resonant with *A Tale of Two Cities*, *Trilby* presents time spent in Paris as a trial by fire that finally emphasizes the value of more sober-minded, domestically grounded life in England. While Svengali, Trilby, and Little Billee lose their self-possession, another British artist—the "realist" Taffy Wynne—comes to represent the achievement of a stable selfhood over and against the novel's figures of temptation. His creativity remains tethered to the "sense of all that [is] sweet and beautiful in nature"; he ultimately marries a British woman who, Du Maurier assures us, speaks no French, and they move into a "quiet little English country home."[40] Taffy's story allows Du Maurier to conclude his long exploration of seductive Paris by idealizing domesticity as a site of refuge: "And there we will leave them to their useful, humdrum, happy domestic existence—than which there is no better that I know of, at their time of life—and no better time of life than theirs!"[41] The narrative takes place abroad, but the happy ending is firmly grounded back in England.

Trilby's popular reception ignored the ending. In the commercial culture that embraced Du Maurier's work, his warning about the loss of self-control was drowned out by fascination with the sexually permissive atmosphere the novel portrays in the Parisian scenes in which characters watch each other bathe, pose nude, and dress in drag.[42] And American responses to the novel were particularly invested in forgetting its anxious withdrawal into imagery of home and homeland. One remarkable *Trilby* parody, for instance, imagined its main characters leaving the cultural stability of England for the excitement of America. "The Last Chapter of Trilby," which appeared in *Puck*, described itself as written "without the author's consent or knowledge" and asked what would happen if the novel's protagonists could cross the Atlantic and see how Trilbymania had captured the American public. This conspicuously unauthorized version replaced Du Maurier's final scene of domestic bliss with an image of Svengali falling in love with American consumption.

In America, the cast of *Trilby* finds that the novel's faddishness has drowned out the narrative itself: citations of the book are everywhere, but nobody has actually read it. And the parody goes on to highlight Du Maurier's lack of control over his novel by making fun of the intertwined investment in realist aesthetics and Britishness that define its conclusion. "The Last Chapter" portrays *Trilby*'s British artists returning to Paris instead of England and becoming obsessed with depicting real American scenes. But they represent "authentic" US culture by painting models dressed in fake Native American clothes "made by a prosperous manufacturer in Norwalk, Connecticut."[43] In this retelling, the faith in realism that grounds Taffy's safe voyage back to England pushes him further and further from any stable social mooring.

Svengali, however, finds a new home amid the artificial charms of mass consumption. He enjoys fake French wine, dresses in an imitation French suit bought from a tailor on the "rue de Bowerie," and finds fellow feeling in the advertising media of Manhattan: "He had fine offers in America, too, from certain merchants in Baxter Street, New York, who wished him to hypnotize incredulous or irresolute passers-by. But, no;—he had preferred to smoke his big cigar of the Havana, and to walk along lower Broadway where he could look up at the signs and feel himself at home."[44] The home that *Puck* imagines for the outcast Svengali turns Du Maurier's most memorable sign of malicious seduction into a symbol of consumerism's ability to transform the social body, drawing the public into a collectivity defined by the appeal of commodities as opposed to the "authenticities" of national cultures. This American Svengali no longer stands for an overrefined aestheticism—losing himself in billboards rather than the etherealities of music—but for a far more commonplace arena of creativity and public responsiveness.

In a way that parallels the relation between the American marketplace and Dickens, however, this departure from *Trilby*'s fears about the attractiveness of culture is less out of step with Du Maurier's work than it seems at first sight. To turn Svengali into a figure of commercial exuberance is to stress an attraction to self-loss and sensual indulgence that pervades *Trilby*, and that Du Maurier will explore further in his next and final novel, *The Martian*. If the American rewriting of *Trilby* runs counter to the author's conclusion, in other words, it brings to the surface a curiosity about the disintegration of self-control and moral vision that is central to the narrative as a whole. *The Martian* will return to this theme of authorial erasure much more explicitly, depicting the life of a deceased celebrity writer who owed his fame to the influence of a controlling spirit from Mars. In the grain of the American readers that imagined Svengali as a figure of progress, in sympathy with consumer culture, Du Maurier's follow-up to *Trilby* depicts the act of possession as a profoundly positive and potentially revolutionary event.

Popularity is coded American in *The Martian* but also associated with self-destruction and violent political change. The Svengali-like alien body snatcher helps the author character, Barty Josselin, develop an unassuming style suited for transatlantic popularity, a brevity that Du Maurier describes as "telegraphic."[45] By this time, the perception of American audiences as craving simplicity was fairly standard. But Du Maurier's personal investment in losing his self-composure to this demographic stands out. On his deathbed in 1896, Du Maurier would announce that "popularity has killed me at last," echoing Dickens's late fascination with celebrity and self-mortification.[46] At the same time, Du Maurier's posthumously published novel fantasized about mass readership as a loss of selfhood and popularity gained at the cost of alien invasion and premature death. *The Martian* stresses this connection between literary celebrity and literal undoing by opening with a stark announcement of the young author's recent passing: "Barty Josselin is no more." Both Du Maurier's last words and his final novel suggest an intimate relationship between reaching the largest possible audience and losing an individuated life.

Du Maurier's interest in transatlantic popularity leads him to treat *Trilby*'s phobias as occasions for joy. Where Svengali makes Trilby a celebrity to satiate his greed and resentment, the Martian invades others' privacy for the benefit of a broader realization, working to create novels that will "touch" and "charm" on a mass scale, even if their simplicity might disqualify them from greatness.[47] This reversal of *Trilby*'s anxieties resonates with its American misreading, looking to the violation of self-possession that Svengali represents as a positive event. Both Du Maurier and his American parodists, then, share an interest in thinking beyond individuality in the light of an expanding commercial culture. And they both appear to have been underwhelmed by the intertwined ideals of home, homeland, and reasonable, realist judgment that *Trilby* offered as a happy ending.

Trilbymania is worth remembering for the vivid connections it made between the not-so-great and the appeal of American life. The enthusiastic welcoming of *Trilby* into American consumer culture, and the rewritings of its characters as deeply moved by modern US circumstances, became another symbolic site—alongside the cool Yankee and the reactions to

American popular literature—that identified objects said to lack greatness with American communal identity. At least one contemporary review related the American mania for *Trilby* to Du Maurier's deft handling of US cultural insecurity. "What could suit us better, at this particular century-end, when we are ashamed of America and afraid to acknowledge faith in our own culture?" the article asked, and it claimed that *Trilby* included subtle references to American culture to fan its hesitant national pride. "We give Mr. Du Maurier a sly wink and duly acknowledge his little artificial flies cast upon American water. We all jump at them. The Ben Bolt business, the indirect quotations from Lowell, some rollicking Americanisms and references to characteristic American centers: all these have their commercial value."[48]

Still more reviewers attributed *Trilby*'s American success to a vague quality short of greatness. Citing William Dean Howells's description of great literature as the "cream" eventually rising to the top of national culture, one article put *Trilby* in its place as a popular fad: "Mr. Howells says that any writing which is popular must have virtue; but there is a kind of reserve force in some literature which bides its time and conquers in the end. Trilby is having a great popularity now, but it has not the staying power nor the ability for a classic."[49] But, as noted by one commentator on American playwright Paul Potter's stage adaptation of *Trilby*, the novel conveyed a special something in its own right. "[Mr. Potter] skimmed the cream off the book" for his theatrical version, the reviewer claimed, capturing "the atmosphere of [*Trilby*]—that refreshing ozone, which was perhaps the book's greatest success."[50] The imagery of atmosphere allowed critics and everyday readers to have it both ways, praising *Trilby* without committing to an ultimate judgment of its value.

In Henry James's analysis, the atmospheric quality of *Trilby* was a direct result of his good friend Du Maurier's unassuming mode of authorship. The undeniable appeal of *Trilby*, James wrote, "all belongs to the sociable, audible air, the irresponsible, personal pitch of a style so talked and smoked, so drawn, so danced, so played, so whistled and sung, that it never occurs to us even to ask ourselves whether it is written."[51] A later *Harper's Weekly* article, referring to James's review, elaborates: "the idea of a literary style never occurs to Du Maurier's reader. Literature itself, in its own realm, seems to have been displaced by all the arts and by the throbbing pulse of life."[52] Whether imagined as ozone, as a smoky air, or a throbbing pulse, the pull of *Trilby* seemed to have nothing to do with masterful authorship, even as it offered something more immediate and more approachable. This was celebrity short of authorship, an ideal figure for a popular culture fascinated by its own ambivalence.

In transatlantic context, American commercial culture was taken as a sign of national identity and also a kind of outer limit of authorship's jurisdiction. Manias of merchandising made popular texts visible in ways that clearly exceeded their authors' moral visions. Irreverent responses that took shape in dialogue with ad media measured celebrity writers' ideals against less conservative, and less individuated, voices. It seems no accident, then, that the books that sold the best in nineteenth-century America all thematized the influence of mass culture, *Uncle Tom's Cabin* offering a theory of mass-mediated politics, *Ben-Hur* representing the pleasure-seeking crowd, Dickens's works contemplating text in urban space, and *Trilby* imagining celebrity as a form of possession. Along with the distinct moral issues and subjects of interest these novels addressed, they fed a fascination with consumerist culture that held unique intensity in a nation so often associated with modern commerce in popular discourse.

And it also seems fitting that the two most successful British novelists in late nineteenth-century America wrote works that entertained fantasies of mass circulation as the limit of authorial control. Their interest in collective forms of creativity resonated with an American public invested in differing from the English authors it consumed en masse. The resolutely unserious and profit-driven sphere of consumerism is a far cry from the "free circulation, the free manipulation, the free composition, decomposition, and recomposition of fiction" that Foucault imagined as a shattering protest against political order. But the cool reading of British fiction in the American mass marketplace can be seen as presenting a popular version of what Foucault calls the "romantic" distaste for the author as a privileged social symbol. American responses to British best sellers flaunted noncommittal, cool detachment as they drew on cultural insecurity and the imagery of advertising to manipulate, decompose, and recompose the models of individual self-possession that Victorian novels had to offer.

CHAPTER 4

Questionable Americans Abroad

Where figures of Britishness inspired adoration and animosity in American settings, American characters in British contexts evoked a different set of mixed feelings. This chapter explores a series of English and American narratives that featured Yankees overseas: Tom Taylor's *Our American Cousin* (1858), Joseph Jefferson's popular stage adaptation of *Rip Van Winkle* (1861), Anthony Trollope's *The American Senator* (1877), and Mark Twain's *A Connecticut Yankee in King Arthur's Court* (1889). Across these popular texts, Yankee figures share a unique, recurring problem. They offer strong critiques of British cultural norms they cannot quite understand, *but nobody really cares*. I have been arguing that reactions to mainstream novels shaped a kind of ambivalent Americanism, in which national identity seemed mediocre but also more appealing than the most obvious points of connection offered by best-selling fiction: interiorized selfhood, domestic happiness, religious awakening. Stories featuring Yankees in England tended to emphasize this mediocrity, which left their criticisms of Britishness without much bite.

But even while Yankee outsiders were, as a rule, laughable—Twain's Connecticut Yankee botching his attempt to modernize England, Trollope's American senator blundering through British society, Joseph Jefferson's rendition of Rip Van Winkle channeling absentmindedness, and Tom Taylor's American cousin playing the gluttonous buffoon—these figures also came to represent an attraction that was both hard to understand and hard to deny. According to nineteenth-century popular culture, absurd Yankees inspire feelings of identification and self-doubt that might disrupt the smooth functioning of British social life. As Twain describes it, the American abroad is something like an elephant, "not revered or respected, but admired and feared as something different."[1] *A Connecticut Yankee* portrays transatlantic influence in extreme terms of love and hate: before the knights of King

Arthur's court decide to kill the American, they thoroughly enjoy his scheme to retrain them as advertisers and traveling salesmen.

Trollope's more realistic narrative of an American in England depicts this disruptive quality through a confrontation over the cherished British institution of the foxhunt. On a visit to observe British social life, the American senator Elias Gotobed gets hung up on the ritualized hunt, disparaging the custom in ways that irritate, anger, and finally exhaust his hosts. But while the British traditionalists all sense the foxhunt's deep social value, it bothers them that they can't seem to defend it on reasonable grounds: "among them all," Trollope writes, "they didn't quite see how they were to confute the Senator's logic. They could not answer it satisfactorily, even among themselves."[2] *The American Senator* celebrates the hunt indirectly, devoting a good deal of space to describing its charms in detail. Over the course of the novel, though, the uncertainty raised by the "aggravating, interfering, and most obnoxious" American is never entirely resolved.[3]

Twain's and Trollope's late-century narratives revisit notions of Americanness abroad that the 1860s theatrical hits *Our American Cousin* and *Rip Van Winkle* helped establish. At work in both the depiction of the cousin, Asa Trenchard, and the discussion surrounding the uniquely realistic technique the American actor Joseph Jefferson developed for his portrayal of Rip Van Winkle was the idea that the United States reflected an unpalatable but nonetheless undeniable *realism*. This was a common attitude in the transatlantic nineteenth century, extending from Alexis de Tocqueville's *Democracy in America* (1835), which figured the United States as the vanguard of an imminent, disappointing future, to Thomas Carlyle's "Shooting Niagara" (1867), which compared English democratic reform to being swept down the iconic American waterfall. Many agreed that American culture seemed to be an incontrovertible force. By embodying the idea of the imminent, disappointing United States in comic Yankee characters, the 1860s popular stage worked to associate this force with ridiculous failures of judgment and self-composure.

In a somewhat contradictory way, these representations of Americanness outlined a version of realism that is achieved by missing the point, falling short of common sense, or otherwise goofing up well-regulated selfhood. Like the American readers who undermined popular novels by misconstruing them in public, Yankee characters disrupted social situations in meaningful ways by misunderstanding them. The uncertainties surrounding

American figures in England went beyond questions of national difference, engaging as well with the meaning of amateur participation itself. American characters helped writers ask why misunderstanding might be hard to dismiss, why the Yankee's cool inability to go with the flow was not only frustrating but also fascinating to watch.

FROM ASA TRENCHARD TO RIP VAN WINKLE

One of the ways in which Tom Taylor's *Our American Cousin* foregrounds the Yankee's likeability is by contrasting two forms of comic relief: the social awkwardness of the visiting American "cousin," Asa Trenchard, and the inanity of the absentminded aristocrat, Lord Dundreary. As self-centered as Trenchard is generous, Dundreary spends most of the play lost in a web of misunderstanding. His sole kind action is brought about by Trenchard, who forces Dundreary to help advance a young soldier's career by stealing and refusing to return his beloved hair dye, an outward sign of the aristocrat's conceit. According to the British playwright Taylor, where the British lord is laughably insincere, the American is laughably frank. When Trenchard describes himself as "a rough sort of customer" who has a "cool head" and "don't know much about the ways of great folks," one of his English hosts admits, "Well, I do think you are honest."[4] This explicitly not-great Yankee embodies a crude sincerity over and against Dundreary's refined selfishness.

Since *Our American Cousin* is not often read today, a brief plot summary might be helpful: Sir Edward Trenchard, the baronet of Trenchard Manor, is in deep financial trouble when he gets word of a visit from his American cousin, Asa, a distant relative whom Edward's great-uncle Mark had made a beneficiary of his will after a falling out with his English family members. Over the course of Asa's visit, the American saves Sir Edward from an extortion plot by revealing a hidden "release" on his mortgage; fends off advances from a rich-husband-seeking young woman, Augusta; helps Edward's daughter, Florence, by forcing Dundreary to arrange a promotion for her fiancée; and transfers his fortune to Mark's granddaughter, Mary, with whom he has fallen in love. The play ends with Asa and Mary's engagement and with Asa politely promising to keep various characters' secrets: that Dundreary dyes his whiskers, that Augusta professed her love for Asa, and that the butler, Binny, is a heavy drinker.

Significantly, Trenchard's representative Americanness depends on his falling short of an ideal. Upon hearing that the American cousin plans to visit, Augusta exclaims, "How delightfully romantic! I can imagine the wild young hunter. An Apollo of the prairie" (6). She repeats the idealized image just before Trenchard makes his first appearance: "I can imagine the wild young hunter, with the free step and majestic mien of the hunter of the forest" (10). But when the American shows up, speaking in a nasal twang, causing a stir by attempting to kiss one of his cousins, and mistaking a request for his card for an invitation to play seven-up, Augusta is forced to think again. "He's not at all romantic," she laments (11). Even though Augusta's ideals are comically unrealistic, they set up Asa's realism as a form of disappointment.

Instead of romantic heroism, Trenchard stands out for his cartoonish appetite and his distaste for British culture. He announces on arrival that he has just "worried down half a dozen ham sandwiches, eight or ten boiled eggs, two or three pumpkin pies and a string of cold sausages," which will hold off his hunger until dinnertime (12). He complains that his hosts have no "pork and beans" or "clam chowder," and when he tries a British cocktail, he spits it out in disgust (12). Trenchard then mixes some American-style drinks—a mint julep and a "Jersey Lightning"—that are so strong they cause Dundreary to keel over at the end of the scene. In his own de-idealized way, Trenchard is a force of nature. He is louder, hungrier, and more self-assured than any other character on the stage. And, for his British observers, this forcefulness inspires feelings of both disdain and respect.

As Augusta puts it later on in the play, "I am so tired, ma, of admiring things I hate . . . What am I to be enthusiastic about with that American?" Since Trenchard is as wealthy as he is goofy, Augusta's money-driven mother counsels patience, responding: "Oh! I hardly know yet, my dear. We must study him" (20). This pair's willingness to mix hatred with admiration is clearly motivated by greed, but, as the narrative unfolds, conflicting feelings about the American become more interesting. The most obvious example comes from Florence, who has nothing but disdain for Trenchard in the opening act, but who, by the play's conclusion, has learned to respect the clumsy American. After Trenchard helps Florence's love interest gain a sailor's commission and gives her cousin, Mary, much-needed financial support, Florence changes her tune: "And they call that man a savage; well, I only wish we had a few more such savages in England" (27).

Florence's wish revives the romantic hope that seemed to die in the opening act, as Trenchard fell so remarkably short of their idealization of American ruggedness. In this way, the American cousin comes to represent a very different romanticism than the "Apollo of the forest." He is, instead, a character whose goodness stems from *inability:* his inability to play the games of calculation and subtle maneuvering that define the aristocrats' social interactions in Taylor's drama. When Trenchard is bluntly insulting to Augusta's self-seeking mother, she points out his ignorance: "I am aware, Mr. Trenchard, you are not used to the manners of good society, and that, alone, will excuse the impertinence of which you have been guilty" (37). In the broader perspective of the play, however, this lack of sophistication is a mark in the American's favor.

As Trenchard describes himself, he is a "rude, ill-mannered block," but his heart is "worth something" (38). While *Our American Cousin* draws on the sentimental celebration of heart over head to describe Yankee appeal, a slightly different distinction will become more central to representations of Americans abroad—not the refinement of sympathy, but the honesty of crude awareness. A symbol of this blunt-force realism is the axe that Trenchard wields throughout much of the play's last act. As he uses the weapon to smash open a drawer containing crucial evidence for the extortion plot, Trenchard calls attention to its Americanness by referring to it as his "Yan-key." In the distance between the appropriateness of a key and the necessity of an axe, *Our American Cousin* figures the unsophisticated realism that came to define representations of Yankees abroad. The drawer-smashing American disrupts social life for the better, without entirely passing over into the realm of the respectable.

As Joseph Jefferson, the American actor who became famous for his portrayal of Asa Trenchard, recalled, this sense of goodness short of respectability also characterized the play itself. *Our American Cousin* was rejected by several producers before ending up in the possession of Laura Keene, whose New York theater finally debuted it. Jefferson wrote in his autobiography that "while [*Our American Cousin*] possessed but little literary merit, there was a fresh, breezy atmosphere about the characters and the story attracted me very much."[5] Jefferson's comment is a reminder that the exploration of unpolished appeal that informed Yankee imagery was more than national caricature. This portrayal of Americanness echoed contemporary interest in cultural forms that attract despite notably lacking refined forms of merit.

In pointing to a vague "atmosphere" that validates an otherwise inartistic narrative, Jefferson's take on *Our American Cousin* connects the staging of Asa Trenchard to the attitude that shaped the culture of cool reading.

The Yankee typology of *Our American Cousin* is especially significant, since it helped launch Jefferson's transatlantic fame, which would center on portraying characteristically American figures both at home and abroad. While he recognized the play's shortcomings, the immediate success it had in New York got Jefferson thinking about the national and international celebrity he would eventually enjoy. "As the curtain descended the first night on that remarkably successful play," he recalled, "visions of large type, foreign countries, and increased remuneration floated before me, and I resolved to be a star if I could" (222–23). And indeed, he soon became one of the most famous actors of the period by portraying another Yankee figure in a way that resonated with his performance in *Our American Cousin*. His Rip Van Winkle was the first successful dramatic version of Washington Irving's story, and one of the longest-running plays of the nineteenth century.

Jefferson chose the part of Rip with the express intention of becoming a characteristically American star. As he recounted stumbling across the idea to revive Irving's novella, "Rip Van Winkle! There was to me magic in the sound of the name as I repeated it. Why, was not this the very character I wanted? An American story by an American author was surely just the theme suited to an American actor" (225). Although determined to reinvent this classic role, Jefferson knew that the narrative alone did not hold sufficient interest to be a hit. He claimed that nothing from the previous stage versions he had seen "gave me the slightest encouragement that I could get a good play out of any of the existing materials" (226). "The tale was purely a narrative. The theme was interesting, but not dramatic" (225). In order to turn this Americana into an effective play, Jefferson fashioned it into a kind of character study and experiment in acting, focusing less on the action than on the style with which he portrayed Rip.

According to contemporary reviewers, what made Jefferson's performance stand out was his unique manner of representing befuddled and confused states of consciousness. In the process of inventing an American persona for transatlantic consumption, Jefferson perfected the art of seeming lost. His *Rip Van Winkle* reimagined the state of ridiculous outsiderhood that *Our American Cousin* had portrayed. And, while *Rip Van Winkle* was not a story of an American abroad, its 1865 London debut provoked reactions that resonated with the contradictory feelings that surround Asa Trenchard in Taylor's play. As one British reviewer wrote of a scene in which Rip's wife attacks him with a broom for coming home drunk, "[Rip] is incorrigible, he is continually guilty of insincerity, and he is thoroughly selfish, but so quietly droll and invariably good-tempered, that Mrs. Van loses an ally among the audience. . . . Mr. Jefferson's acting is so perfectly natural that the feelings of the audience go with him entirely."[6]

Jefferson's American figure epitomized the appeal of the ridiculous. Inebriated for the entire play, Rip allowed Jefferson to foreground the languidness for which he was known. He worked hard to present an exaggeratedly loose body, as the stage directions in his play text suggest. In scene after scene, Rip "lounges," "drops" into chairs, "slinks" and "creeps" away, sits "indolently" with his hands behind his head, and, of course, "sinks" and "falls to the ground" to sleep.[7] New York reviews of *Rip Van Winkle* described Jefferson as "ductile as dough" and noted that his "backbone" seemed to be made of "jelly."[8] Along with the physical fluidity went a distinctive style of speech aimed to portray Rip's constant confusion. Using a soft voice that was said to have captivated his audiences, Jefferson performed Rip as continually absorbed by his muddled consciousness, rambling to himself, losing and finding again his train of thought throughout the play.

One of the main threads connecting this *Rip Van Winkle* to the broader discourse of Americanness is its evocation of the undeniably real. Even though audiences might find little to admire in the Yankee character, its reviewers often claimed, the natural, believable quality of the performance earned Rip the crowd's sympathy. "A more thoroughly original impersonation," London's *Era* reported, "has never won the unanimous approval of a metropolitan audience."[9] Many noted Jefferson's departure from conventional, more flamboyant comedic style; in the place of burlesque and rant, his Rip was said to offer "touches of nature," a "subtle and truthful physiognomy," and a "refined psychological exhibition."[10] A counterpart to Asa Trenchard's honesty, this realism is believable to the extent that it reveals a subject unworthy of admiration. As the *Era* put it, the "pathetic" charm of Jefferson's Rip has everything to do with his "moments of weakness . . . which are in constant occurrence."[11] From his loose body to his weak mind, Rip was presented to the transatlantic public as constantly falling short of self-possession, and in the process representing something overwhelmingly real.

Again in line with *Our American Cousin,* the nationally coded realism that viewers saw in *Rip Van Winkle* took shape as, in part, a celebration of appetite. Placing a habitual drinker in a plot that *didn't* feature his self-destruction was a marked departure for audiences on both sides of the Atlantic. In the year leading up to Rip's London debut, for example, regular attendees of the Adelphi Theatre would have witnessed *The Workmen of Paris; or, The Drama of the Wine Shop,* which revolved around a murder committed by a drunk man. Two months before *Rip Van Winkle* opened, they would have seen the theater's stock low comedian J. L. Toole as Joe Bright, a fireman and reformed drinker who returns to brandy and is "suddenly converted from a comparatively rational being into an ungovernable savage, ready to commit any deed of violence."[12] Against this moralistic backdrop, American characters like Trenchard and Rip stood out as figures that broke the rules but somehow got away with it, pushing the audience to sympathize beyond the margins of decency.

The air of license and celebration surrounding the Americanness of *Rip Van Winkle* was well suited to the changing atmosphere of the West End theater district. As Jim Davis and Victor Emeljanow explore in their study of London's playgoing audiences, by the "sensational" 1860s, the West End was being transformed into a center of pleasure seeking and consumerist entertainment. Where Londoners could elsewhere find theaters that seemed part of neighborhoods "seeking theatrical expression" of their shared values, the West End was more like "a theme park constructed in order to promulgate values which would attract audiences from elsewhere."[13] The attractions included not only theaters featuring light repertoire but also a wide variety of bars and brothels. A performance in which an American figure makes the margins of appropriate behavior seem pleasant played well in a neighborhood dedicated to self-indulgence.

For at least one reviewer, *Rip Van Winkle* on the West End represented the ideal play for a less-than-ideal audience. "The success of Mr. Jefferson," the *Pall Mall Gazette* claimed, "is as cheering as it is undoubted. It is cheering because it proves that even a common public, with taste vitiated by a long course of alcoholic stimulants, can relish the delicate moderation of truth."[14] The undeniable truth of Jefferson's muddled, confused Rip, in other words, is perfect for a muddled and confused West End audience. Shifting here along with London's geography of consumption is the popular connection between Americanism and the less-than-ideal. In the distance between *Our American Cousin* and *Rip Van Winkle*, Yankee realism moves from Asa Trenchard's goofy goodness to Rip's pleasantly detached, impaired awareness. Jefferson helped shape the Yankee stereotype by cutting out the expectation that the character will serve as a force of moral correction, emphasizing instead the link between confusion and consumption. This was a subtler image than Trenchard's axe-wielding detective work. But Rip's "delicate moderation of truth" still depended on linking America with the charm of imprecision.

OUR AMERICAN SENATOR

In Anthony Trollope's 1875 novel, *The American Senator*, the imprecise, unsophisticated American is more confusing than confused. The American abroad in England, Senator Elias Gotobed, shares much with his Yankee predecessor Asa Trenchard. He can't seem to understand the British customs he has traveled overseas to study, and his blunt honesty offends his hosts despite his seemingly good intentions. But even though the American's name—Gotobed—strikes a comic tone, Trollope reimagines the Yankee as a figure of agitation rather than comic relief. His extended analysis of the feelings Gotobed evokes resonates more with the response to Rip, with whom the audience sympathizes against their better judgment, than with the laughter at Asa Trenchard. The American senator deeply bothers his British acquaintances because they find it impossible to dismiss him entirely.

Gotobed's main offense is his lack of appreciation for foxhunting, the social custom that connects the novel's disparate cast of characters. Trollope portrays the hunt as a vital source of communal cohesion, an activity through which wealthy lords and ladies, attorneys, clerks, small-scale farmers, and hired hands enact and celebrate their shared stake in Britishness. In Trollope's rural England, a gentleman might be popular among his social inferiors for financially supporting the upkeep of hunting dogs for communal use: "He not only rode well to hounds but paid twenty-five pounds annually to the hunt, which entitled him to feel quite at home in his red coat."[15] After one hunting sequence that Trollope describes in painstaking detail, the narrator makes it clear that the custom appeals to all the local inhabitants, regardless of social position: "The fox had been killed close to Norrington, and the run was remembered with intense gratification for many a long day after. 'It's that kind of thing that makes hunting beat everything else,' said Lord Rufford, as he went home. That day's sport certainly had been 'tanti,' and Glomax and the two counties boasted of it for the next three years" (385). Attended by crowds and remembered long after in county folklore, foxhunting functions as an elaborate point of pride not only for its wealthy participants but also for the greater populace that Gotobed has arrived in England to study.

The American senator will have many issues with British life, but none more thoroughgoing than his inability to understand the hunt. When his host, country squire John Morton, takes Gotobed foxhunting, his complaints and confusions are relentless. Unable to understand why anyone would spend time taking care of foxhounds for no pay, Gotobed remarks, "If he could make a living out of it I should respect him . . . though it's like knife-grinding or handling arsenic,—an unwholesome sort of profession" (43). The senator's inflexible practicality leaves him incapable of seeing how, in Morton's words, the keeper of the hounds is "the greatest man in the country on hunting days" (43). The American's density sets up a clash between the rational and the picturesque, in which the rational observer is portrayed as lacking not only basic social aptitude but basic politeness: "The Senator was certainly ungracious," the narrator explains. "Nothing he saw produced from him a single word expressive of satisfaction" (45).

Gotobed's wrongheadedness is further stressed by a subplot in which the senator supports an Englishman's lawsuit against the foxhunt's organizers. An angry tenant farmer named Goarly poisons one of the hunt's foxes in protest against the foxes killing his fowl, then decides to sue for damages. To everyone but Gotobed, Goarly's actions are indefensibly and almost inconceivably antisocial. There is a "general feeling that Goarly ought to be extinguished" (50). But Gotobed deeply admires the outcast: "He liked Goarly for killing the fox, and he liked him more for going to the law with Lord Rufford" (78). Gotobed loves Goarly's apparent independent-mindedness and his disruption of a ritual that makes no sense. When Morton explains the foolishness of pursuing a lawsuit so at odds with public opinion, Gotobed holds up Goarly as a hero: "Then I respect that man the more. . . . He's one against two hundred, and he insists upon his rights. Those men standing round and wiping their eyes, and stifled with grief because a fox had been poisoned, as though some great patriot had died among them in the service of his country, formed one of the most remarkable phenomena, sir, that ever I beheld in any country" (49). Gotobed's financial backing of Goarly's suit wins the senator a good deal of local notoriety. And as tensions build around the court case pitting the small farmer against the extremely wealthy Lord Rufford, it begins to seem as if the suit will become a watershed event, symbolizing the people's agitation against the ruling classes. The rapport between the American and this symbol of popular resistance recalls the Americanism espoused by parliamentary activists such as Richard Cobden and John Bright as they pushed for democratic reforms throughout the 1860s. For Trollope, however, the partnership between Gotobed and Goarly is a sign not of progress but of wrongheadedness.

The lawsuit goes out with a whimper when Goarly's opponents threaten to expose unflattering secrets about him and he drops the charges. Gotobed, it seems, has backed the wrong side, supporting a scoundrel in an ill-conceived fight against communal feeling. This public embarrassment appears to validate the many characters that have met Gotobed with frustration and disdain. But Trollope instead uses this plot point as a way of exploring the Yankee's ongoing appeal. Resonant with the foxhunting fans who could not "answer the senator's logic, even amongst themselves," the British public continues to treat Gotobed as an irritating but also compelling curiosity. This feeling is most apparent when, toward the novel's conclusion, Gotobed puts on a lecture in London entitled "The Irrationality of Englishmen." The lecture attracts a huge interest: "Every ticket had been taken for weeks" (402).

Even as the sold-out crowd becomes increasingly hostile to the American critic, the audience is unable to refute his long list of claims, from the evils of primogeniture to the backwardness of selling military commissions. According to the novel, there is something more American than British about Gotobed's lack of interest in the crowd's reaction: "He was impelled by that intense desire to express himself which often amounts to passion with us, and sometimes to fury with Americans, and he hardly considered much what reception his words might receive" (402). Trollope places the senator's frankness in a broader context of mutual fascination and mistrust between Americans and the English: "The intelligence of the American, displayed through the nose, worries the Englishman. The unconscious self-assurance of the Englishman, not always unaccompanied by a sneer, irritates the American" (401). The back-and-forth between Gotobed and his listeners reflects a clash between communal feeling and more detached perspectives.

Trollope leaves this confrontation unresolved. As insults begin to fly at Gotobed from the back rows, the attendant police officers become increasingly nervous about the "uncanny gathering of roughs about the street" outside. Gotobed launches into his tirade on foxhunting as the tension comes to a head. He claims that no American could hope to understand it: "I shall omit this story as I know it will be impossible to make my countrymen believe that a hundred harum-scarum tomboys may ride at their pleasure over every man's land, destroying crops and trampling down fences ... and that no one can either stop them or punish them" (408). At this, the lecture hall becomes so unruly that the organizers decide to cancel the proceedings, "thinking that something worse might occur" (410). Gotobed's English audience grumbles, yells, and threatens, but no one gets the chance to answer his criticisms directly.

It is significant that, while public opinion is set strongly against the American senator, his rejection is never finalized. Gotobed fits nineteenth-century conventions of Americanness by playing a disruptive role on the margins of social belonging.

The angry mob that greets him is far different from the pleasure-seeking audience of *Rip Van Winkle*, but the crowds' interaction with American figures relate. Both groups plainly see the deficiency in their Yankee counterparts, and both remain semi-attached to the character: drawn to Rip despite his moral failings, deeply bothered by Gotobed even though his sentiments seem unconscionably off-base. As Trollope writes, Americans "worry" the English by disturbing their national sense of self-importance (401). On an even more basic level, however, their presence disrupts the experience of self-coherence. The Yankees represent difference that is too clear to ignore, but not extreme enough to dismiss as entirely foreign. From the derisive sympathy that met Rip Van Winkle to the inability to dismiss Senator Gotobed, Americans abroad inspired feelings that pulled in two ways at once.

MARK TWAIN'S AMERICAN YANKEE

Unsurprisingly, though, for the most part English popular culture remained focused on England. While British interest in Yankee figures helps emphasize how American characters came to stand for a kind of realistic, but also deficient, social perspective, the Yankee would take on more complex leading roles in American texts. No one made the nineteenth-century Yankee more iconic than Mark Twain, for whom the national character was both a major subject matter and a role he played very deliberately in public. As Randall Knoper claims in his study of Twain's performance style, the author's famously deadpan lectures explored the Yankee characteristics that Joseph Jefferson had popularized—the "style of seemingly unconscious humor" that depended on the speaker appearing somewhat lost and confused in a flow of thought not quite adequate to the subject at hand.[16] Like Jefferson, Twain depicted the American type as a kind of compelling inadequacy.

And, like Jefferson's, Twain's performances were praised not just for their humor but also for their psychological realism. Knoper relates that "Twain impersonated a vacant-minded, rambling, drawling, incoherent bumpkin. As Twain told his manager, James Redpath, 'I rely for my effects on a simulated unconsciousness and intense absurdity.'" Reviews of Twain's lectures often described them as "untheatrical, undramatic, moderate, quiet, subdued." This version of the Yankee, in other words, worked to erase the distance between absurdity and American reality. "Ultimately," Knoper continues, "the elements of effect, artifice, mimicry, burlesque, and variety could be viewed as embedded within an unselfconscious drawl and a bodily absorption, lessening the sense of vulgarity or theatricality, and heightening the sense of an artlessly unveiled self."[17] Knoper points out that this version of Americanism hinged on the repackaging of working-class performance styles for more genteel audiences. I would add that it also reinforced the idea that American culture will charm its audience despite its ultimate lack of respectability.

Twain's performances of the unconsciously comedic, mildly vulgar American on stage certainly anticipated the rough-edged, good-natured American types he attempted to portray in his most lastingly famous characters. But his most subtle exploration of the link between Americanness and absurd unsophistication took shape in a later novel far more self-consciously ridiculous than *The Adventures of Tom Sawyer* (1876) or *Adventures of Huckleberry Finn* (1884): *A Connecticut Yankee in King Arthur's Court*, published in 1889. In this text, the premise of time travel as well as international distance—the protagonist falls asleep in nineteenth-century Connecticut and wakes up under a tree in Arthurian England—allows Twain to focus intently on questions of sophistication. Hank Morgan, the American at the center of novel, is a petty and ultimately unsuccessful schemer; but set against a court society Twain describes as the "crude" and "simple" interactions of "more or less tame animals," the Yankee often seems to be the most respectable person in the room.[18]

While Morgan stands for a realistic and democratic worldview in contrast to the superstitious and monarchical British, the story insists that this form of realism, in the end, lacks the emotional appeal it would need to convince. Over the course of the novel, Morgan comes extremely close to affecting what he describes as a bloodless revolution in Arthur's England. After winning respect by pretending to cause an eclipse by magic, he succeeds in ending slavery, democratizing taxation, and introducing a long list of social and technological innovations, including public education, the telephone, and steam power. Although he is an agent of progress, the trickery with which he achieves these ends already marks his character as less than heroic. Twain underscores the Yankee's questionable nature at one point by referring to a group of crooked London alderman as having the "spirit of Yankees," perpetrating fraud "of the sort that has given their race a unique and shady reputation among all truly good and holy peoples that be in the earth" (226). The essence of Yankee-dom here is disreputable self-interest.

Even as Morgan exerts a world-historical influence on Arthurian England, he represents social forces it is hard to be proud of. The most vivid recurring symbol of this limitation takes up the theme of advertising that is ubiquitous in the discourse of Americanism at the time. Part of Morgan's modernizing scheme involves training knights to put their wandering to use by carrying advertisements for a variety of products. One knight carries a banner for Persimmon's Soap (120). Another, parodying the American sensation ad campaign for Sozodont toothpaste, holds a sandwich sign that simply says, "Try Noyoudont" (161). Linking what Twain sees as the emptiness of medieval religion with the shallowness of modern American consumerism, Morgan convinces a devout pilgrim who spends his days continually bowing to power a factory for shirts, and he paints every cliff, "bowlder," and wall in England with giant ads for merchandise.

As the Yankee's influence begins to erode, it becomes clear that the forms of progress he represents are not only often ridiculous but also emotionally unsatisfying. Morgan learns this in stages, first finding himself unable to convince King Arthur that limiting military commissions to nobility is absurd. The king simply finds the Yankee irritating, and Morgan drops the subject. Later on, he is surprised when his lecture about real wage growth falls flat with a group of blacksmiths. "It was a crusher," he says of his concluding point. "But alas, it didn't crush. . . . Nothing could unseat their strange beliefs" (317). At the same time, he also has moments in which his antimonarchical convictions weaken. "Well really there *is* something peculiarly grand about the gait and bearing of a king, after all," Morgan admits after watching Arthur address a crowd (366). England is growing on him, while his American influence is wearing thin.

Anti-Yankee sentiment soon turns into epic-scale violence. Morgan declares a republic, retreats into a cave, and withstands a mass assault using dynamite and rigging up an electric fence. By the end of the scene, Morgan looks out at a mass of twenty-five thousand bodies and realizes he has made a mistake: "Ah, what a donkey I was!" he exclaims (412). In a vivid image of Yankee density, it has taken a bloodbath to show Morgan that American modernity is not as emotionally appealing as he had thought. But his cool reaction also suggests that he hasn't quite understood the stakes involved in his goof-up. The novel ends abruptly after the battle, as the court magician Merlin puts Morgan to sleep for thirteen hundred years, sending him back to the nineteenth century. Morgan can finally return to his accustomed life in the United States, but Twain's satire leaves it an open question as to how fulfilling this accustomed life could be. *A Connecticut Yankee* depicts the citizens of Arthurian England as dupes of the nobility and the clergy. But its representative American is woefully inadequate as well. Unable to convince his audience, he also fails to grasp the magnitude of his failure, shrugging off the staggering body count as if he had simply lost a game.

From Twain's performances of an American subject lost in a confused train of thought to Hank Morgan's inability to grasp the failings of his national culture, we have moved from the realistic depiction of inadequacy to the exploration of a shared reality that is inadequately fulfilling. The time travel scenario allows Twain to portray contemporary American life as an inevitable and deeply disappointing future—a coming reality that will undoubtedly let us down. In this context, the misunderstanding that had marked Yankee characters from the start takes on a new meaning. No longer just comic relief, the inability to grasp the situation fully becomes a survival tool as well. Only someone with fundamentally flawed perception, Twain suggests, could be comfortable living in a public culture as reckless and commercially driven as America's without being a little removed from reality. More than any other nineteenth-century Yankee figure, Hank Morgan signifies the need to keep cool: the United States might be in better order than benighted European social forms, but it certainly isn't anything to embrace without reserve.

The inevitability and inadequacy of American social institutions was an old theme. Tocqueville had asked in his 1830s study of American democracy, "Should we not, therefore, consider the gradual development of democratic institutions and customs not as the best but as the only means left to us of being free? And, without loving democratic government, would we not be inclined to adopt it as the most suitable and most honorable remedy against the present ills of society?"[19] Tocqueville believed that centuries of protest against European aristocracies had left them unworkable, making American-style democracy the sad but inevitable future. Embodying this notion in the goofy goodness of Asa Trenchard, the pathetic lovability of Rip Van Winkle, the irritating truth of Elias Gotobed, and the failed revolution of Hank Morgan, the tradition of Yankee caricature gave the abstract ambivalence about American modernity a personal edge. Where books like *Democracy in America* approached the United States from the perspective of an outside observer, depictions of Yankees abroad asked American playgoers and readers to imagine viewing America from within. These figures represented more than just uncertainty about progress; they reflected the impaired and inadequate states of mind one might need to live comfortably in the American future.

Where responses to *Uncle Tom's Cabin* and *Ben-Hur* lent a certain mystique to inadequate American productions, narratives of British figures in the United States and Yankees abroad clarified the notion that it was especially American to be amateurish, inadequate, and dense. But like the ambivalent discourse surrounding best-selling American novels, as this and the preceding chapter have shown, the narratives of transatlantic movement cast this supposed inadequacy in a highly ambivalent light. Americans purposefully misreading Dickens and Du Maurier created vibrant critiques of their ideological assumptions. Qualities like refreshing honesty, bumbling goodness, and overwhelming reality gave the stock Yankee character a disruptive appeal. As the final chapter and the afterword show, the disruptive charm of the American not-so-great would continue to influence American writing through the twentieth and twenty-first centuries. Once popular literary culture had so loudly pronounced the appeal of American inadequacy, the idea would become difficult to ignore, perhaps most of all for American authors with uncompromising aesthetic ambition.

CHAPTER 5

Unknowing American Realism
Uncle Tom's Cabin to Henry James,
James Weldon Johnson, and James Baldwin

Early on in Henry James's *The Portrait of a Lady* (1881), Isabel Archer's uncle claims that popular novels have yet to capture real Americanness. He should know: a successful American businessman long residing in England, he has even *been* the Yankee in a British book. "We once had a lady who wrote novels staying here," he tells his niece. "She afterwards published a work of fiction in which she was understood to have given a representation—something in the nature of a caricature, as you might say—of my unworthy self." The author must not have been paying much attention, he concludes, as she simply repeated the standard "American peculiarities, nasal twang, Yankee notions, stars and stripes."[1] James implies here that he can do it better. His rendering of a New Yorker's fateful misunderstanding of European culture, he suggests, will reflect transatlantic society as it is, free from the Yankee stereotypes of popular art.

But *The Portrait of a Lady* doesn't avoid popular American types as much as transpose them to a new key. Isabel Archer lacks the nasal twang and Yankee notions that performers like Twain and Jefferson had made famous; in groundbreaking detail, however, she embodies the idea that Americans can't quite figure out what is going on. James's rich description of a consciousness with no reliable foothold on the world reimagines the national confusion that was comic relief in Yankee stagecraft as a serious aesthetic opportunity. And the inadequacy of American figures would become central to the narrative form James made his trademark, the "American abroad" novel. From Henry James to James Baldwin, stories about Americans leaving home promoted the idea that to be American is to be fundamentally flawed in a way that is crying out for masterful literary treatment. American authors could become great, in other words, not *despite* a flawed national culture but *because* of it.

This idea led to novels that explore American identities as pathological, whether shaped by the nation's protean lack of social structure; toxic histories of race, gender, or sexuality; or—as in Baldwin's fiction—all of the above. Europe became less a place of escape in this subgenre than a setting in which American characters realize they can't leave their problems behind: the longing for an elsewhere that Isabel Archer is unable to satisfy in England or Italy, the homesickness James Weldon Johnson's ex-colored man feels in Paris, the self-destructive attachments Baldwin's characters can't shake. Underneath all of the racial and ideological difference that divides these three authors, they seem to agree that American society might be best understood as a kind of haunting, destroying the possibility of happiness in ways that can't be evaded even by crossing the Atlantic.

At the same time, the texts of James, Johnson, and Baldwin also seem a bit haunted themselves by the book that most powerfully evokes mainstream American literary taste: while each writer, at one point or another, would single out *Uncle Tom's Cabin* as the epitome of mediocre American art—drawing a line in the sand between lofty aesthetic goals and the feminine fiction that Stowe's novel represented—the abolitionist best seller keeps appearing in their works in complex and conflicted moments. These references range from the ex-colored man's recollections of reading *Uncle Tom's Cabin* as a boy, to Baldwin nicknaming a tragically victimized character "Little Eva," to the more subtle echoes of James's childhood memories that shape his later writings on America. While these authors imagined characters that could not escape their American roots, their works reflected the ongoing impact that *Uncle Tom's Cabin* continued to have, even as the novel had become a popular subject of ridicule by the end of the nineteenth century.

Why would this symbol of feminine literary impact and the power of popular reading have an afterlife in American abroad novels? Focusing on distinctions between high and low culture, we might read this as yet another reflection of Stallybrass and White's "politics and poetics of transgression"—another construction of elevated aesthetics that entails mixed feelings of fascination with and revulsion for the low. With this in mind, it makes sense that James, Johnson, and Baldwin would be compelled to revisit a popular text they viewed as beyond the pale of great art. Approaching the question through the lens of racial identity, it also makes sense that for Johnson and Baldwin the work of asserting themselves as African American writers amid a deeply racist culture would entail antagonism with *Uncle*

Tom's Cabin's ubiquitous and controversial portrayals of black characters. Baldwin's complicated relationship with *Uncle Tom's Cabin* in particular suggests both the mixed feelings of transgression and the struggle with norms of black representation: he read Stowe's novel so obsessively as a child that his mother confiscated his copy, and he abhorred *Uncle Tom's Cabin* enough as an adult to describe it as a work of "inhumanity."[2]

Ideals of cultural hierarchy and issues of personal identity are both in question where *Uncle Tom's Cabin* reappears in later American fiction. Indeed, Stowe's novel troubles James, Johnson, and Baldwin in large part because it asserts so boldly that the value of artwork and the social position of the author cannot be understood as separate things. By framing her novel as an expression of feminine sympathy, aimed at inciting similar feelings in the white women of the North, Stowe had made perhaps the most memorable connection between a specific location in social space and the power of novel reading in all of American literature. As I have been arguing, however, by the late nineteenth century one of the most glaring facts about *Uncle Tom's Cabin* was that it showcased how texts are shaped by forces beyond authorial control. After decades of rewriting, ridicule, and criticism, *Uncle Tom's Cabin* had come to stand not only for the potential of a feminine counterculture but also for questionable quality, racist caricature, and gauzy emotionalism. For late-century observers, Stowe's novel was an image of a highly personal form of authority very visibly falling short.

For writers invested in confronting American failure, *Uncle Tom's Cabin*'s ambitions and shortcomings had special appeal. It was not only *Uncle Tom's Cabin*'s representativeness of American taste but also its status as a partially failed work that made it difficult for James, Johnson, and Baldwin to dismiss. This chapter argues that their late antagonisms with Stowe's novel helped these respective authors navigate a contradiction that, as Amy Kaplan points out in her analysis of American realism, had become central to the male-dominated discourse of literary authority by the end of the nineteenth century. Kaplan reads realism as a response to the felt loss of social intelligibility, driven at once by growing class conflict and the increasing prevalence of mass cultural forms. In this context, she argues, the realism of James, William Dean Howells, and others took up the contradictory task of "represent[ing] the commonplace and the ordinary, at a time when such knowledge no longer seemed available to common sense."[3] This idea of artistic success sees failure as in some ways part of the job.

Baldwin announces this brand of heroic failure in the epigraph to *Another Country* (1962), a passage taken from James's "New York" preface to his novella *Lady Barbarina*. Referring to the new wave of Americans in Europe, James had remarked that "they strike one, above all, as giving no account of themselves in any terms already consecrated by human use; to this inarticulate state they probably form, collectively, the most unprecedented of monuments; abysmal the mystery of what they think, what they feel, what they want, what they suppose themselves to be saying."[4] For Baldwin, this epigraph describing American types as ultimately opaque, even to the observing author, marks the beginning of a novel fascinated by the seemingly crumbling social fabric of the contemporary United States. *Another Country* follows James in linking modern America with the limits not only of his characters' self-awareness but also of his own authorial vision.

There was plenty of room for contradiction in the ways both Baldwin and James announced the limitations of their authorship while also depicting their characters' inner lives with incredible depth and virtuosity. And this is part of the point about their fascination with *Uncle Tom's Cabin:* American abroad novels kept returning to Stowe's text for what it suggested about the contradictory connection between artistic failure and American insight. The male literary figures considered here wrote at a conscious cultural distance from Stowe. They sought reputations as serious professional artists, the kind of notoriety that Mark McGurl, in his study of the art novel after James, refers to as "elevated discursive status."[5] They also distanced themselves from the feminine modes of domesticity and maternal sympathy that had strongly shaped *Uncle Tom's Cabin*. But they couldn't shake the feeling that the cultural forms Stowe represented—the feminine and the mass mediated—might be better suited for capturing the Yankee emptiness they hoped to express.

STOWE TO JAMES

In an 1868 *Nation* article entitled "The Great American Novel"—one of the first ever uses of the term—James's fellow literary realist John W. DeForest reserved high praise for *Uncle Tom's Cabin*. Although "there were very noticeable faults in the story," DeForest claimed, Stowe's best seller had come the closest of any book to the great American novel. DeForest's two criteria are geographic range and verisimilitude; he celebrates *Uncle Tom's Cabin* for its "national breadth" and for presenting recognizable types. "Such Northerners as Mrs. Stowe painted we have seen," he argues, "and we have seen such Southerners, no matter what the people south of Mason and Dixon's line may protest; we have seen such negroes, barring, of course, the impeccable Uncle Tom."[6] This assessment relies on a straightforward model of representation. This approach to both Stowe and the great American novel takes for granted America's status as a social world with a solid existence, simply waiting for the right observer to express it in print.

James couldn't disagree more. For James, the power of *Uncle Tom's Cabin* lay in its ability not to describe the various social spheres that made up the United States but to blur their outlines. James writes that there was "for that triumphant work no classified condition; it was no sort of reader as distinct from any other sort." He recalls experiencing Stowe's novel as "gathering in alike the small and the simple and the big and the wise."[7] As James continues, it becomes clear that he was fascinated not only with *Uncle Tom's Cabin*'s manner of defying the boundaries among social groups but also with how it transgressed the more abstract line between American fiction and American consciousness. Where DeForest respects Stowe's representational accuracy, James admires her novel's infectious quality.

Famously, James notes that *Uncle Tom's Cabin* "knew the large felicity of gathering in alike the small and the simple and the big and the wise, and had above all the extraordinary fortune of finding itself, for an immense number of people, much less a book than a state of vision."[8] According to the young observer, Stowe's power to shape the public imagination here has nothing to do with the accuracy of her American types. James refers to his encounter with *Uncle Tom's Cabin* as a "brave beginning" of his aesthetic sense precisely because the narrative seemed to compel its audience members even while calling attention to its failure of verisimilitude. His memory of watching Little Eva's fall from the steamboat on stage in New York sums up the disconnect between *Uncle Tom's Cabin*'s clear shortcomings and elusive overall effect:

> Why should I have duly noted that no little game on [Eva's] part could well less have resembled or simulated an accident, and yet have been no less moved by her reappearance, rescued from the river but perfectly dry, in the arms of faithful Tom, who had plunged in to save her, without either so much as wetting his shoes, than if I had been engaged with her in a reckless

romp? I could count the white stitches in the loose patchwork, and yet could take it for a story rich and harmonious; I could know we had all intellectually condescended and that we had yet the thrill of an aesthetic adventure; and this was a brave beginning for a consciousness that was to be nothing if not mixed and a curiosity that was to be nothing if not restless.[9]

James's *Uncle Tom's Cabin* doesn't appeal by representing facts that preexist the text; it appeals by offering a feeling of depth that remains in tension with the perception of the superficial, amateur, and ridiculous. A "loose patchwork" capable of transforming into "rich" experience for the viewer, and a text that the audience condescends to while it thrills them, Stowe's novel sparks James's interest in aesthetic production as sleight of hand.

This passage exudes the mix of condescension and envy that elsewhere shapes James's engagements with mass cultural forms. David Kurnick's recent study, *Empty Houses,* has explored how James never stopped fantasizing about writing the theatrical hit he never could. Nancy Bentley's scholarship on American literary realism and mass culture emphasizes that, for James and many of his contemporaries, fascination with and disdain for amusement parks, Wild West shows, and early cinema as emblems of a disintegrating communal world provided both the impetus and inspiration for imagining new forms of social analysis.[10] But focusing on James's special interest in *Uncle Tom's Cabin* suggests how his discomfort with the novel as a medium took shape not so much through a longing for a mass audience or an interest in new, destabilizing forms of popular culture but through his suspicion that the appeal of best-selling fiction lay in its allowing the audience to have it both ways: to see the shoddiness of the production while also being convinced of its experiential value.

By the time James was recalling his early experiences with *Uncle Tom's Cabin* in *A Small Boy and Others* (1913), this exaggerated form of ambivalence had become central not only to his aesthetic ideals but also to the manic style of social criticism he developed toward the end of his career, most notably in *The American Scene* (1907). A collection of articles written for the *North American Review, Harper's,* and the *Fortnightly Review* over the course of his 1904–1905 trip through the United States, *The American Scene* attempted to express what James saw as a national culture made incoherent by immigration, democratic leveling, and the rapid growth of urban space. Like the Americans abroad that James would describe as absolute mysteries, the Americans he observed at home seemed to him to reflect a fundamental emptiness brought about by the lack of tradition and the presence of rapid change. "It is the huge democratic broom that has made the clearance," James wrote, "and that one seems to see brandished in the empty sky." The condescending, xenophobic expatriate paints a bleak picture of the national scene.[11]

But, along the way, James offers the reader a running commentary on his mixed feelings that recalls his memory of *Uncle Tom's Cabin*. The nickname he gives himself—the "restless analyst"—anticipates his later recollection of how his "nothing if not restless" sensibility was born while watching Stowe's novel on stage. And the tension that defines *The American Scene* reflects the same dynamic of trying to name a feeling of richness in excess of the object's failure that James would express in his discussion of *Uncle Tom's Cabin*. In Newport, Rhode Island, James asks, "Of what, in the bright air, for the charmed visitor, were the softness and sweetness of impression made? I had again to take it for a mystery" (38). But the metropolitan sprawl of his native New York brings out this elusive feeling more than any other setting. In Manhattan, James experiences what he calls "a kind of fluidity of appreciation—a mild, warm wave that broke over the succession of aspects and objects according to some odd inward rhythm, and often, no doubt, with a violence that there was little in the phenomena themselves flagrantly to justify" (3).

Much of the restlessness that shapes *The American Scene* surrounds James's efforts to explain this experience of being violently moved beyond what seems to be a reasonable response. James sees the United States as an inferior product, "a welter of object and sounds in which relief, detachment, meaning, perished utterly and lost all rights" (83). Observing the "inconceivable aliens" entering New York through Ellis Island, he remarks how "this sense of dispossession . . . haunted me so" (86). At one especially critical point, the "crudities and vulgarities" of national culture prompt James to ask "if the cash-register, the ice-cream freezer, the lightning-elevator, the boy's paper, and other such overflows, do truly represent the sum of [America's] passions" (312). Channeling one of his literary heroes, Matthew Arnold, James has no shortage of slights for the homeland he views as gaudy and trivial.

Elitism and xenophobia, though, tell only half the story of *The American Scene*. James spends as much time wondering at his inability to dismiss the

United States entirely as he does dismissing the new nation. In brief moments, even what James sees as America's most abhorrent qualities—its homogeneity and its emptiness—can inspire him to a kind of ecstasy. Writing of the "ache of envy" he felt toward America's "spirit" while walking through New York, James admitted that "one was in presence, as never before, of a realized ideal and of that childlike rush of surrender to it and clutch at it.... It made the whole vision unforgettable, and I am now carried back to it, I confess, in musing hours, as to one of my few glimpses of perfect human felicity. It had the admirable sign that it was, precisely, so comprehensively collective—that it made so vividly, in the old phrase, for the greatest happiness of the greatest number" (104). Sliding back and forth across disdain and elation, James presents himself as the ultimate ambivalent subject, for whom America was at once a profound disappointment and a glimpse of perfection.

The American Scene thus shares the contradictory feelings that, I have been arguing, so often shaped encounters with popular American culture. And it is telling that James's articulation of this divided consciousness reappears as he recalls the "birth" of his sensibility in front of *Uncle Tom's Cabin*. For him, seeing Stowe's novel on stage was a lesson in the kind of self-observation it would take to be an American; James felt as if he and the rest of the audience were watching themselves as much as the play: "the point exactly was that we attended this spectacle just in order *not* to be beguiled, just in order to enjoy with ironic detachment and, at the very most, to be amused ourselves at our sensibility should it prove to have been trapped and caught."[12] James's persona of the restless analyst in his writings on the United States owes a lot to his understanding of this origin scene, in which he glimpsed the violent force with which popular American culture can trap observers into believing something they know to be frivolous and fake.

In contrast to the works of Johnson and Baldwin, which engage with *Uncle Tom's Cabin* by name, *The American Scene* registers its presence only indirectly. But with gendered imagery that anticipates both Johnson's *Autobiography of an Ex-Colored Man* and Baldwin's *Another Country,* James associates the bleak but powerfully alluring American atmosphere with best-selling fiction and with femininity gone awry. As men have retreated into commerce, he claims, women have "pounced" on American culture, and, "outside business, she has made it over in her image" (346). He compares the dazzling heterogeneity of New York to "the abundance of some ample childless mother who consoles herself for her sterility by an unbridled course of adoption" (186). James makes sense of his mixed feelings about the United States in part by relating them to a feminized greed for attention and affection.

Alongside what James sees as the unnatural empowerment of women goes the exaggerated force of popular novels. For an aesthete and social critic, James has remarkably little to say about the consumption of cultural forms in *The American Scene*, but, at one point, the immensity and sameness of the United States calls to his mind "the vast vogue of some infinitely-selling novel, one of those happy volumes of which the circulation roars, periodically, from Atlantic to Pacific . . . in the manner . . . of a blazing prairie fire; with as little possibility of arrest from 'criticism' in the one case as from the bleating of lost sheep in the other. Everything, so to speak, was monotonized, and the whole social order might have had its nose, for the time, buried, by one leveling doom, in the pages that, after the break of the spell, it would never know itself to mention again" (306). Here, the collective spirit that he elsewhere describes as a form of perfection appears as a destructive, doom-dealing type of witchcraft—the strange violence of popular fiction.

This indecisiveness is James's answer to the contradiction of the realist moment: in order to be an effective critic in an era that has made arrest from criticism impossible, the only viable solution might be to replicate the problem. That is, social representation might have to accept its status as a failure and hope to be compelling by some quality other than verisimilitude. James certainly might have envied best-selling authors because he wished to be adored by a large audience, too; but, more fundamentally, he envied their show of creative force. Drawing on nothing insightful enough to be memorable, popular fiction showcased the ability to cast a "spell" on its audience, compensating for its inadequacy by violently holding public attention. Cutting against the grain of contemporary descriptions of mass audiences as easily led sheep—a notion that James would echo elsewhere—here he focuses instead on the elusive power of best-selling books.[13]

As an unquestionably accomplished man of letters, James wrote of his "amateurism," his "incoherent ideas," and his states of confusion from a comfortable height (314). But the persistence with which he casts doubt on his powers of judgment in *The American Scene* suggests a sincere intellectual crisis. In trying to express the Yankee character, James had become a kind of stock Yankee himself: the visiting tourist who can't seem to understand what is really going on. James is imagining himself as yet another victim of the way American social contexts wreck the coherence of individual experience. Again anticipating Johnson and Baldwin, James depicts what he sees as the American ruin of "private life" through the metaphor of vanishing domestic space. "One is . . . tempted to ask," he remarks, "if the hotel-spirit may not just *be* the American spirit most seeking and most finding itself" (102). The collective, anti-individualist nature of American existence seems apparent in its departure from home life as well as its practices of mass reading.

Later on, discussing the "strange perversity" of the American house "with almost no one of its indoor parts distinguishable from any other," James suggests that perverse domestic space sums up the nation's hostility to the individual. These homes "testify . . . to the prevailing 'conception of life'; they correspond, within doors, to the as inveterate suppression of almost every outward exclusory arrangement. The instinct is throughout, as we catch it at play, that of minimizing, for any 'interior,' the guilt or odium or responsibility, whatever these may appear, of its *being* an interior . . . denying its right to exist" (167). As Bentley notes, *The American Scene* is riddled with James's realization that "the literary culture that has defined his own life and mind has been eclipsed."[14] The vanishing interior space here signifies not just new architectural fashions but also, more to the point, the felt loss of a coherent individual experience capable of witnessing and aptly describing the social world.

The compromised home presents a far different spatial metaphor than those most often associated with American realism. In their fascination with the removed, thoughtful interior space of the author's study, Bentley points out, nineteenth-century literary figures such as William Dean Howells, Edith Wharton, and James Russell Lowell explored the ideal of authorship as privileged social analysis. Magazine columns like *Harper's* "Editor's Study" and books like Lowell's *My Study Windows* (1871) reinforced the link between professional novel writing and a detached, comprehensive point of view.[15] But the inhospitable interiors James describes in *The American Scene* imply a less confident version of the author's role. With characteristic ambivalence, James leaves his feelings about this shift unclear. On the one hand, he refers to the new American interior as a disappearance of "responsibility"; on the other, he describes it as a removal of the guilt that goes along with the privatizing act of cordoning off an interior space. James's America is both a loss and a relief.

What would authorship look like if it originated not from a peaceful study but a de-individualizing interior? The restlessness and ambiguity that shapes *The American Scene* suggests that James doesn't have an answer. But his understanding of *Uncle Tom's Cabin* as a text that achieved a kind richness without reflecting any particular analytical merit offered a prominent point of departure. It is one of the many reversals of the *Uncle Tom's Cabin* phenomenon: while Stowe hoped that her antislavery novel could transform American politics by reorienting it toward the feminine moral compass of the home, the phenomenon ended up suggesting how aesthetics might work in the absence of stable interiority—how realism might leave the comfort of the study. James saw American popular culture as a mess of bad feminine influence, groundless change, and "alien" encroachments; but its most famous best seller showed how these negative qualities might be overcome by something like literary magic.

The American Scene makes explicit the question of authorship's changing role in American contexts that James had long engaged with in novels that asked what it meant for Americans to leave home. One of the main ways in which James had, from early in his career, implied the inferiority of the new world to the old was through narratives featuring Americans who find themselves somehow inadequate to European social contexts. *Roderick Hudson*'s (1875) eponymous main character travels to Italy, is undone by frustrations, and drowns. *The American*'s (1877) Christopher Newman fails miserably at marrying the European girl he loves; she enters a convent and refuses to see him before he gives up and returns to America. Daisy Miller flails through her naïve misunderstandings of the social hierarchy and eventually dies of "Italian fever" in Rome. These early novels seem to suggest that the United States forms individuals who are remarkably unfit for life beyond its borders.

But this sentiment shifts subtly in *The Portrait of a Lady*, which is less about an American falling flat in sophisticated Europe than about the impossibility of leaving America behind. The plot is a web of expatriates: the promising, dreamy young woman Isabel Archer is invited to Europe by her American aunt, who spends most of her time in Italy but is married to a wealthy American businessman who lives in the English countryside. After refusing two proposals—one from the progressive-minded Lord Warburton and another from Caspar Goodwood, the son of another rich American businessman—Archer ends up trapped in a loveless marriage with Gilbert Osmond, another American expatriate, which was arranged by the scheming, cold Madame Merle, who sounds French but is actually an American living abroad. With the notable exception of Lord Warburton, all of the central characters are from the United States. Although set in Europe, this American abroad novel is an extended survey of peculiarly American types.

And these American stories all seem to revolve around ill-disposed domestic space. Archer meets her rich expatriate uncle, Daniel Touchett, for the first time in an odd addition to the private inner rooms of his English country house, where "the wide carpet of turf that covered the level hilltop seemed but the extension of a luxurious interior."[16] This zone between inside and outside introduces a novel that is obsessed with family homes that depart from the norm. The Touchetts, for instance, lead a divided life, Daniel and his son, Ralph, staying on their English estate while Daniel's wife spends most of her time in Italy. Ralph's observation that "his father, as he often said to himself, was the more motherly; his mother, on the other hand, was paternal" makes it clear that James sees this family as playing out the loss of a traditional order.

Anticipating the "hotel-spirit" that James will come to see as the essence of American life, Archer grew up in a home that was more like an inn. Her grandmother's Albany home reflected its owner's boundless hospitality by offering "to a certain extent the appearance of a bustling provincial inn kept by a gentle old landlady who sighed a great deal but never presented a bill" (32). As if retreating from this bustling, semipublic space into her own private, interior experience, Archer finds an odd, unused study room and adopts it as hers, the "mysterious apartment which lay beyond the library . . . called, traditionally, no one knew why, the office" (33). Unlike realism's "author's studies," spaces that make room for detached, thoughtful observation of the social world, this office encourages Archer to indulge in groundless fantasy. "If the sidelights had not been filled with green paper she might have looked out upon the little brown stoop and the well-worn brick pavement. But she had no wish to look out, for this would have interfered with her theory that there was a strange, unseen place on the other side" (33).

This domestic backstory introduces the quality that will make Archer's narrative so unique and eventually tragic: her endless fascination with the unseen and the potential, the unreal things she considers crucial to her freedom. Transplanted to Europe, her thoughts proceed in "a thousand ridiculous zigzags," "a tangle of vague outlines which had never been corrected by the judgement [*sic*] of people speaking with authority" (53). Her two refusals of marriage proposals turn the preservation of this vagueness into a kind of moral principle. As she tells Lord Warburton, marrying him would feel like giving up the freedom to imagine her life:

> "It's getting—getting—getting a great deal. But it's giving up other chances."
> "Other chances for what?"
> "I don't mean chances to marry," said Isabel, her colour quickly coming back to her. And then she stopped, looking down with a deep frown, as if it were hopeless to attempt to make her meaning clear. (118–19)

Archer's inability to let go of her early infatuation with open-ended possibility not only shuts down Lord Warburton's proposal, it also makes it impossible for her to explain herself to others.

In this way, *The Portrait of a Lady* marks a movement away from James's considerations of Americans as having bad taste—Roderick Hudson's overwrought romanticism, Christopher Newman's dull utilitarianism, Daisy Miller's lack of sophistication—toward his exploration of America as an experiment in subjectivity. Archer's faith in her sense of possibility will ultimately make her an easy target for the American-born schemers Gilbert Osmond and Madame Merle. But James doesn't present Archer's weakness as a character flaw that might be corrected by a more critical perspective. Instead, he suggests that her groundless, elusive interiority is beyond the reach of analysis: "Altogether, with her meagre knowledge, her inflated ideals, her confidence at once innocent and dogmatic . . . her combination of the delicate, desultory, flame-like spirit and the eager and personal creature of conditions: she would be an easy victim of scientific criticism if she were not intended to awaken on the reader's part an impulse more tender and more purely expectant" (54). Archer here represents the sense of real loss offset by dubious gains that James will later describe as the American predicament. The vanishing of any stable foothold amid the stream of individual consciousness leaves the would-be critic helplessly floundering. But in the place of stable selfhood and critical intelligence, *The Portrait of a Lady* offers a feeling of sympathy with the groundless character that James describes as more valuable and "pure."

It might seem strange to read a novel that stands out for its incredibly dense, florid descriptions of inner life as an anti-individualist text. But its insistence on the continual slipping away of self-absorption suggests that, along with Dickens, Du Maurier, and Stowe herself, James was drawn to the American scene as a place in which self-coherence might dissolve in a pleasurable and productive way. As figured by the strange domestic spaces that define Archer, she has been freed from the responsibility, or even the guilt, of achieving a stable interiority. The tragic conclusion of her story suggests that this open-endedness can be read as a kind of failure. But James is far more interested in the loss of selfhood as an opportunity, both for his characters to play out unpredictable lives and for his interest in authorship that goes beyond the purview of critical intelligence, even as it explores its subject's motivations with a painstaking thoroughness. As he would in *The American Scene,* the "restless analyst" sees American social emptiness as an occasion for performing authorship without the responsibility of critical authority.

The Portrait of a Lady thus can be seen as an attempt to create a perfectly ambivalent reader: an observer who clearly sees the meagerness and the inflation of Archer's inner life but is nevertheless carried away by its restless and groundless density—we might say its richness here, recalling the vocabulary with which James described the elusive quality that *Uncle Tom's Cabin* held despite its meager, threadbare construction. The "flame-like" spirit that James ascribes to Archer is far less violent than the blazing forest fire to which he compares the appeal of best-selling American novels. But Archer's characterization and the portrayal of popular reading in *The American Scene* both share an overriding interest. For James, they illustrate how America's demolition of the private, knowing subject requires being of two minds at once: one knowing better and one carried away.

To oversimplify a bit, we might see these two poles as representing the two forces that James struggled to balance over the course of his long career: artistic self-determination and the demands of the marketplace. As Michael Anesko details in his publication history of James's comprehensive New York Edition, James found endless frustration but also feelings of gratitude in his many experiences of market failure. "Like so many other works by James," Anesko writes, the collection's history "exemplifies, as the author himself once had occasion to remark, 'that benefit of *friction with the market* which is so true a one for solitary artists too much steeped in their mere personal dreams.'"[17] The complex negotiations and compromises involved in compiling the New York Edition offer a concrete case of the balance that James attempted to strike in his fiction, which asked how a masterful rendering of American life might require some level of relinquishing authorial control.

We might take James seriously, then, when he claims that his sensibility was born as he watched *Uncle Tom's Cabin* in a New York theater. In attempting to portray Archer sympathetically, James made a symbolic return to the split selfhood that the *Uncle Tom's Cabin* phenomenon had brought into the foreground of his young consciousness. And he asked his readers to follow him there, to ignore the flaws of Archer's character in the name of a vague sense of "expectation." *The Portrait of a Lady*'s attempt at depicting a more believable Yankee figure sought to capture an identity that could move its audience without taking on the vaguely guilty responsibility of understanding itself. And the failure of *Uncle Tom's Cabin* to achieve the status of serious, respectable, representational art served as a strange inspiration. As an image of popular aesthetics, *Uncle Tom's Cabin* signified not only (as Stowe had hoped) the feminine, domestic purification of American politics but also the life that novels might take on when severed from any requirement of representing a coherent analysis of national culture. The unique interior spaces of *The Portrait of a Lady* subtly reflect James's intuition that the American scene Stowe hoped to expose and the one her novel revealed were dramatically different locales.

STOWE TO JOHNSON

It might be argued that African American and white readers would experience a novel about slavery in ways that are impossible to compare. But part of what turned *Uncle Tom's Cabin* into a phenomenon was its ability to stand for many things at once: not just a plea for sympathy or a portrayal of racial injustice but also an exploration of gender politics, the relation of home and nation, and the power of popular cultural expression. Even as race meant incommensurate things to Henry James, James Weldon Johnson, and James Baldwin, their reactions to Stowe's novel show how, for each, the text symbolized both the failings and the possibilities that seemed to shape American popular culture broadly conceived—a vague social territory to which they each felt it necessary and difficult to relate. To be sure, though, when it comes to questions of blackness and whiteness, the difference of social privilege is glaring: James ignored the political urgency of *Uncle Tom's Cabin* almost entirely; Johnson, for his part, famously portrayed reading Stowe's book as a major, disillusioning rite of passage for people of color, through which young African Americans learn how they are viewed by the white majority. As the fictional subject of Johnson's *The Autobiography* explains, *Uncle Tom's Cabin* "opened my eyes to who I was and what my country considered me; in fact, it gave me my bearing."[18]

Readers who confuse Johnson with the ex-colored man often repeat this description of *Uncle Tom's Cabin* as if it stated a fact from Johnson's childhood; but, in the fictional context of the *Autobiography*, this seemingly straightforward scene of reading is more like a wry joke. Nothing defines Johnson's ex-colored man more than his complete lack of bearings: after drifting through a failed attempt at college, a stint as a cigar roller in Florida, a short career as a piano player in New York and Europe, and an extended trip to the American South to connect with his African American roots, he finally decides to pass as white and start a family in Manhattan, a decision he remains unsure about at the novel's end. The link that Johnson makes between the ex-colored man's protean sense of "bearing" and his encounter with *Uncle Tom's Cabin* is thus more Jamesian than seems at first sight. For the ex-colored man, Stowe's novel is a gateway not to self-knowledge or racial identity but to a life spent chasing their elusiveness.

As if to symbolize this subversive reading of Stowe, Johnson transforms one of *Uncle Tom's Cabin*'s most memorable images of loyalty, white paternalism, and stable selfhood into something like its opposite in the *Autobiography*. Many scholars have noted that the gold coin necklace that the ex-colored man receives from his absentee white father echoes the gift given to Uncle Tom by George Shelby, his master's son. This coin associates the ex-colored man's link to the white world with both Stowe's moral vision and her novel's most nonthreatening black character. Accordingly, the necklace has been read to signify the ex-colored man's ultimate acceptance of white cultural authority over and above any other.[19] But where Uncle Tom's coin signifies the mutual love between slave and master and George Shelby's promise to reclaim him from his new owners, the ex-colored man's necklace ties him to a father who seems to care little about being a father and for whom the ex-colored man has next to no affection. Stowe's coin is a reminder of Uncle Tom's fixed identity within a household and a family (however temporarily upended by the plot); Johnson's refers to the lack of familial stability.

The ex-colored man's coldness toward his father underscores the young man's detachment from his domestic life but also, as Johnson describes it, from the overwrought emotions often associated with domestic fiction and stagecraft. When the ex-colored man is twelve, his father returns for a brief visit which leaves the son feeling sure about his absence of feeling. "Somehow I could not arouse any considerable feeling of need for a father," the ex-colored man recalls. "I could not rise to this dramatic or, better, melodramatic climax" (23). The failure of melodrama to capture this familial scene marks this as a moment of genre distinction as well as emotional distance. Although this narrative of identity confusion begins, in a way, with *Uncle Tom's Cabin,* here it takes a sharp turn away from Stowe's vision of an American society grounded in domestic feeling. Johnson's critique of Stowe goes beyond the standard notion that sentimentality oversimplifies complex social realities. In turning her symbol of filial love into a sign of its absence, the *Autobiography* pursues a mode of realism that might do justice to a fundamental emptiness at the center of an unstable American identity.

If the *Autobiography* departs from *Uncle Tom's Cabin*'s faith in domestic bliss with relative ease, however, it has more trouble shaking the image of American popular culture's appeal. Like Isabel Archer, the ex-colored man drifts from his unconventional childhood home through a series of odd domestic spaces, none more crucial to the plot than the converted Manhattan house in which he discovers the power of popular music. Part hotel, part club, the brownstone is decorated like a nineteenth-century home: "the floor of the parlor was carpeted; small tables and chairs were arranged about the room; the windows were draped with lace curtains" (64). But it also caters to more modern tastes, with ragtime performances on the first floor, a "chop suey" restaurant in the basement, and walls "covered with photographs or lithographs of every colored man in America who had ever 'done anything'" (64).

A classically trained piano player, the ex-colored man is especially struck by the amateur musicians who perform at the club. The ragtime artists will eventually inspire him to develop his own mix of classical and modern style, but at first they cause him to reflect on the more general significance of popular expression. "Whatever new thing the *people* like is pooh-poohed; whatever is *popular* is spoken of as not worth while. The fact is, nothing great or enduring, especially in music, has ever sprung full-fledged and unprecedented from the brain of any master; the best he gives to the world he gathers from the hearts of the people." For the ex-colored man, music reflects a "universal appeal" which he understands as "one strong element of greatness" (62). Just as Stowe had tied together a version of domestic happiness with a vision of how popular aesthetics might change the world, Johnson's alternative home implies a theory of American popular expression's value. And this space provides the ex-colored man a renewed sense of purpose as he dedicates himself to connecting with his African American identity by weaving ragtime into his repertoire.

But these bearings don't remain steady for very long. Almost immediately, the ex-colored man's fantasy of black community is interrupted by a figure of popular novel reading. As his hybrid performances of classical and ragtime begin to attract slumming white audiences as well as the club's regular African American clientele, one white fan draws his attention. "She was an exceedingly beautiful woman of perhaps thirty-five," Johnson writes, "she had glistening copper-colored hair, very white skin and eyes very much like Du Maurier's conception of Trilby's 'twin gray stars.' When I came to know her I found that she was a woman of considerable culture; she had traveled in Europe, spoke French, and played the piano well" (75). Just when the ex-colored man seems to be on the verge of finding a coherent racial identity, this image of white womanhood and best-selling fiction appears to trouble the waters: "my finer feelings entirely overcame my judgment," he claims (75).

From here, it becomes increasingly unclear whether the central conflict in the *Autobiography* is the struggle to define a complex racial identity or the struggle to understand the power of popular appeal. The ex-colored man is saved from his overwhelming feelings for the Trilby-esque woman by an abrupt and violent turn of events in which another of her love interests shows up and shoots her in a fit of passion. But the Trilby sequence sets up a tension between the stability of selfhood and the disruptive force of popular fiction that continues to define the plot. The *Autobiography* becomes an American abroad novel when the ex-colored man travels to Europe with a white patron, passing himself for white as he performs for parties in Paris, London, and Berlin. And the backdrop of Europe allows the ex-colored man to perceive the American predicament that he can't leave behind. Here the lack of a solid identity that might have helped him adopt a new life overseas instead makes him homesick. He soon makes up his mind to return to the

United States to better acquaint himself with the black identity from which he has always felt uncomfortably detached.

"I made up my mind to go back into the very heart of the South," the ex-colored man explains, "to live among the people, and drink in my inspiration first-hand" (86). His search for racial belonging is paralleled by his ambition to harness the appeal of "the people's" expression. The more he looks for popular music to inspire him, however, the more he finds a social landscape that seems, disappointingly, stuck in the fantasy life of commercially successful fiction. He doesn't need to describe the people he encounters, he writes, "for log cabins and plantations and dialect-speaking darkies are perhaps better known in American literature than any other single picture of our national life. Indeed, they form an ideal exclusive literary concept of the American Negro to such an extent that it is almost impossible to get the reading public to recognize him in any other setting" (102). *Uncle Tom's Cabin* is the elephant in the room here: up to this point, the ex-colored man has attempted to locate an alternative social vision to Stowe's alignment of home life and racial representation; after this scene of disillusionment, he comes to see this ideal as impossible to realize precisely because of novels like Stowe's.

The *Autobiography*'s tenuous conclusion turns away from the fantasy of collective African American domestic space and cultural expression embodied in the Manhattan club. Disappointed with the South, the ex-colored man returns to New York, where he ends up marrying a white woman with whom he plays Chopin duets instead of ragtime. But the closing lines of the narrative suggest that this final domestic and cultural arrangement is no more satisfying than any other. Wondering what he could have made of himself had he stuck with his ambition to express the popular black "heart" through music, he admits that he "cannot repress the thought, that, after all, I have chosen the lesser part, that I have sold my birthright for a mess of pottage" (127). Despite the ex-colored man's search for the perfect home—which leads him from the Manhattan social club, to a Paris apartment, back to a marriage in New York—he can't settle on a satisfying relationship to mainstream American life. Johnson's much-criticized choice to conclude the narrative by having the ex-colored man pass for white is a flight from the complexities of racial identity and also from popular fiction.

The ex-colored man's concluding uncertainty reflects his failure not only to become unburdened by his racial identity but also to leave behind the decentering attitude of cool reading. In the end, he is unable to live comfortably apart from his ambivalence about American popular culture. The *Autobiography* ends by imagining the possibility of longing for an American scene that is too groundless to relate to in any fulfilling way.

STOWE TO BALDWIN

Baldwin's comprehensive critique of American racial, romantic, and sexual relations adds a new urgency to the idea that national culture makes happiness nearly impossible for all, regardless of social status, sexual orientation, or racial identity. And in the end it is hard to disentangle his disdain for American popular fiction from his nearly absolute pessimism about human connection. Consider, for instance, the echo of his famous dismissal of *Uncle Tom's Cabin* in the violent interracial relationship at the center of *Another Country* (1962). Baldwin's early essay "Everybody's Protest Novel" takes Stowe to task for reducing black characters to sentimental archetypes; but he also accuses contemporary African American texts—his example is Richard Wright's *Native Son* (1940)—of promoting a similarly reductive image of black identity, featuring characters who are wholly consumed with "hatred and fear," like Wright's Bigger Thomas. Baldwin claims that neither side writes with "devotion to the human being, his freedom and fulfillment."[20]

Baldwin figures failed fiction as a kind of pathological attraction: "the contemporary Negro novelist and the dead New England woman are locked together in a deadly, timeless battle . . . and, indeed, within this web of lust and fury, black and white can only thrust and counter-thrust, long for each other's slow, exquisite death."[21] Transplanted into *Another Country,* this passage might serve as a description of the dysfunctional relationship that anchors the opening section, between Rufus, an angry and confused young man resonant with Bigger Thomas, and Leona, a white woman from the South who is nicknamed "Little Eva." When Rufus takes Leona to a Harlem house party, the host's vaguely menacing asides set up the violent sexual scene about to take place. "See that Little Eva has a good time," he suggests, and later, "How you coming with Eva? . . . Blast Little Eva with some pot. Let her get her kicks" (381). Rufus then lashes out at this image of white femininity as if they are thrown into a life-or-death struggle: "Under his breath," Baldwin writes, "he cursed the milk-white bitch and groaned and rode his weapon between her thighs" (384). Like the black novelist Baldwin imagined locked in rage with the New England woman, Rufus responds to his white love interest with a violence that drowns out any potential for human exchange. Leona, too, reflects Baldwin's sense of American culture as trauma. She has come to New York to leave behind a relationship that ended with her abusive husband claiming custody of their child, but her underestimation of Rufus's anger at white America makes her vulnerable to becoming a victim yet again. As if to banish mediocre fiction from his text, early on Baldwin has Rufus commit suicide while Little Eva loses her sanity, wandering the freezing New York streets in search of her lost baby. Her story marks a clear departure from the ideals Stowe projected onto her own Little Eva: the healing power of white sympathy and the feminine influence exerted through domestic space seem to have no influence in Baldwin's New York.

As Leona moves in with Rufus, who continues to abuse her, she comes to seem even more like a powerless version of Little Eva. Where the locks of Eva's blonde hair curl around Simon Legree's fingers, causing him to recall his mother's love in a fit of remorse, Leona's whiteness only infuriates Rufus. As Baldwin describes their final violent scene, "he twisted his fingers in her long pale hair and used her in whatever way he felt would humiliate her most" (412). In ways that echo the misogyny that runs throughout Baldwin's work (the title character of *Giovanni's Room* [1956], for instance, suggests that women enjoy being beaten because they have limited inner lives), the depiction of this failed relationship seems to revel in the drawn-out demolition of Stowe's sentimental fantasy. But this is still only the beginning of the novel. If Rufus seems akin to Bigger Thomas in being consumed by rage, his early death is a sign that Baldwin intends to write a different kind of book than *Native Son*. Focused on the aftermath of Rufus's suicide, *Another Country* is less about the all-consuming force of black anger than about how those in the grips of American history might create something positive out of devastation.

In other words, moving away from Rufus and Leona marks a point at which, in Baldwin's terms, bad fiction ends and a novel devoted to the "freedom of the human being" might begin. But in order to understand the unique concept of freedom that Baldwin saw as realizable in American contexts, it helps to revisit his earlier exploration of American self-discovery abroad, *Giovanni's Room*. Where James's and Johnson's texts imply the trope of masculine flight from an overly feminized American culture, *Giovanni's*

Room literalizes this fantasy of escape: the novel revolves around a young American's flight from his impending marriage into the gay subculture of Paris. With thoroughly mixed feelings, the American, David, leaves behind the American dream of hetero-domestic happiness for the more uncharted life symbolized by the room in the novel's title. Like many literary Americans abroad, however, David finds himself unable to locate happiness in his flight from American life; Giovanni's room is no place to live, a fact the narrative begins to drive home by opening with news of Giovanni's impending execution (he has murdered his ex-boss in a fit of passion).

This sensational crime is only an extreme instance of the larger instability that characterizes David's relationship with Giovanni throughout the book, an emotional unviability that Baldwin explores through the metaphor of strange domestic space. "What kind of life can we have in this room?—this filthy little room," David asks Giovanni as he considers returning to his fiancée. "What kind of life can two men have together, anyway?"[22] The room is too cramped for two and, as if in a state of suspended animation, crowded with dust, dirty clothes, and signs of halted plans: half-removed wallpaper, paintbrushes, packed suitcases (289). Hardly one of American literature's many male utopian spaces, Giovanni's room symbolizes an interior experience that has become glaringly unlivable.

Baldwin implies that much of David's confusion has to do with sexual shame; but he also portrays the American abroad, in the grain of Isabel Archer and the ex-colored man, as someone whose bigger issue is one of national culture. As David sums up his time in France: "Perhaps, as we say in America, I wanted to find myself. This is an interesting phrase, not current as far as I know in the language of any other people, which certainly does not mean what it says but betrays a nagging suspicion that something has been misplaced. I think now that if I had had any intimation that the self I was going to find would turn out to be only the same self from which I had spent so much time in flight, I would have stayed at home" (236). To be American in this assessment is to be unable to shake the feeling that your selfhood has been lost, a feeling that becomes especially acute for those who attempt to find a coherent inner life. The freedom to explore new geographical and sexual territory amounts to little for David because of the empty national ethos that he feels he can't leave behind.

This begins to explain why Giovanni's intricate critiques of American culture sound, at times, so much like Henry James. Horace Porter has argued that the plot of *Giovanni's Room* resonates with James's early novel *The American,* but I would suggest that the imagery reflects a broader engagement with James's work.[23] And it certainly revisits the language of *The American Scene.* Giovanni describes the difference between Europeans and Americans (to whom he refers as a different "species") with the Jamesian notion that privacy has been destroyed in the United States. In Giovanni's more explicitly misogynist and sexually frank worldview, this privacy would have allowed David to be comfortable marrying his fiancée while continuing to have affairs with men (286). And the more David realizes that he can't be happy with either the dream of hetero-normative marriage or the escape of Giovanni's room, the more he sees this national lack of interiority as the definitive, and devastating, fact of his life. France teaches David that he can't leave America: "perhaps home is not a place but simply an irrevocable condition," he finally suggests (294). *Giovanni's Room* thus traces the development of a discomforting form of freedom: escape from the false hope of escaping an unfulfilling homeland.

Baldwin continues to explore this negative freedom in *Another Country,* through the struggles of its various characters to make sense of Rufus's catastrophic story. Rufus's memory connects the novel's sprawling cast of characters to the knowledge that America's destructive history cannot be escaped, a reality that Baldwin describes by taking the lack of privacy that James observed to a new extreme. New York "was so familiar and so public," Baldwin writes, "that it became, at last, the most despairingly private of cities" (571). For James, the American scene is knitted together by a common emptiness; for Baldwin its underlying reality is acute, isolating pain: "This note of despair, of buried despair, was insistently, constantly struck."[24] And the cardinal rule of Baldwin's American ethics is that this despair can't be ignored; it needs to be acknowledged as a force that has torn people apart before anything like real human relationships can take shape.

For this reason it is not Eva's childish purity but the absolute devastation of another of *Uncle Tom's Cabin*'s characters—the "tragic mulatta," Cassy—that ends up playing the most vivid role in *Another Country.* Cassy is Stowe's reflection of transformation through despair, a character whose backstory includes decades of sexual slavery and the desperate act of killing her own child to spare her a life of bondage. Stowe's Cassy has too many similarities to *Another Country*'s Cass to be merely coincidental, leaving us to ask why Baldwin would write a white mother of two who finds it nearly impossible to live her life as an echo of the tragic slave. On Simon Legree's plantation, Cassy intimidates the otherwise hardened slave owner by laughing "wildly" and seeming to be on fire with "smoldering embers of womanhood"; and she ultimately escapes from his house by pretending to be a ghost in the attic. Cass's struggle is not with the evils of slavery but with the claustrophobia of bad fiction and domestic ideals: her husband, Richard, has found success writing superficial novels that Cass doesn't respect. When Richard becomes physically abusive, Cass's story becomes a literal representation of the violence exerted by inadequate writing.

The more Baldwin's Cass feels threatened by the parallel fantasies of mediocre novels and domestic happiness, the more she begins to sound like Stowe's Cassy. She starts up an affair with another man and a rocky friendship with Rufus's sister, Ida, but Cass's restlessness also affects her appearance. Suddenly, she seems to "blaze, nearly, with some private, barely contained passion"; she "discovers the wildness of herself," and, echoing Cassy's wild laughter in *Uncle Tom's Cabin,* begins laughing "with her head thrown back" (605, 657). Most strikingly, both women resist their confinement by haunting their respective homes: Cassy plays a ghost in Legree's attic, and Cass warns Richard that she has been living "in this house like a ghost for months" (698). *Another Country* might seem to have dismissed *Uncle Tom's Cabin* by humiliating "Little Eva," but these recurring traces of Cassy imply an unresolved relationship between the two texts.

Ultimately, I think, these echoes of Stowe help Baldwin express a quality that is crucial not only to his work but also to the broader culture of response: the sense of potentiality that surrounds disappointing things. Cass will return to her suffocating domestic life, the novel's conclusion implies. But the Cassy-esque wildness and ghostliness she displays along the way signifies the inability of her home life to capture her character completely. She rejoins her life under the sign of protest and partial participation—knowing full well that it doesn't come near to exhausting the potentiality she represents. That Baldwin identifies with this partial detachment is suggested by the second character that learns to compromise with the inadequate culture in Cass's house, the bohemian novelist Vivaldo. In contrast to Richard, Vivaldo struggles uncompromisingly throughout the book to write a novel truer to life than typical American fiction. While at a party at Cass and Richard's house filled with superficial, smarmy book agents and television producers, however, he decides, against his previous intent, to write for mainstream audiences.

Baldwin describes this artistic compromise as jumping into less-than-ideal water: "he himself felt, in a way he had not felt before, that it was time for him to take the plunge. This was the water, the people in this room; it impressed him, certainly, as far from fine, but it was the only water there was" (513). Like Cass, Vivaldo is of two minds about joining the house of bad fiction. They both see no alternative in contemporary America; and they both know that its norms and expectations can't possibly do justice to the potentiality they feel. They are making what I would argue is an especially American bargain, opting into a shared culture that seems brimming with possibility first and foremost because it is so obviously inadequate.

Baldwin is making a kind of compromise here, too, surprisingly open to Stowe's imagery just as his characters are jumping into mainstream American culture. It seems as if Baldwin is willing to loosen the genre boundary between sentimental fiction and the work of serious realism in considering the meaning of Cass's house. Baldwin's excoriation of *Uncle Tom's Cabin* described clichés as forms of inhumanity. *Another Country* suggests otherwise: "Nobody lives without clichés," Cass's lover, Eric, claims while trying to convince her to return home to Richard (714). In other words, there is no escape from bad writing. There might be events—Baldwin describes them with a religiously informed concept of love—indicating a better life that has yet to arrive. But if this potential energy tasks American novels with portraying various states of expectancy, as *Another Country* does, there is no reason to rule out the possibility that this as yet unarticulated existence might be signified by a work of fiction clearly inadequate to its subject. Driving toward an elusive goal, Cassy's restless wildness is an apt image for the loose connection between novels that accept their provisional status and novels that fall short of their subjects without meaning to.

The uneven reception of Baldwin's work attests to the uncertain status of authorship conceived as heroic failure. While neither academic nor popular critics would treat Baldwin with what I would call *coolness*—the acceptance that low quality and strong appeal can go hand in hand—many contemporary readers expressed the hope that his not-yet-realized artistic potential might embody inspiring ambition. One of the recurring themes of Baldwin criticism in both the African American and mainstream press was that he represented a formidable thinker and powerful essayist who fell short of arriving at his full potential as a novelist. African American novelist and critic Leon Forrest was voicing a widely held take on Baldwin when, in a review of *Just above My Head* (1979), he accused Baldwin of unprofessionalism. "Rather than profundity of character development in his main figures," Forrest wrote, "Baldwin gives us the graphic details of their sexual flings, which are by and large poorly, even amateurishly rendered."[25]

Objections to Baldwin's sex scenes tend to imply, with varying degrees of subtlety, the homophobia that shaped his mixed reception. Eldridge Cleaver's excoriation of Baldwin in *Soul on Ice* (1968) stands out for its directness. But, as Rachel Corbman points out in her article on *Giovanni's Room* and the black press, discomfort with Baldwin's sexuality was expressed as well in far less overt ways, such as his representation in a 1964 cartoon that the *Chicago Defender* reprinted from artist and activist Elombe Brath's satirical coloring book, *Color Us Collud!* Depicting Baldwin as exaggeratedly effeminate, the cartoon asked its readers to "color him funny."[26]

But there was a profoundly positive side to reflections on Baldwin's "failings" as well. In a noteworthy review of *Another Country*, editorialist James Finn chalks up Baldwin's shortcomings to his huge creative ambitions for the novel: "What seems to be the case," Finn claims, "is that Baldwin has yet to find the artistic form that will reveal the mystery, that will uncover the truth he knows is there."[27] In other words, what many readers see as the uneven quality of Baldwin's narratives signifies his broader struggle to twist the novel into a vehicle that might contain truths about American experience. This state of expectancy opens up a way of relating Baldwin's high art fiction with the best-selling novels readers treated coolly: the artist struggling with genre might benefit from popular fiction's apparent ability to transcend the glaring shortcomings of form, format, and authorship.

The version of *Uncle Tom's Cabin* most relevant here is not the roundly criticized book of "Everybody's Protest Novel" but the object of fascination Baldwin describes in *The Devil Finds Work*. Here, he recalls his childhood obsession with Stowe's text: "I had read *Uncle Tom's Cabin* compulsively, the book in one hand, the newest baby on my hipbone. I was trying to find out something, sensing something in the book of some immense import for me: which, however, I knew I did not really understand."[28] Baldwin goes on to recall his mother confiscating the novel and placing it out of his reach on a high shelf, only later to have a change of heart. "Then, my mother, as she herself puts it, 'didn't hide it anymore,' and, indeed, from that moment, though in fear and trembling, began to let me go."[29] As a boy, Baldwin felt that Stowe's text left open an expansive world of significance beyond the confines of the home. *Another Country* suggests that, even as he grew into one of the novel's harshest critics, he never entirely left behind the sense that American popular culture gestured weakly toward a fulfillment that has not yet arrived.

The aesthetic mode most suitable to this cultural world is not the detachment of the privileged observer but the detachment of the subject split by ambivalence—the American traveler powerfully attracted to the scene that also repels him; the ex-colored man uncertain that he ever should have left; the wife who can't decide between going or staying; the novelist repulsed by the waters in which he swims. James, Johnson, and Baldwin were not just, as Kaplan suggests, attempting to represent an American community that no longer seemed to be "available to common sense"; they described a national scene not only as the aftereffect of destructive forces but also in the process of transformation.[30] Along with the cool readers of best-selling fiction, they helped articulate the mixed feelings of partial participation as a state of expectancy, loaded with equal parts potentiality and disappointment. These moments of Stowe's voice intruding on high literary culture show how this version of expectancy made it difficult to draw the line between the failures of popular fiction and the failures of the art novel.

Understanding how the creativity of readers who can't quite buy in became a crucial source of the novel's meaning suggests the extent to which the genre was a form of invitation. Particularly in American contexts, shaped by the sense that democracy was a world-historical experiment, the novel hosted a drama of public access: its appearance as an unfinished but hugely significant thing inspired anonymous voices to chime in where it seemed like salvation was on the line. Baldwin's eschatological view of race and American community throws this unique quality of popular novels into the foreground. *Uncle Tom's Cabin* has a meaningful place in his vision of the struggle between good and evil because, along with many of the voices considered here, he felt that anything approximating national salvation would involve the destruction of the self-enclosures and contentment that shape the present moment. Perhaps no book like an inadequate best seller could better express the partial, unfinished creativity of an unfulfilled mass public.

At this moment, that is. As Baldwin wrote, the fractured audiences of twentieth-century modernism and various genre fictions were making it increasingly difficult for any novel to signify the American social body as a whole. Literary culture would never recover the association with national community that it held in the era of *Uncle Tom's Cabin;* meanwhile, the emergence of cinema and youth-oriented music scenes would revolutionize expressions of coolness in ways well beyond the scope of this study. As part of this attitude's early development, however, the American response to nineteenth-century popular fiction bears out Alan Liu's claim that "cool has a history, and its core experience, however inchoate and unknown to itself, is *of* history."[31] The ambivalent Americanism that cool reading outlined in US contexts pushed vaguely against individualism, intellectualism, and notions of personal happiness from within a specific historical narrative: in responding to novels, American readers were struggling to come to terms with the disjunction between national ideals and national reality.

This is not to say that the United States has any particular monopoly on cool as a cultural style, but that the social space and the attitude have, at times, held a special relationship. Remembering how the popular novel worked to articulate this relationship directs attention to the ways in which the genre channeled a certain variety of disappointment—not the literary disappointment that the great American novel had yet to be written, nor the modernist distaste for popular forms, but the feeling that disappointing objects somehow best expressed the unique potential of national community. This means that a range of bad qualities, from stupidity to callousness, took on the ability to signify deep national pride. But it also means that the relationship between mediocre expression and partially detached audiences took on a critical edge that studies of American culture and its ongoing global presence have yet to explore in full.

AFTERWORD

The Novel and America Abroad Now

A quick glance into twenty-first-century fiction shows that the fascination with American mediocrity is still going strong. In Chimamanda Ngozi Adichie's *Americanah* (2013), for instance, disillusionment with the United States drives the central love plot between Nigerian characters Ifemelu and Obinze. After years spent consuming American novels, TV shows, and mix tapes and pursuing American ways of life—Ifemelu spends most of the story studying and working in the United States before returning to Lagos—their relationship concludes the book as a contrast to their previous, unsatisfying romantic ties. Ifemelu's "relentlessly upbeat" American ex-boyfriend, Curt, reflects the appealing dullness of his national culture: he is "admirable and repulsive," Adichie explains, "in a way that only an American of his kind could be." "He believed in good omens and positive thoughts and happy endings to films," traits she finds at once endearing and frustratingly fake.[1] In the grain of cool reading, Ifemelu is acutely aware that she is attracted to a deeply flawed product of American culture.

But *Americanah* differs from the classic narrative of lost illusions (leave home with big dreams, return with more realistic expectations). Adichie explores deep ambivalence about the United States not as an obstacle or a diversion on a path to self-discovery but as a productive, enabling condition. When Ifemelu returns to Nigeria, she tells Obinze: "The best thing about America is that it gives you space. I like that you buy into the dream, it's a lie but you buy into it and that's all that matters."[2] This is a somewhat contradictory claim, as if the promises of American culture were believable enough to bring a kind of disruptive freedom into Ifemelu's life but unbelievable enough to inspire self-fashioning that is more creative and locally centered than its flawed source of inspiration. Ifemelu ends up not leaving home for America but bringing the space of America back to Nigeria.

Obinze is finally moved to disrupt his life as well, leaving a marriage he describes as "a kind of floating along contentment" for a less settled relationship with Ifemelu.[3]

Adichie is not alone among contemporary novelists in depicting American culture as most productive where it seems to lack authority and depth. Michael Chabon revisits the pop art movement's fascination with American comic books in *The Amazing Adventures of Kavalier and Clay*, in which the Holocaust escapee Joe Kavalier, student of Prague's Academy of Fine Arts, first impresses his comic book–loving New York cousin by drawing the sound of a fart. Kavalier's entryway into American culture is marked by his realization that "half bad is maybe better than beauteeful [sic]."[4] And his grand, final scene channels the power of the half bad: after a twisting and traumatic plot in which Joe ends up living for years as a recluse, unable to reconnect with his friends and family ("So many times I wanted to," he later admits. "I would call you and hang up the phone. I would write letters but didn't send them. And the longer I waited, the harder it became to imagine"), he literally reappears as a comic book hero.[5] In a stunt announced anonymously in the newspaper, drawing a crowd, he swings from the Empire State Building in an iridescent gold suit and mask.

When Joe's estranged wife and cousin later ask why he performed the elaborate stunt, he responds, "I guess this was the point . . . for me to come back. To end up sitting here with you, on Long Island, in this house, eating some noodles."[6] Somehow, the act of thrilling onlookers in a golden bathing suit and boots has enabled the refugee to rejoin the American family he otherwise might not have seen again. It's as if, for the very different novelists Adichie and Chabon, the obvious lack of depth in American cultural forms can push fragile relationships into uncharted zones where they can, at the very least, survive. Neither *Americanah* nor *Kavalier and Clay* depict American culture as the imperializing, monolithic force it is often made out to be. Nor do they stress, along with much recent scholarship in global American studies, how acts of reception can change and localize the meaning of specific texts.[7] Instead, they imply that American popular culture emboldens new social awareness by pulling in two directions at once: by packaging magisterial ideas like happiness and self-transformation in formats that clearly lack authority.

One last example, because few American cultural objects express less authority than the 1992 comedy *Encino Man*, starring Sean Astin and Pauly

Shore, with Brendan Fraser as an unfrozen caveman. The film plays a prominent role in Alberto Fuguet's *The Movies of My Life* (2003). The basic plot of Fuguet's novel is simple: a Chilean American seismologist, Beltrán Soler, is inspired to recall his many encounters with American movies after a conversation on a plane in which his seatmate—a US immigration attorney who will become a love interest—reminisces about her favorite movies. The narrator is hardly an unqualified fan of the United States. Early on, he remarks that his grandfather, also a scientist, had become popular in the United States "in the only way that someone can become popular there: by selling his soul."[8] When his seatmate asks if he has seen *Encino Man*, he quickly denies it, but in such a way that seems to emphasize his growing fascination with both California and the attorney:

> "Have you ever seen *Encino Man*?"
> "No."
> What did she know that I did not? Did she know that, in the end, L.A. was really my destiny and not just a place to change planes? Was she reading my mind? Or was it just simple airplane chat?[9]

This uncertainly leads him through the following chapters detailing his love for films and concluding with a confessional email to the attorney. "I'd like and am afraid and hope" that we will meet again, he writes. "P.S. I did see *Encino Man* . . . I thought it was pretty bad and—nevertheless—enjoyed it."[10] In Fuguet's narrative, one of the most ridiculous movies of the 1990s marks the protagonist's fraught consideration both of a personal attraction that scares and inspires him and—in an overlap emphasized by her occupation—his uncertain attraction to the United States. Along the way, the episodic chapters return again and again to the idea that American culture's lack of depth enables otherwise impossible relationships. This is nowhere expressed more clearly than in Soler's recollection of watching *Jaws* with his estranged father: "My heart didn't stop pounding the entire time. I don't know if it was because of the shark, the pulsating music of John Williams, or the fear of being with my father and not knowing what to say. But you don't have to say much in a theater, just the occasional, 'That was cool, huh?'"[11]

Why the ongoing fascination with the American not-so-great? The echoes of nineteenth-century novel reading in the mixed feelings expressed by these recent texts point to a bridge between genre history and constructs of nationhood that have yet to be fully explored. In different ways, Adichie, Chabon, and Fuguet are sounding out what film historian Miriam Hansen has called the "global vernacular" of American culture. The question to ask about Hollywood cinema, Hansen argues, is what makes it translate so well: "how an aesthetic idiom developed in one country could achieve transnational and global currency." She claims that American movies traveled more effectively than their national counterparts because they had been made to attract a culturally heterogeneous national audience, and they did so by promoting the "promises of mass consumption." Hansen offers several possibilities for what these promises seem to be: the promise of democratizing happiness, the promise of carving out a good life in opposition to "bourgeois" values, the promise of mediating between conflicting versions of modernity.[12]

When we focus on novel history, a different promise comes to the foreground: the assurance that the cultural objects we share will lack final authority. The biggest attraction of American forms, according to nineteenth-century cool readers and contemporary novelists alike, is that they will be insubstantial enough that you might make of them what you will. That is, US culture stands out not only for its accessibility but also for its flimsiness. As Hansen points out, citing Russian film historian Yuri Tsivian, something like a "slumming mentality" often shapes foreign engagements with American productions—a defiant notion that lower spheres of culture might better answer modern needs.[13] This observation suggests that to better understand the meaning of American culture in global contexts, we will need a better sense of the social conflicts that attraction to the less-than-respectable is able to make visible, negotiate, or transform.[14]

I think we have a lot more to learn about these kinds of ambivalent attraction. And I would suggest that the current status of the novel—now, more often than not, a genre that observes a vibrant mass media culture from the sidelines—has renewed its attention to the kinds of mixed feelings that surrounded novel reading in the nineteenth century. I have tried to show how, for nineteenth-century readers and novelists, the flimsiness of American fiction became a sounding board for questions about conflicting feelings, about the uncertain grounds of individualism, and about ambivalence toward national belonging. American culture's flimsiness continues to provoke, for better or worse. Listening more intently to the language surrounding this unsettling quality might help us better understand both the discontents that have shaped our cultural history and the searching that defines its present.

Notes

INTRODUCTION

1. "The Drama," *New York Tribune,* November 30, 1899, 7.
2. "Tendency to Literary Hysteria," *Chicago Herald,* May 1895, 395.
3. Beaumont Fletcher, "Trilby as a Play," *Godey's Magazine,* June 1895, 574.
4. "Recent Literature," *Atlantic Monthly,* March 1879, 407.
5. William Lloyd Garrison, "Uncle Tom's Cabin," *The Liberator,* March 26, 1852, 50.
6. For a thorough account of "great American novel" discourse in the nineteenth century, see Buell, *The Dream of the Great American Novel.*
7. James, *A Small Boy and Others,* 162.
8. See, for instance, Hunt, *Inventing Human Rights;* Armstrong, *How Novels Think;* and Moretti, *The Novel: History, Geography, and Culture.*
9. For these studies connecting novelistic forms and national consciousness, see Fliegelman, *Prodigals and Pilgrims;* Davidson, *Revolution and the Word;* and Tennenhouse, *The Importance of Feeling English.*
10. See Dinerstein, *The Origins of Cool;* MacAdams, *Birth of the Cool;* Gioia, *The Birth (and Death) of the Cool;* Stearn, *American Cool;* and Liu, *The Laws of Cool.* These studies of coolness make it clear that the attitude has had too long and variegated a cultural life to fit into a single story, from the appropriation of African American performance styles by Hollywood and advertising in the late twentieth century (MacAdams, Gioia) to the weak spirit of dissent proliferating through the twenty-first century "information age" (Liu). Most relevant to this book are the ways in which each of these examples of cool, in Liu's terms, gesture toward a "counter-ethos within the dominant ethos" (71) or, as Dinerstein puts it, toward "a resistant mode of being in the world" (5).
11. See Eagleton, *The English Novel;* McKeon, *The Origins of the English Novel, 1600–1740;* and Armstrong, *How Novels Think.*
12. Benjamin, *The Arcades Project,* 212–27.
13. Songtag, "Notes on Camp," 530.
14. LaBruce, "Notes on Camp/Anti Camp."
15. Parfait, *The Publishing History of Uncle Tom's Cabin.* Parfait's analysis of surviving evidence of textual reception—from many cheaply printed editions of *Uncle Tom's*

Cabin to expensive gift books bearing personal inscriptions—testifies to the multiplicity of *Uncle Tom's Cabin*. See especially pp. 87–89.

16. Baym, *Novels, Readers, and Reviewers*, 24.
17. Ibid., 8.
18. Armstrong, *How Novels Think*, especially pp. 20–23.
19. Liu, *The Laws of Cool*, 304.
20. Armstrong, *How Novels Think*, 51.
21. Brantlinger, *The Reading Lesson*, 143.
22. Henry James, "Miss Braddon," in *Notes and Reviews*, 108–9.
23. "Music and the Drama," *Wilkes' Spirit of the Times*, January 16, 1864, 320.
24. Cook, *The Arts of Deception*, 5.
25. "She," *Wilkes' Spirit of the Times*, December 3, 1887, 626.
26. "Sense v. Sensation," *Punch: Or, The London Charavari*, July 21, 1861, 31.
27. "American Sensations," *All the Year Round* 5, no. 106 (May 4, 1861): 131–6.
28. "Certain Dangerous Tendencies in American Life," *Puck*, June 9, 1880, 244.
29. "Literary Comment: The Great American Novel," *Current Literature*, May 1892, 113.
30. James Lane Allen, "The Great American Novel," *The Independent*, September 24, 1891, 3.
31. Frank Bailey Millard, "The Great American Novel," *Philistine: A Periodical of Protest*, August 1898, 100.
32. Higginson, *The New World and the New Book*, 5.
33. "The Great American Novel," *Dial*, December 1, 1896, 2.
34. Buell, *The Dream of the Great American Novel*, 12.
35. "Hold On," *Morning News* (New London, CT), January 5, 1846, 2.
36. "The Morality of 'Cuteness,'" *Knickerbocker*, August 1845, 180.
37. "American Quacks in London," *Medical News*, December 1857, 185.
38. Clapp, *Reminiscences of a Dramatic Critic*, 11.
39. See, for instance, "The Night-Passenger," *Chambers Journal*, April 27, 1867, 260–63; and Spears, *The History of Our Navy*, 2:91.
40. For the elopement story, see "Cool Girl in Kansas," *Washington Post*, September 11, 1898, 21; for the breakfast story, see "Cool," *Washington Post*, June 17, 1906, 14.
41. Radway, *Reading the Romance*, 12; Jameson, *Archaeologies of the Future*.
42. Radway, *A Feeling for Books*; Blair, *Reading Up*.
43. Benjamin, *The Arcades Project*, 358.

1. *UNCLE TOM'S CABIN* AND THE UNPRIVILEGED PUBLIC SPHERE

1. James, *A Small Boy and Others*, 158–9.
2. Douglas, *The Feminization of American Culture*; Baldwin, "Everybody's Protest Novel," 11–18.
3. Cordelia Howard, quoted in Gossett, *Uncle Tom's Cabin and American Culture*, 372.

4. Berlant, *The Female Complaint*, 47.

5. For a thorough discussion of this literary chronology, see Kirkham, "The Writing of Harriet Beecher Stowe's *The Pearl of Orr's Island*."

6. See Merish, *Sentimental Materialism*.

7. "Uncle Tom's Cabin," *National Era*, April 15, 1852.

8. William Allen, "Uncle Tom's Cabin," *Frederick Douglass' Paper*, May 20, 1852.

9. "Uncle Tom's Cabin," *Southern Literary Messenger*, December 18, 1852, 722.

10. "Uncle Tom's Cabin, or, Life among the Lowly," reprinted in *Littell's Living Age*, July 10, 1852, 61.

11. Ibid.

12. "'The Uncle Tom Epidemic," *Literary World*, December 4, 1852.

13. Ibid.

14. Cited in Parfait, *The Publishing History of Uncle Tom's Cabin*, 81.

15. "Uncle Tomitudes," *Putnam's Monthly*, January 1853, 99.

16. Ibid.

17. Douglas, *The Feminization of American Culture*, 8.

18. Quoted in Hedrick, *Harriet Beecher Stowe*, 208.

19. Weld, *American Slavery as It Is*.

20. Stowe, *Uncle Tom's Cabin*, 81. Subsequent references to this volume will be parenthetical in the text.

21. Berlant, *The Female Complaint*, 29.

22. Stowe, *Agnes of Sorrento*, 46. Subsequent references to this volume will be parenthetical in the text.

23. Stowe, "An Appeal to the Women."

24. Quoted in Fields, *Life and Letters of Harriet Beecher Stowe*, 212.

25. Reynolds, *Mightier than the Sword*, 139.

26. For a good overview of the *Uncle Tom's Cabin* exhibit, see Hochman, "*Uncle Tom's Cabin* at the World's Columbian Exposition."

27. EAD, "At the Theatres," *New York Times*, March 10, 1901, 52.

28. "Sweet Singers Wanted," *New York Times*, February 10, 1878, 8.

29. Posters cited in Reynolds, *Mightier than the Sword*, 193, 195.

30. Quoted in Lott, *Love and Theft*, 222.

31. Ibid., 216.

32. "Uncle Tom at Niblo's," *Wilkes' Spirit of the Times*, July 2, 1881, 598.

33. Hochman, *Uncle Tom's Cabin and the Reading Revolution*, 133, 139.

34. "Recent Literature," *Atlantic Monthly*, March 1879, 408–9.

35. Howells, *My Literary Passions*, 63.

36. John William DeForest, "The Great American Novel," *The Nation*, January 9, 1868.

37. Newton, *A Burlesque on Uncle Tom's Cabin*.

38. Henrique Vivian Messetti, *Little Eva's Temptation: A Musical Comedy Farce (Suggested by Uncle Tom's Cabin)* (Unpublished typescript, 1928).

39. Hughes, "Colonel Tom's Cabin," 577.

2. BEN-HUR

1. Wallace, *Lew Wallace*, 2:1000.
2. "News of the Theaters," *Chicago Daily Tribune*, December 2, 1899, 16.
3. "Chronicle and Comment," *Bookman*, April 1905, 117.
4. "Dramatizing the Christian Religion," *Life*, December 14, 1899, 516.
5. Gregory S. Jackson, "What Would Jesus Do?," 642.
6. "How 'Ben Hur' Came to Be Written," *Current Literature*, February 1907, 178–79.
7. Quoted from an advertisement in the *Athenaeum*, September 24, 1891, 387.
8. "General Lew Wallace: A Notable Career," *Our Day*, February 1905, 13.
9. John R. Spears, "How Books Sold," *New York Times*, December 28, 1901, BR5.
10. "The Book Table," *Outlook*, December 17, 1919, 514.
11. "Gotham Critics on Ben Hur," *Chicago Tribune*, December 2, 1899, 16.
12. "Chronicle and Comment," *Bookman*, April 1905, 113.
13. "The Drama," *New York Tribune*, November 30, 1899, 7; "Lew Wallace," *Herald of Gospel Liberty*, May 4, 1905, 274.
14. Edward A. Dithmar, *New York Times*, November 19, 1899, 18.
15. Wallace, *Lew Wallace*, 2:931–32.
16. Wallace, *Ben-Hur*, 83. Subsequent references to this edition will be parenthetical in the text.
17. "Dramatic and Musical: 'Ben-Hur' as a Play at the Broadway Theatre," *New York Times*, November 30, 1899, 7.
18. Letter to Paul Hamilton Hayne, quoted in Wallace, *Lew Wallace*, 2:950.
19. Oliver B. Bunce, "The Cash Value of a Book Review," *North American Review*, August 1899, 223–24.
20. "Gotham Critics on Ben Hur," *Chicago Daily Tribune*, December 2, 1899, 16.
21. "'Ben-Hur' Hissed in London," *Washington Post*, April 6, 1902, 3; "Brief Comment," *Current Literature*, May 1892, 153–55.
22. "How 'Ben-Hur' Came to Be Written," *Current Literature*, February 1907, 178.
23. "The Drama," *New York Tribune*, November 30, 1899, 7.
24. Kristeva, *The Powers of Horror*; Benjamin, "Surrealism," 214; Agamben, *Profanations*, 68–69;.
25. Rimbaud, *A Season in Hell*, 7.
26. "Philosophy between Puffs," *New York Times*, June 20, 1893, 8.
27. Harry Franklin Covington, [Untitled], *Nassau Literary Magazine*, March 1891, 562.
28. Ibid., 46.
29. "Drama: An After-Theatre Symposium," *Life*, May 3, 1900, 384.
30. "At the Play and with the Players," *New York Times*, December 3, 1899, 18.
31. "A Remarkable Play," *Overland Monthly and the Out West*, July 1900, 38.
32. Benjamin E. Smith, "The 'Ben-Hur' Chariot-Race," *St. Nicholas*, November 1900, 45.

33. Ibid.

34. "'Ben-Hur' Again in Glory: The Drury Lane Production at the New York Theatre," *New York Times*, September 22, 1903, 6.

35. "Ben-Hur Roasted," *Billboard*, March 21, 1903, 11.

36. From a *London Times* review cited in "'Ben-Hur' Hissed in London," *Washington Post*, April 6, 1902, 3.

37. "'Ben-Hur' Passes Over to the Movies," *New York Times*, January 7, 1923, SM4.

38. Ibid.

39. "The Domestic Ideal," *Puck*, August 26, 1891, 16.

40. "A Question of Propriety," *Washington Post*, April 12, 1902, 6.

41. Ibid.

42. Aunt Jane, "The Autobiography of a Country Spinster," *The Independent*, August 13, 1906, 626.

43. Ibid.

44. "'Ben-Hur' Passes Over to the Movies," SM4.

45. For an overview on *Ben-Hur* branded merchandise, see Solomon, "Fugitive Sources, *Ben-Hur*, and the Popular Art 'Property.'"

46. Lewis Wallace, Harper & Brothers, Mark Klaw and A. L. Erlanger v. William S. Cleveland, Northern Illinois Circuit Court of the United States, Case No. 26027, 35. National Archives and Records Administration-Chicago.

3. BRITISH AUTHORSHIP, AMERICAN ADVERTISING

1. Trollope, *Domestic Manners of the Americans*, 183.

2. Arnold, *Culture and Anarchy*, xxiv.

3. Stallybrass and White, *The Politics and Poetics of Transgression*, 3.

4. Ibid., 25.

5. Giles, *Transatlantic Insurrections*, 1.

6. Foucault, "What Is an Author?," 211.

7. "An Advertising Genius," *Frank Leslie's Popular Monthly*, May 1902, 24.

8. "Pedal Advertising," *National Police Gazette*, October 9, 1880, 12; on Barnum's Americanness, see "Yankee Advertising," *Youth's Companion*, October 21, 1915, 574.

9. Wicke, *Advertising Fictions*.

10. Foucault, "What Is an Author?," 221–22.

11. Hauranne, *A Frenchman in Lincoln's America*, 2:22.

12. "Pictures and Placards—The Humbug Gallery," *New York Ledger*, October 24, 1863, 4.

13. "Ellis, Beadle Novel Man," *New York Sun*, June 24, 1900, 63.

14. Armstrong, *How Novels Think*.

15. Dickens, *A Tale of Two Cities*, 209. Subsequent references to this volume will be parenthetical in the text.

16. Dickens's letters, cited in McGill, *American Literature and the Culture of Reprinting*, 114.

17. Dickens, *American Notes*, x.

18. Ibid., 176, 133, 267.

19. "Dickens Is Coming!," *New York Observer and Chronicle*, October 17, 1867, 334.

20. "Dickens in America," *Putnam's Magazine*, January 1868, 112.

21. "Charles Dickens and His Worshipers," *The Independent*, April 29, 1869, 4.

22. "Buz," *Dolby and Father* (New York: P. S. Wynkoop and Son, 1868).

23. "A Thanksgiving Story: After the Manner of Dickens," *Puck*, November 23, 1887, 205.

24. "The Philosophy of Advertising," *Once a Week*, August 1, 1865, 163–65.

25. Smith, *Advertise*, 122.

26. Dickens, *Somebody's Luggage*, 24. Subsequent references to this work will be parenthetical in the text.

27. Payne, *The Reenchantment of Nineteenth-Century Fiction*, 146–51.

28. Charles Dickens to George Tennant, January 9, 1857, in *The Letters of Charles Dickens*, 8:424.

29. Dickens to Wilkie Collins, *Letters*, 8:535.

30. Miller, *Charles Dickens: The World of His Novels*, 293.

31. Ibid., 179.

32. Ibid., 308–9.

33. See Poovey, "Speculation and Virtue in *Our Mutual Friend*," in *Making a Social Body*, 155–81; and Gallagher, "The Bio-Economics of *Our Mutual Friend*," in *The Body Economic*, 86–117.

34. Dickens, *Our Mutual Friend*, 781. Subsequent references to this volume will be parenthetical in the text.

35. See, for example, Rothenberg, "Articulating Social Agency," and Farrell, "The Partners' Tale."

36. Dickens, "The Young Man from the Country."

37. McGill, *American Literature and the Culture of Reprinting*, 115.

38. Kerr, *The Cloven Foot*, 15.

39. Ibid., 121.

40. Du Maurier, *Trilby*, 6.

41. Ibid., 242.

42. On the prurience of Trilbymania, see Jenkins, "Trilby: Fads, Photographers."

43. H. L. Wilson, "'Trilby': Being the Last Chapter, Written without the Author's Consent or Knowledge, by Another," *Puck*, April 3, 1895, 100–101.

44. Ibid., 101.

45. Du Maurier, *The Martian*, 383.

46. Du Maurier, quoted in Jenkins, "Trilby: Fads, Photographers," 228.

47. Du Maurier, The Martian, 2.

48. "Du Maurier's Latest Story," *The Independent*, October 25, 1894, 17.

49. Mary Abbot, "Tendency to Literary Hysteria," *Current Literature*, May 1895, 395.

50. Beaumont Fletcher, "Trilby as a Play," *Godey's Magazine*, June 1895, 570–79.

51. Henry James, "George du Maurier," *Harper's Weekly*, April 14, 1894.
52. "George du Maurier," *Harper's Weekly*, October 17, 1896, 1023C.

4. QUESTIONABLE AMERICANS ABROAD

1. Twain, *A Connecticut Yankee*, 60.
2. Trollope, *The American Senator*, 96.
3. Ibid.
4. Taylor, *Our American Cousin*, 24. Subsequent references to this volume will be parenthetical in the text.
5. Jefferson, *The Autobiography of Joseph Jefferson*, 193. Subsequent references to this volume will be parenthetical in the text.
6. "Theatres," *Era*, October 8, 1865, 11.
7. "Rip Van Winkle, as Played by Joseph Jefferson" (New York: Dodd, Mead and Co., 1896), 43, 51, 55, 56, 64, 134.
8. Reviews quoted in McArthur, *The Man*, 138.
9. "Theatres," *Era*, October 8, 1865, 11.
10. Ibid.; "The Acting of Mr. Jefferson," *Pall Mall Gazette*, August 16, 1865, 10–11; "The Adelphi," *London Times*, September 6, 1865, 12.
11. [Untitled], *Era*, October 8, 1865, 11
12. Information on the Adelphi repertoire comes from the Adelphi Theatre Project site, www.emich.edu/public/english/adelphi_calendar; review of Toole's performance as Joe Bright from *London Times*, July 3, 1865, 5.
13. Davis and Emeljanow, *Reflecting the Audience*, 173.
14. "The Acting of Mr. Jefferson," 11.
15. Trollope, *The American Senator*, 5. Subsequent references to this volume will be parenthetical in the text.
16. Knoper, *Acting Naturally*, 6.
17. Ibid., 65.
18. Twain, *A Connecticut Yankee in King Arthur's Court*, 50. Subsequent references to this volume will be parenthetical in the text.
19. Tocqueville, *Democracy in America*, 369.

5. UNKNOWING AMERICAN REALISM

1. James, *Portrait of a Lady*, 58–59.
2. Baldwin, "Everybody's Protest Novel," 12.
3. Kaplan, *The Social Construction of American Realism*, 13.
4. James, *Literary Criticism*, 1218.
5. McGurl, *The Novel Art*, 4.
6. John William DeForest, "The Great American Novel," *The Nation*, January 9, 1868, 27–29.
7. James, *A Small Boy and Others*, 167.

8. Ibid.
9. Ibid., 177.
10. See Kurnick, *Empty Houses;* and Bentley, *Frantic Panoramas.*
11. James, *The American Scene,* 55. Subsequent references to this volume will be parenthetical in the text.
12. James, *A Small Boy and Others,* 171.
13. See, for example, James's assessment of Mary Braddon's popularity in "Miss Braddon," in *Notes and Reviews* 108–9.
14. Bentley, *Frantic Panoramas,* 302.
15. Ibid., 42.
16. James, *Portrait of a Lady,* 18. Subsequent references to this volume will be parenthetical in the text.
17. Anesko, *Friction with the Market,* 143–44.
18. Johnson, *The Autobiography of an Ex-Colored Man,* 27. Subsequent references to this volume will be parenthetical in the text.
19. See Miskolcze, "Intertextual Links: Reading *Uncle Tom's Cabin* in James Weldon Johnson's *The Autobiography of an Ex-Colored Man.*" To Miskolcze, the necklace signifies the "legacy of white paternalism" that continued to hold sway in the twentieth century.
20. Baldwin, "Everybody's Protest Novel," 11–19.
21. Baldwin, *Another Country,* 381. Subsequent references to this volume will be parenthetical in the text.
22. Baldwin, *Giovanni's Room,* 337. Subsequent references to this volume will be parenthetical in the text.
23. See Porter, *Stealing the Fire.*
24. Baldwin, *Another Country,* 571. Subsequent references to this volume will be parenthetical in the text.
25. Leon Forrest, "Graphic Gospel According to James Baldwin" *Chicago Tribune,* September 16, 1979, sec. 7 p. 1.
26. Baldwin cartoon from Brath, *Color Us Cullud!,* reprinted in the *Chicago Daily Defender,* March 16, 1964, A5. For a discussion of *Giovanni's Room* and the black press, see Corbman, "Next Time, the Fire."
27. James Finn, quoted in Francis, *The Critical Reception of James Baldwin,* 106.
28. Baldwin, "The Devil Finds Work," 487.
29. Ibid.
30. Kaplan, *The Social Construction of American Realism,* 122.
31. Liu, *The Laws of Cool,* 306.

AFTERWORD

1. Adichie, *Americanah,* 242.
2. Ibid., 536.
3. Ibid., 588.

4. Chabon, *Kavalier and Clay*, 89.
5. Ibid., 588.
6. Ibid.
7. See, for example, the recent essay collection, edited by Edwards and Gaonkar, *Globalizing American Studies*.
8. Fuguet, *The Movies of My Life*, 21.
9. Ibid., 54.
10. Ibid., 164.
11. Ibid., 199.
12. Hansen, "The Mass Production of the Senses," 60, 68, 70.
13. Ibid., 62.
14. Some recent scholarship on American culture abroad has notably begun to explore this kind of attraction to the less-than-respectable. See, for example, Koolman, *Fabricating the Absolute Fake*, which details how the superficial idealism of American music and cinema sparks productive dialogue about national belonging in Holland.

Bibliography

Adichie, Chimamanda Ngozi. *Americanah*. New York: Anchor Books, 2013.
Anesko, Michael. *Friction with the Market: Henry James and the Profession of Authorship*. New York: Oxford University Press, 1986.
Armstrong, Nancy. *How Novels Think: The Limits of Individualism from 1719–1900*. New York: Columbia University Press, 2005.
Arnold, Matthew. *Culture and Anarchy: An Essay in Political and Social Criticism*. New York: Macmillan, 1883.
Baldwin, James. *Another Country*. In *Baldwin: Early Novels and Stories*, edited by Toni Morrison. New York: Library of America, 1998. First published 1962 by the Dial Press.
———. "The Devil Finds Work." In *Collected Essays*, edited by Toni Morrison. New York: Library of America, 1998.
———. "Everybody's Protest Novel." In *Collected Essays*, edited by Toni Morrison. New York: Library of America, 1998. First published 1949 by the *Partisan Review*.
———. *Giovanni's Room*. In *Baldwin: Early Novels and Stories*, edited by Toni Morrison. New York: Library of America, 1998. First published 1956 by the Dial Press.
Baym, Nina. *Novels, Readers, and Reviewers: Responses to Fiction in Antebellum America*. Ithaca, NY: Cornell University Press, 1984.
Benjamin, Walter. *The Arcades Project*. Translated by Howard Eiland and Kevin McLaughlin. Cambridge, MA: Harvard University Press, 1999.
———. "Surrealism: The Last Snapshot of the European Intelligentsia." In *Selected Writings*, vol. 2, 211–17. Translated by Rodney Livingstone. Edited by Michael W. Jennings, Howard Eiland, and Gary Smith. Cambridge, MA: Belknap Press, 1999.
Bentley, Nancy. *Frantic Panoramas: American Literature and Mass Culture, 1870–1920*. Philadelphia: University of Pennsylvania Press, 2009.
Berlant, Lauren. *The Female Complaint: The Unfinished Business of Sentimentality in American Culture*. Chapel Hill, NC: Duke University Press, 2008.
Birdoff, Harry. *The World's Greatest Hit: "Uncle Tom's Cabin."* New York: S. F. Vanni, 1947.
Blair, Amy L. *Reading Up: Middle-Class Readers and the Culture of Success in the Early Twentieth-Century United States*. Philadelphia: Temple University Press, 2011.

Brantlinger, Patrick. *The Reading Lesson: The Threat of Mass Literacy in Nineteenth-Century British Fiction*. Bloomington: Indiana University Press, 1998.

Brath, Cecil Elombe. *Color Us Collud! The American Negro Leadership Official Coloring Book*. Harlem, NY: Black Standard Publishing, 1964.

Buell, Lawrence. *The Dream of the Great American Novel*. Cambridge, MA: Harvard University Press, 2014.

Chabon, Michael. *The Amazing Adventures of Kavalier and Clay*. New York: Picador, 2000.

Cook, James W. *The Arts of Deception: Playing with Fraud in the Age of Barnum*. Cambridge, MA: Harvard University Press, 2001.

Corbman, Rachel. "Next Time, the Fire in Giovanni's Room." *Zeteo* (Spring 2012). http://zeteojournal.com/archives/spring-2012-issue/.

Daly, Nicholas. *Sensation and Modernity in the 1860s*. Cambridge: Cambridge University Press, 2013.

Davidson, Cathy. *Revolution and the Word: The Rise of the Novel in America*. Oxford: Oxford University Press, 1988.

Davis, Jim, and Victor Emaljanow. *Reflecting the Audience: London Theatregoing, 1840–1880*. Iowa City: University of Iowa Press, 2005.

Dickens, Charles. *American Notes*. New York: Penguin, 2000. First published 1842 by Chapman and Hall.

———. *Our Mutual Friend*. New York: Penguin, 1997. First published in book form 1865 by Chapman and Hall.

———. *Somebody's Luggage*. London: Chapman and Hall, 1862.

———. *A Tale of Two Cities*. New York: Penguin, 2000. First published 1859 by Chapman and Hall.

———. "The Young Man from the Country." *All the Year Round*, March 1, 1862, 540–42.

Dinerstein, Joel. *The Origins of Cool in Postwar America*. Chicago: University of Chicago Press, 2017.

Douglas, Ann. *The Feminization of American Culture*. New York: Farrar, Straus and Giroux, 1998.

du Maurier, George. *The Martian*. New York: Harper and Brothers, 1896.

———. *Trilby*. Hertfordshire, UK: Wordsworth Classics, 1995. First published as a book 1894 by Harper and Brothers.

Eagleton, Terry. *The English Novel: An Introduction*. Malden, MA: Blackwell, 2005.

Edwards, Brian, and Dilip Gaonkar, eds. *Globalizing American Studies*. Chicago: University of Chicago Press, 2010.

Farrell, John P. "The Partners' Tale: Dickens and *Our Mutual Friend*." *ELH* 66, no. 3 (1999): 759–99.

Fields, Anne, ed. *Life and Letters of Harriet Beecher Stowe*. Boston: Houghton Mifflin, 1898.

Fliegelman, Jay. *Prodigals and Pilgrims: The American Revolution against Patriarchal Authority, 1750–1800*. Cambridge: Cambridge University Press, 1985.

Foucault, Michel. "What Is an Author?" In *Aesthetics, Method, and Epistemology*, edited by James D. Faubion, 204–11. New York: New Press, 1998.
Francis, Consuela. *The Critical Reception of James Baldwin, 1963–2010*. New York: Camden House, 2014.
Fuguet, Alberto. *The Movies of My Life: A Novel*. Translated by Ezra E. Fitz. New York: HarperCollins, 2003.
Gallagher, Catherine. *The Body Economic: Life, Death, and Sensation in Political Economy and the Victorian Novel*. Princeton, NJ: Princeton University Press, 2006.
Giles, Paul. *Transatlantic Insurrections: British Culture and the Formation of American Literature, 1730–1860*. Philadelphia: University of Pennsylvania Press, 2001.
Gioia, Ted. *The Birth (and Death) of the Cool*. New York: Fulcrum, 2009.
Gossett, Thomas. *"Uncle Tom's Cabin" and American Culture*. Dallas: Southern Methodist University Press, 1985.
Hansen, Miriam. "The Mass Production of the Senses: Classical Cinema as Vernacular Modernism." *Modernism/Modernity* 6, no. 2 (April 1999): 59–67.
Hauranne, Ernest Duvergier de. *A Frenchman in Lincoln's America*. Translated by Ralph H. Bowen. 2 vols. Chicago: Lakeside Press, 1975. First published 1866 as *Huit Mois en Amérique* by Librairie Internationale, Paris.
Hedrick, Joan D. *Harriet Beecher Stowe: A Life*. New York: Oxford University Press, 1994.
Hochman, Barbara. *"Uncle Tom's Cabin" and the Reading Revolution*. Amherst: University of Massachusetts Press, 2011.
———. "Uncle Tom's Cabin at the World's Columbian Exposition." *Libraries and Culture* 41, no. 1 (Winter 2006): 82–108.
Howells, William Dean. *My Literary Passions*. New York: Harper and Brothers, 1895.
Hughes, Langston. "Colonel Tom's Cabin." In *The Plays to 1942: "The Mulatto" to "The Sun Do Move."* Vol. 5 of *The Collected Works of Langston Hughes*, edited by Leslie Catherine Sanders and Nancy Johnston, 574–77. Columbia: University of Missouri Press, 2002.
Hunt, Lynn. *Inventing Human Rights*. New York: W. W. Norton, 2007.
Jackson, Gregory S. "'What Would Jesus Do?': Practical Christianity, Social Gospel Realism, and the Homiletic Novel." *PMLA* 121, no. 3 (May 2006): 641–61.
James, Henry. *The American Scene*. New York: Harper and Brothers, 1908.
———. *Literary Criticism: French Writers, Other European Writers, the Prefaces to the New York Edition*. New York: Library of America, 1984.
———. *Notes and Reviews*. Cambridge, MA: Dunster House, 1921.
———. *Portrait of a Lady*. Edited by Robert D. Bamberg. New York: Norton, 1975 [1881].
———. *A Small Boy and Others*. New York: Harpers, 1913.
Jameson, Fredric. *Archaeologies of the Future: The Desire Called Utopia and Other Science Fictions*. London: Verso, 2005.
Jefferson, Joseph. *The Autobiography of Joseph Jefferson*. New York: Century, 1889.
Jenkins, Emily. "Trilby: Fads, Photographers, and 'Over-Perfect Feet.'" *Book History* 1 (1998): 221–67.

Johnson, James Weldon. *The Autobiography of an Ex-Colored Man*. In *Collected Writings*, edited by William L. Andrews, 1–124. New York: Library of America, 2000.

Kaplan, Amy. *The Social Construction of American Realism*. Chicago: University of Chicago Press, 1988.

Kerr, Orpheus C. [Robert Henry Newell]. *The Cloven Foot*. New York: Carleton, 1870.

Kirkham, E. Bruce. "The Writing of Harriet Beecher Stowe's *The Pearl of Orr's Island*." *Colby Quarterly* 16, no. 3 (September 1980): 158–65.

Knoper, Randall. *Acting Naturally: Mark Twain and the Culture of Performance*. Berkeley: University of California Press, 1995.

Koolman, Jap. *Fabricating the Absolute Fake: America in Contemporary Pop Culture*. Amsterdam: Amsterdam University Press, 2013.

Kristeva, Julia. *The Powers of Horror: An Essay on Abjection*. Translated by Leon S. Roudiez. New York: Columbia University Press, 1982.

Kurnick, David. *Empty Houses: Theatrical Failure and the Novel*. Princeton, NJ: Princeton University Press, 2001.

LaBruce, Bruce. "Notes on Camp/Anti Camp." http://brucelabruce.com/2015/07/07/notes-on-camp-anti-camp/.

Liu, Alan. *The Laws of Cool: Knowledge Work and the Culture of Information*. Chicago: University of Chicago Press, 2004.

Lott, Eric. *Love and Theft: Blackface Minstrelsy and the American Working Class*. Oxford: Oxford University Press, 2013.

Loughran, Trish. *The Republic in Print: Print Culture in the Age of U.S. Nation Building, 1770–1870*. New York: Columbia University Press, 2007.

MacAdams, Lewis. *Birth of the Cool: Beat, Bebop, and the American Avant Garde*. New York: Free Press, 2001.

McArthur, Benjamin. *The Man Who Was Rip Van Winkle: Joseph Jefferson and Nineteenth-Century American Theater*. New Haven, CT: Yale University Press, 2007.

McGill, Meredith. *American Literature and the Culture of Reprinting, 1834–1853*. Philadelphia: University of Pennsylvania Press, 2007.

McGurl, Mark. *The Novel Art: Elevations of American Fiction after Henry James*. Princeton, NJ: Princeton University Press, 2001.

McKeon, Michael. *The Origins of the English Novel, 1600–1740*. Baltimore: Johns Hopkins University Press, 2002.

Meer, Sarah. *Uncle Tom Mania: Slavery, Minstrelsy, and Transatlantic Culture in the 1850s*. Athens: University of Georgia Press, 2005.

Merish, Lori. *Sentimental Materialism: Gender, Commodity Culture, and Nineteenth-Century American Literature*. Durham, NC: Duke University Press, 2000.

Miller, J. Hillis. *Charles Dickens: The World of His Novels*. Bloomington: Indiana University Press, 1969.

Miskolcze, Robin. "Intertextual Links: Reading *Uncle Tom's Cabin* in James Weldon Johnson's *The Autobiography of an Ex-Colored Man*." *College Literature* 40, no. 1 (Winter 2013): 121–38.

Moretti, Franco, ed. *The Novel: History, Geography, and Culture.* Princeton, NJ: Princeton University Press, 2007.

Parfait, Claire. *The Publishing History of "Uncle Tom's Cabin."* Burlington, VT: Ashgate, 2007.

Payne, David. *The Reenchantment of Nineteenth-Century Fiction: Dickens, Thackeray, George Eliot, and Serialization.* New York: Palgrave, 2005.

Poovey, Mary. *Making a Social Body: British Cultural Formation, 1830–1864.* Chicago: University of Chicago Press, 1995.

Porter, Horace A. *Stealing the Fire: The Art and Protest of James Baldwin.* Middletown, CT: Wesleyan University Press, 1990.

Radway, Janice. *A Feeling for Books: The Book-of-the-Month Club, Literary Taste, and Middle-Class Desire.* Chapel Hill: University of North Carolina Press, 1997.

———. *Reading the Romance: Women, Patriarchy and Popular Literature.* 2nd ed. Chapel Hill: University of North Carolina Press, 1991. First published in 1984.

Reynolds, David. *Mightier than the Sword: "Uncle Tom's Cabin" and the Battle for America.* New York: W. W. Norton, 2012.

Rimbaud, Arthur. *"A Season in Hell" and "The Drunken Boat."* Translated by Louise Varese. New York: New Directions, 2011.

Rothenberg, Molly Anne. "Articulating Social Agency in *Our Mutual Friend*: Problems with Performances, Practices, and Political Efficacy." *ELH* 71 (2004): 719–49.

Smith, William. *Advertise: How? When? Where?* London: Routledge, Warne, and Routledge, 1863.

Solomon, Jon. "Fugitive Sources, *Ben-Hur*, and the Popular Art 'Property.'" *RBM: A Journal of Rare Books, Manuscripts, and Cultural Heritage* 9, no. 1 (2008): 67–78.

Sontag, Susan. "Notes on Camp." *Partisan Review* (Fall 1964): 515–30.

Stallybrass, Peter, and Allon White. *The Politics and Poetics of Transgression.* Ithaca, NY: Cornell University Press, 1986.

Stearn, Peter. *American Cool: Constructing a Twentieth-Century Emotional Style.* New York: New York University Press, 1994.

Stowe, Harriet Beecher. *Agnes of Sorrento.* 3rd edition. Boston: Ticknor and Fields, 1862.

———. "An Appeal to the Women of the Free States of America on the Present Crisis in Our Country." *Provincial Freeman*, March 25, 1854.

———. *Uncle Tom's Cabin.* Edited by Elizabeth Ammons. New York: Norton, 2010. First published 1852 by John P. Jewett.

Taylor, Tom. *Our American Cousin.* Bedford, MA: Applewood, 2006. Facsimile reproduction of playtext from the 1858 performance at Laura Keane's Theater, New York.

Tennenhouse, Leonard. *The Importance of Feeling English: American Literature and the British Diaspora, 1750–1850.* Princeton, NJ: Princeton University Press, 2016.

Tocqueville, Alexis de. *Democracy in America.* New York: Penguin, 2003. First published in two volumes from 1835–1840 by Librarie de Charles Gosselin, Paris.

Tompkins, Jane. *Sensational Designs: The Cultural Work of American Fiction, 1790–1860*. Oxford: Oxford University Press, 1986.
Trollope, Anthony. *The American Senator*. Detroit: Craig and Taylor, 1877.
Trollope, Frances. *Domestic Manners of Americans*. London: Gilbert and Rivington, 1832.
Twain, Mark [Samuel Clemens]. *A Connecticut Yankee in King Arthur's Court*. New York: Harper and Brothers, 1889.
Wallace, Lew. *Ben-Hur: A Tale of the Christ*. London: Sampson, Low, Marston, Searle, and Rivington, 1881.
———. *Lew Wallace: An Autobiography*. 2 vols. New York: Harper and Brothers, 1906.
Weld, Theodore. *American Slavery as It Is*. New York: Anti-Slavery Society, 1939.
Wicke, Jennifer. *Advertising Fictions: Literature, Advertisement, and Social Reading*. New York: Columbia University Press, 1988.

Index

Adichie, Chimamanda Ngozi, 149–50
advertising, 78–103; authorship and, 80–103; and P. T. Barnum, 18; of *Ben-Hur*, 74–75; and "cool," 5; as mark of Americanness, 19; and sensationalism, 83–85, 89; of *A Tale of Two Cities*, 82–84; of *Trilby*, 99–100
Agnes of Sorrento (Stowe), 8, 31–34, 42–46
amateurism, 2–13; and James Baldwin's reception, 146; in *The Diary of an Ex-Colored Man*, 137; and Henry James, 129; as national characteristic, 2–4, 106, 119; and *Uncle Tom's Cabin*, 8–10, 52, 126; and Lew Wallace, 9, 12, 67–75
Another Country (Baldwin), 124, 140–46
Armstrong, Nancy, 5, 13
Arthur, T. S., 16

Baldwin, James, 10, 30, 122, 135; *Another Country*, 124, 140–46; *The Devil Finds Work*, 146; *Giovanni's Room*, 141–43
Barnum, P. T., 18, 81
Baym, Nina, 12
Bellamy, Edward, 18
Ben-Hur (Wallace), 1–3, 6–9, 18, 57–77; satire of, 69–70, 76
Ben-Hur (film), 57–58
Benjamin, Walter, 5–6, 11, 13, 27, 61–62; *Arcades Project*, 6, 27; "On the Work of Art in the Age of Mechanical Reproduction," 6
Bentley, Nancy, 14, 126, 130
Berlant, Lauren, 32, 41
Black Crook, The, 14, 17, 47, 60

Blair, Amy, 26
Braddon, Mary Elizabeth, 14, 16–17; *Aurora Floyd*, 17; *Lady Audley's Secret*, 17, 60
Brantlinger, Patrick, 16
Brown, William Wells, 40
Buell, Lawrence, 14, 21

Chabon, Michael, 150
Child, Lydia Maria, 40
Clapp, Henry Austin, 24
Collins, Wilkie, 14, 16
cool, 4, 23–25; and advertising, 81; as anti-individualism, 32, 79, 99; and camp, 7; and celebrity, 12, 79; as characteristically American, 9, 37, 77, 109; as form of detachment, 5–9; and Lew Wallace, 67–68; and Yankee characters, 4, 10, 23–25, 49, 72
Cook, James W., 18

Daly, Augustin, 17; *Around the World in Eighty Days*, 17; *Under the Gaslight*, 14
Daly, Nicholas, 15
DeForest, John, 20, 53, 124
Dial, 22
Dickens, Charles, 2, 9, 12, 79; *All the Year Round*, 20, 89, 95; *American Notes*, 78, 86; *The Frozen Deep*, 92; *Our Mutual Friend*, 81, 92–98; parodies of, 87–88, 97; *Somebody's Luggage*, 89–91; *A Tale of Two Cities*, 2, 18, 82–98
Douglas, Ann, 30–32
Douglass, Frederick, 47

Dumas, Alexandre, 22
Du Maurier, George, 1, 9, 98; *The Martian*, 100–101. See also *Trilby*

Eagleton, Terry, 5
Eliot, T. S., 96
Encino Man, 151

Foucault, Michel, 81–82
Frank, Thomas, 5
Frank Leslie's, 81
Fraser, Brendan, 151
Frederick Douglass' Paper, 35
Fuguet, Alberto, 151–52

Garfield, James, 59
Garrison, William Lloyd, 2, 40
genre, 3–5, 9–13; and advertising, 79–82; and approachability, 5; and *Ben Hur*, 9, 59–60; in constructions of realism, 137–47; and consumerism, 34–35; historicity of, 25–27; and readership, 12
Giles, Paul, 80
Great American Novel, 20–23, 124

Hansen, Miriam, 152
Harper and Brothers, 59
Harper's Weekly, 16, 82
Hauranne, Ernest Duvergier de, 83
Higginson, Thomas Wentworth, 2, 20
Hochman, Barbara, 8
Howard, Cordelia, 31
Howells, William Dean, 2, 19, 102
Hughes, Langston, "Colonel Tom's Cabin," 8, 55–56
Hugo, Victor, 22

Jackson, Gregory, 58
James, Henry, 10, 29, 102, 125, 135; *The American Scene*, 126–31; literary reviews by, 17, 102; *The Portrait of a Lady*, 121, 131–35; *A Small Boy and Others*, 126
Jameson, Fredric, 25–26
Jefferson, Joseph, 10, 104, 108–12

Johnson, James Weldon, 10, 122, 135; *The Autobiography of an Ex-Colored Man*, 136–40

Kaplan, Amy, 14
Kerr, Orpheus C. (Robert Henry Newell), 9, 97
Knickerbocker, The, 23
Kurnick, David, 126

Labruce, Bruce, 7
Life Magazine, 58, 69
Lippard, George, 16
Liu, Alan, 13; *The Laws of Cool*, 13
Lott, Eric, 8

Marx, Karl, 27
McGill, Meredith, 96
McGurl, Mark, 14
McKeon, Michael, 5
Merish, Lori, 34

Nassau Literary Magazine, 69
Newell, Robert Henry (Orpheus C. Kerr), 9, 97
New York Ledger, 18
New York Times, 47, 63, 67
New York Tribune, 1

Our Mutual Friend (Dickens), 81, 92–98
Outlook, 60

Pall Mall Gazette, 111
Parfait, Claire, 9, 37
Payne, David, 91
Poe, Edgar Allen, 6
Puck, 20, 46, 72–73
Punch (London), 19
Putnam's Monthly, 38, 87

Radway, Janice, 25

sensationalism, 9, 14–20; and advertising, 83–85, 87
sentimentalism, 34
Shore, Pauly, 150–51

Sontag, Susan, 6; "Notes on Camp," 6
Southern Literary Messenger, 35
Stallybrass, Peter, 78–79, 122
Stowe, Harriet Beecher, 1, 8; *Agnes of Sorrento,* 8, 31–34, 42–46. See also *Uncle Tom's Cabin*
surrealism, 61–62; and profanation, 66–67
St. Nicholas (magazine), 70

Tale of Two Cities, A (Dickens), 2, 18, 82–98
Taylor, Tom, 10, 104; "Our American Cousin," 10, 106–8
Tocqueville, Alexis de, 119
Tourgeé, Albion, 2
Trilby (Du Maurier), 1–3, 18, 98–103, 138; anonymous sequel, 9; parodies of, 99–100
Trollope, Anthony, 10, 104; *The American Senator,* 10, 104, 112–15

Twain, Mark (Samuel Clemens), 10, 104; *A Connecticut Yankee in King Arthur's Court,* 10, 104–5, 115–19

Uncle Tom's Cabin, 1–3, 6–10, 18, 24, 29–56, 122–48; Eva's role in, 40–44; popular response to, 31–39, 46; theatrical productions of, 46–56

Wallace, Lew, 1, 9, 12. See also *Ben-Hur*
Weld, Theodore, 40
White, Allon, 78–79, 122
Whitman, Walt, 23
Wicke, Jennifer, 82
Wilde, Oscar, 6
Wilkes' Spirit of the Times, 17
Wright, Richard, 140

CPSIA information can be obtained
at www.ICGtesting.com
Printed in the USA
LVHW09s1339280818
588389LV00001B/247/P